# Apache HTTP Server 2.2

# Official Documentation

## Server Administration

## Volume I

*Fultus*™ *Books*

# Apache HTTP Server 2.2
## Official Documentation

## Server Administration

## Volume I

ISBN-10: 1-59682-191-4
ISBN-13: 978-1-59682-191-0

Cover design and book layout by Fultus Corporation

*Published by Fultus Corporation*

Publisher Web: *www.fultus.com*
Linbrary - Linux Library: *www.linbrary.com*
Online Bookstore: *store.fultus.com*
email: *production@fultus.com*

# Apache HTTP Server 2.2
# Official Documentation List

| Version | Title | Edition | ISBN- 10 | ISBN- 13 |
|---------|-------|---------|----------|----------|
| Apache Web Server 2.2 | Apache HTTP Server 2.2 **Vol.I. Server Administration** | paperback | 1-59682-191-4 | 978-1-59682-191-0 |
| | | eBook (pdf) | 1-59682-195-7 | 978-1-59682-195-8 |
| | Apache HTTP Server 2.2 **Vol.II. Security & Server Programs** | paperback | 1-59682-192-2 | 978-1-59682-192-7 |
| | | eBook (pdf) | 1-59682-196-5 | 978-1-59682-196-5 |
| | Apache HTTP Server 2.2 **Vol.III. Modules (A-H)** | paperback | 1-59682-193-0 | 978-1-59682-193-4 |
| | | eBook (pdf) | 1-59682-197-3 | 978-1-59682-197-2 |
| | Apache HTTP Server 2.2 **Vol.IV. Modules (I-V)** | paperback | 1-59682-194-9 | 978-1-59682-194-1 |
| | | eBook (pdf) | 1-59682-198-1 | 978-1-59682-198-9 |
| *http://www.linbrary.com/apache-http/* | | | | |

# Table of Contents

# List of Figures

# Foreword

**The Apache Software Foundation Announces
the 15th Anniversary of the Apache HTTP Web Server**

*Tuesday Feb 23, 2010*

**ASF Flagship Project is World's Most Popular Web Server, Powering More than 112
Million Websites.**

**FOREST HILL, MD, 23 February, 2010** -- The Apache Software Foundation (ASF) --
developers, stewards, and incubators of 138 Open Source projects -- today announced the
15th anniversary of the Apache HTTP Web Server.

The ASF's first project became the world's most popular Web server software within the first
six months of its inception. The Apache HTTP Server today powers nearly 112 million
Websites world-wide.

A triumph for the all-volunteer Foundation, the Apache HTTP Server reliably delivers
petabytes of data across the world's most demanding uses, including real-time news
sources, Fortune 100 enterprise portals, cloud computing clusters, financial services
platforms, mission-critical military intelligence applications, aerospace communications
networks, and more. The server software can be downloaded, modified and installed by
anyone free of charge.

### History

The Apache Server started as a fork (an independent development stream)
of the NCSA httpd, a Web server created by Rob McCool at the National Center for
Supercomputing Applications. Further development to the server ceased after McCool's
departure from NCSA in 1994, so an online community of individuals was formed to
support and enhance its software via email collaboration. The founding members of that
community (the Apache Group) included Brian Behlendorf, Roy Fielding, Rob Hartill,
David Robinson, Cliff Skolnick, Randy Terbush, Robert Thau, and Andrew Wilson.

Within less than a year of the Apache Group's formation, the Apache server surpassed
NCSA httpd as the #1 server on the Internet.

In March 1999, members of the Apache Group formed The Apache Software Foundation to
provide organizational, legal, and financial support for the Apache HTTP Server. An

additional goal for the Foundation was to serve as a neutral, trusted platform for the development of community-driven software.

## Growth, the "Apache Way"

Beyond the Apache HTTP Server, dozens of ASF projects – from build tools to Web services to cloud computing and more – lead the way in Open Source technology.

At the ASF, community plays a vital role in the collaborative development of consensus-driven, enterprise-grade solutions. The number of projects led by the Apache community has grown from the singular Apache HTTP Server at the ASF's inception in 1999 to nearly 140 projects today.

The ASF's commitment to fostering a collaborative approach to development has long served as a model for producing consistently high quality software and helping advance the future of open development. Through its leadership, robust community, and meritocratic process known as the "Apache Way", the ASF continues to gain recognition as one of the most successful influencers in Open Source.

Through the Apache Way, the ASF is able to spearhead new projects that meet the demands of the marketplace and help users achieve their business goals. With the Apache Incubator mentoring more projects than ever before, the ASF continues to meet the growing demand for quality Open Source products.

*"Community Over Code"*: among the Foundation's core tenets is open collaboration through respectful, honest, technically-focused interaction. The ASF's success is testament to its outstanding community efforts that serve as best practices widely embraced by organizations and individuals alike.

*"If it didn't happen on-list, it didn't happen"*: building upon the transparency-oriented culture of the Apache Group, whose collaboration took place on email lists, millions of messages are archived on Apache publicly-accessible mailing lists, documenting the ASF's achievements over the past decade.

*"Meritocracy in Action"*: the ASF's tagline reflects an average of 10,000 code contributions (commits) made each month. The ASF is responsible for millions of lines of code by more than 2,000 ASF Committers and countless contributors across the Open Source landscape. Nearly 500 community-driven modules have been developed to extend functionality of the Apache HTTP Server alone.

## Milestones

February 23, 1994: Individual patch authors around the world are invited to join the "new-httpd" mailing list to discuss enhancements and future releases of NCSA httpd. The Apache name was chosen for this new effort within the first few days of discussion, along with basic rules for email-based collaboration and a mission to replace the existing server with a standards-based, open source, and extensible software system.

March 15, 1994: Apache-style voting created (+1, 0, -1; with '-1' meaning 'no', '0' meaning 'neutral', and '+1' meaning 'yes.')

March 18, 1994: First Apache Group release (Apache 0.2)

Apache server v.1.0 was released in December 1995. Four years later, Apache HTTP Server v.1.3.0 was released, and rapidly becoming the most popular Web server on the planet.

Apache HTTP Server v.2.0 alpha was released in March 2000, with the first general availability release two years later. V.2.0 remained best-of-breed sever until the release of v.2.2.0 in December 2005, and is widely deployed across the Internet.

In February 2009, the Apache HTTP Server became the first Web server software in history to surpass the 100 million Website milestone.

The most current, best-of-breed, stable version of the Apache HTTP Server is v.2.2.14, released September 2009. Developers seeking to test new features and preview what will become stable Version 2.4 are able to do so today with the development of v.2.3.5.

Earlier this month, after ten years and more than forty revisions, the Apache HTTP Server v.1.3.x officially reached end of life status with the release of v.1.3.42. Future patches to v.1.3.x will be for critical security updates only.

The Apache HTTP Server remains the world's most beloved Web server, forming the backbone of nearly 70% of all sites on the Internet.

### Availability

The Apache HTTP Server is available for a variety of operating systems, including Unix, Linux, GNU, FreeBSD, Netware, Solaris, Windows, Mac OS X, OS/2, TPF, and eCS. In addition, the Apache HTTP Server is redistributed through many proprietary software packages such as WebSphere, Oracle RDBMS, Kylix, NetWare, and Delphi, as well as numerous Linux distributions.

All ASF projects, including the Apache HTTP Server, are available free of charge under the Apache Software License v.2.0. To download, or for more information, visit *http://httpd.apache.org/*

### About The Apache Software Foundation (ASF)

Established in 1999, the all-volunteer Foundation oversees more than seventy leading Open Source projects, including Apache HTTP Server — the world's most popular Web server software. Through The ASF's meritocratic process known as "The Apache Way," more than 300 individual Members and 2,000 Committers successfully collaborate to develop freely available enterprise-grade software, benefiting millions of users worldwide: thousands of software solutions are distributed under the Apache License; and the community actively participates in ASF mailing lists, mentoring initiatives, and ApacheCon, the Foundation's official user conference, trainings, and expo. The ASF is funded by individual donations and corporate sponsors including Facebook, Google, HP, Microsoft, Progress Software, SpringSource, and Yahoo! For more information, visit *http://www.apache.org/*.

*Posted at 02:00PM Feb 23, 2010 by Sally in Milestones*
*https://blogs.apache.org/foundation/entry/the_apache_software_foundation_announces2*

# Part I.

# Release Notes

# Chapter 1.
# Upgrading to 2.2 from 2.0

In order to assist folks upgrading, we maintain a document describing information critical to existing Apache users. These are intended to be brief notes, and you should be able to find more information in either the *New Features* document, or in the src/CHANGES file.

This document describes only the changes from 2.0 to 2.2. If you are upgrading from version 1.3, you should also consult the *1.3 to 2.0 upgrading document*[1].

## 1.1. Compile-Time Configuration Changes

The compilation process is very similar to the one used in version 2.0. Your old configure command line (as found in build/config.nice in the installed server directory) can be used in some cases. The most significant change required will be to account for changes in module names, in particular for the authentication and authorization modules. Some details of changes:

- mod_imap has been renamed to mod_imagemap
- mod_auth has been split up into mod_auth_basic, mod_authn_file, mod_authz_user, and mod_authz_groupfile
- mod_access has been renamed to mod_authz_host
- mod_auth_ldap has been renamed to mod_authnz_ldap
- Upgraded to require the APR 1.0 API.
- Updated bundled PCRE version to 5.0

## 1.2. Run-Time Configuration Changes

Your existing version 2.0 config files and startup scripts can usually be used unchanged in version 2.2. Some small adjustments may be necessary for particular configurations as discussed below. In addition, if you dynamically load the standard modules using the LoadModule directive, then you will need to account for the module name changes mentioned above.

---

[1] *http://httpd.apache.org/docs/2.0/upgrading.html*

If you choose to use the new default configuration file for version 2.2, you will find that it has been greatly simplified by removing all but the most essential configuration settings. A set of example configuration settings for more advanced features is present in the `conf/extra/` directory of the installed server. Default configuration files are installed in the `conf/original` directory.

Some runtime configuration changes that you may notice:

- The *apachectl* option `startssl` is no longer available. To enable SSL support, you should edit `httpd.conf` to include the relevant `mod_ssl` directives and then use `apachectl start` to start the server. An example configuration to activate `mod_ssl` has been included in `conf/extra/httpd-ssl.conf`.

- The default setting of `UseCanonicalName` is now `Off`. If you did not have this directive in your config file, you can add `UseCanonicalName On` to retain the old behavior.

- The module `mod_userdir` will no longer act on requests unless a `UserDir` directive specifying a directory name is present in the config file. To restore the old default behavior, place the directive `UserDir public_html` in your config file.

- The directive `AuthDigestFile` from `mod_auth_digest` has been merged with `AuthUserFile` and is now part of `mod_authn_file`.

## 1.3. Misc Changes

- The module `mod_cache`, which was experimental in Apache 2.0, is now a standard module.

- The module `mod_disk_cache`, which was experimental in Apache 2.0, is now a standard module.

- The module `mod_mem_cache`, which was experimental in Apache 2.0, is now a standard module.

- The module `mod_charset_lite`, which was experimental in Apache 2.0, is now a standard module.

- The module `mod_dumpio`, which was experimental in Apache 2.0, is now a standard module.

## 1.4. Third Party Modules

Many third-party modules designed for version 2.0 will work unchanged with the Apache HTTP Server version 2.2. But all modules must be recompiled before being loaded.

# Chapter 2.

# Overview of new features in Apache 2.0

This document describes some of the major changes between the 1.3 and 2.0 versions of the Apache HTTP Server.

## 2.1. Core Enhancements

### Unix Threading

On Unix systems with POSIX threads support, Apache can now run in a hybrid multiprocess, multithreaded mode. This improves scalability for many, but not all configurations.

### New Build System

The build system has been rewritten from scratch to be based on `autoconf` and `libtool`. This makes Apache's configuration system more similar to that of other packages.

### Multiprotocol Support

Apache now has some of the infrastructure in place to support serving multiple protocols. `mod_echo` has been written as an example.

### Better support for non-Unix platforms

Apache 2.0 is faster and more stable on non-Unix platforms such as BeOS, OS/2, and Windows. With the introduction of platform-specific *multi-processing modules* (MPMs) and the Apache Portable Runtime (APR), these platforms are now implemented in their native API, avoiding the often buggy and poorly performing POSIX-emulation layers.

### New Apache API

The API for modules has changed significantly for 2.0. Many of the module-ordering/-priority problems from 1.3 should be gone. 2.0 does much of this automatically, and module ordering is now done per-hook to allow more flexibility. Also, new calls have been added that provide additional module capabilities without patching the core Apache server.

## IPv6 Support

On systems where IPv6 is supported by the underlying Apache Portable Runtime library, Apache gets IPv6 listening sockets by default. Additionally, the `Listen`, `NameVirtualHost`, and `VirtualHost` directives support IPv6 numeric address strings (e.g., `"Listen [2001:db8::1]:8080"`).

## Filtering

Apache modules may now be written as filters which act on the stream of content as it is delivered to or from the server. This allows, for example, the output of CGI scripts to be parsed for Server Side Include directives using the `INCLUDES` filter in `mod_include`. The module `mod_ext_filter` allows external programs to act as filters in much the same way that CGI programs can act as handlers.

## Multilanguage Error Responses

Error response messages to the browser are now provided in several languages, using SSI documents. They may be customized by the administrator to achieve a consistent look and feel.

## Simplified configuration

Many confusing directives have been simplified. The often confusing `Port` and `BindAddress` directives are gone; only the `Listen` directive is used for IP address binding; the `ServerName` directive specifies the server name and port number only for redirection and vhost recognition.

## Native Windows NT Unicode Support

Apache 2.0 on Windows NT now uses utf-8 for all filename encodings. These directly translate to the underlying Unicode file system, providing multilanguage support for all Windows NT-based installations, including Windows 2000 and Windows XP. *This support does not extend to Windows 95, 98 or ME, which continue to use the machine's local codepage for filesystem access.*

## Regular Expression Library Updated

Apache 2.0 includes the *Perl Compatible Regular Expression Library*[1] (PCRE). All regular expression evaluation now uses the more powerful Perl 5 syntax.

---

[1] *http://www.pcre.org/*

## 2.2. Module Enhancements

**mod_ssl**

New module in Apache 2.0. This module is an interface to the SSL/TLS encryption protocols provided by OpenSSL.

**mod_dav**

New module in Apache 2.0. This module implements the HTTP Distributed Authoring and Versioning (DAV) specification for posting and maintaining web content.

**mod_deflate**

New module in Apache 2.0. This module allows supporting browsers to request that content be compressed before delivery, saving network bandwidth.

**mod_auth_ldap**

New module in Apache 2.0.41. This module allows an LDAP database to be used to store credentials for HTTP Basic Authentication. A companion module, mod_ldap provides connection pooling and results caching.

**mod_auth_digest**

Includes additional support for session caching across processes using shared memory.

**mod_charset_lite**

New module in Apache 2.0. This experimental module allows for character set translation or recoding.

**mod_file_cache**

New module in Apache 2.0. This module includes the functionality of mod_mmap_static in Apache 1.3, plus adds further caching abilities.

**mod_headers**

This module is much more flexible in Apache 2.0. It can now modify request headers used by mod_proxy, and it can conditionally set response headers.

**mod_proxy**

The proxy module has been completely rewritten to take advantage of the new filter infrastructure and to implement a more reliable, HTTP/1.1 compliant proxy. In addition, new <Proxy> configuration sections provide more readable (and internally faster) control of proxied sites; overloaded <Directory "proxy:..."> configuration are not supported. The module is now divided into specific protocol support modules including proxy_connect, proxy_ftp and proxy_http.

### `mod_negotiation`

A new `ForceLanguagePriority` directive can be used to assure that the client receives a single document in all cases, rather than NOT ACCEPTABLE or MULTIPLE CHOICES responses. In addition, the negotiation and MultiViews algorithms have been cleaned up to provide more consistent results and a new form of type map that can include document content is provided.

### `mod_autoindex`

Autoindex'ed directory listings can now be configured to use HTML tables for cleaner formatting, and allow finer-grained control of sorting, including version-sorting, and wildcard filtering of the directory listing.

### `mod_include`

New directives allow the default start and end tags for SSI elements to be changed and allow for error and time format configuration to take place in the main configuration file rather than in the SSI document. Results from regular expression parsing and grouping (now based on Perl's regular expression syntax) can be retrieved using `mod_include`'s variables $0 .. $9.

### `mod_auth_dbm`

Now supports multiple types of DBM-like databases using the `AuthDBMType` directive.

# Chapter 3.

# Overview of new features in Apache 2.2

This document describes some of the major changes between the 2.0 and 2.2 versions of the Apache HTTP Server. For new features since version 1.3, see the *2.0 new features* document.

## 3.1. Core Enhancements

**Authn/Authz**

The bundled authentication and authorization modules have been refactored. The new `mod_authn_alias` module can greatly simplify certain authentication configurations. See *module name changes*, and *the developer changes* for more information about how these changes affects users and module writers.

**Caching**

`mod_cache`, `mod_disk_cache`, and `mod_mem_cache` have undergone a lot of changes, and are now considered production-quality. `htcacheclean` has been introduced to clean up `mod_disk_cache` setups.

**Configuration**

The default configuration layout has been simplified and modularised. Configuration snippets which can be used to enable commonly-used features are now bundled with Apache, and can be easily added to the main server config.

**Graceful stop**

The `prefork`, `worker` and `event` MPMs now allow `httpd` to be shutdown gracefully via the `graceful-stop` signal. The `GracefulShutdownTimeout` directive has been added to specify an optional timeout, after which `httpd` will terminate regardless of the status of any requests being served.

**Proxying**

The new `mod_proxy_balancer` module provides load balancing services for `mod_proxy`. The new `mod_proxy_ajp` module adds support for the `Apache JServ Protocol version 1.3` used by *Apache Tomcat*[1].

---

[1] *http://jakarta.apache.org/tomcat/*

### Regular Expression Library Updated

Version 5.0 of the *Perl Compatible Regular Expression Library*[2] (PCRE) is now included. `httpd` can be configured to use a system installation of PCRE by passing the `--with-pcre` flag to configure.

### Smart Filtering

`mod_filter` introduces dynamic configuration to the output filter chain. It enables filters to be conditionally inserted, based on any Request or Response header or environment variable, and dispenses with the more problematic dependencies and ordering problems in the 2.0 architecture.

### Large File Support

`httpd` is now built with support for files larger than 2GB on modern 32-bit Unix systems. Support for handling >2GB request bodies has also been added.

### Event MPM

The `event` MPM uses a separate thread to handle Keep Alive requests and accepting connections. Keep Alive requests have traditionally required httpd to dedicate a worker to handle it. This dedicated worker could not be used again until the Keep Alive timeout was reached.

### SQL Database Support

`mod_dbd`, together with the `apr_dbd` framework, brings direct SQL support to modules that need it. Supports connection pooling in threaded MPMs.

## 3.2. Module Enhancements

### Authn/Authz

Modules in the aaa directory have been renamed and offer better support for digest authentication. For example, `mod_auth` is now split into `mod_auth_basic` and `mod_authn_file`; `mod_auth_dbm` is now called `mod_authn_dbm`; `mod_access` has been renamed `mod_authz_host`. There is also a new `mod_authn_alias` module for simplifying certain authentication configurations.

### mod_authnz_ldap

This module is a port of the 2.0 `mod_auth_ldap` module to the 2.2 `Authn/Authz` framework. New features include using LDAP attribute values and complicated search filters in the `Require` directive.

---

[2] *http://www.pcre.org/*

**mod_authz_owner**

> A new module that authorizes access to files based on the owner of the file on the file system

**mod_version**

> A new module that allows configuration blocks to be enabled based on the version number of the running server.

**mod_info**

> Added a new ?config argument which will show the configuration directives as parsed by Apache, including their file name and line number. The module also shows the order of all request hooks and additional build information, similar to httpd -V.

**mod_ssl**

> Added a support for *RFC 2817*[3], which allows connections to upgrade from clear text to TLS encryption.

**mod_imagemap**

> mod_imap has been renamed to mod_imagemap to avoid user confusion.

## 3.3. Program Enhancements

*httpd*

> A new command line option -M has been added that lists all modules that are loaded based on the current configuration. Unlike the -l option, this list includes DSOs loaded via mod_so.

*httxt2dbm*

> A new program used to generate dbm files from text input, for use in RewriteMap with the dbm map type.

## 3.4. Module Developer Changes

**APR 1.0 API**

> Apache 2.2 uses the APR 1.0 API. All deprecated functions and symbols have been removed from APR and APR-Util. For details, see the *APR Website*[4].

---

[3] *http://www.ietf.org/rfc/rfc2817.txt*
[4] *http://apr.apache.org/*

## Authn/Authz

The bundled authentication and authorization modules have been renamed along the following lines:

- `mod_auth_*` -> Modules that implement an HTTP authentication mechanism
- `mod_authn_*` -> Modules that provide a backend authentication provider
- `mod_authz_*` -> Modules that implement authorization (or access)
- `mod_authnz_*` -> Module that implements both authentication & authorization

There is a new authentication backend provider scheme which greatly eases the construction of new authentication backends.

## Connection Error Logging

A new function, `ap_log_cerror` has been added to log errors that occur with the client's connection. When logged, the message includes the client IP address.

## Test Configuration Hook Added

A new hook, `test_config` has been added to aid modules that want to execute special code only when the user passes `-t` to *httpd*.

## Set Threaded MPM's Stacksize

A new directive, `ThreadStackSize` has been added to set the stack size on all threaded MPMs. This is required for some third-party modules on platforms with small default thread stack size.

## Protocol handling for output filters

In the past, every filter has been responsible for ensuring that it generates the correct response headers where it affects them. Filters can now delegate common protocol management to `mod_filter`, using the `ap_register_output_filter_protocol` or `ap_filter_protocol` calls.

## Monitor hook added

Monitor hook enables modules to run regular/scheduled jobs in the parent (root) process.

## Regular expression API changes

The `pcreposix.h` header is no longer available; it is replaced by the new `ap_regex.h` header. The POSIX.2 `regex.h` implementation exposed by the old header is now available under the `ap_` namespace from `ap_regex.h`. Calls to `regcomp`, `regexec` and so on can be replaced by calls to `ap_regcomp`, `ap_regexec`.

**DBD Framework (SQL Database API)**

With Apache 1.x and 2.0, modules requiring an SQL backend had to take responsibility for managing it themselves. Apart from reinventing the wheel, this can be very inefficient, for example when several modules each maintain their own connections.

Apache 2.1 and later provides the `ap_dbd` API for managing database connections (including optimised strategies for threaded and unthreaded MPMs), while APR 1.2 and later provides the `apr_dbd` API for interacting with the database.

New modules SHOULD now use these APIs for all SQL database operations. Existing applications SHOULD be upgraded to use it where feasible, either transparently or as a recommended option to their users.

# Chapter 4.

# The Apache License, Version 2.0

Apache License
Version 2.0, January 2004
*http://www.apache.org/licenses/*

TERMS AND CONDITIONS FOR USE, REPRODUCTION, AND DISTRIBUTION

1. **Definitions**

   "License" shall mean the terms and conditions for use, reproduction, and distribution as defined by Sections 1 through 9 of this document.

   "Licensor" shall mean the copyright owner or entity authorized by the copyright owner that is granting the License.

   "Legal Entity" shall mean the union of the acting entity and all other entities that control, are controlled by, or are under common control with that entity. For the purposes of this definition, "control" means (i) the power, direct or indirect, to cause the direction or management of such entity, whether by contract or otherwise, or (ii) ownership of fifty percent (50%) or more of the outstanding shares, or (iii) beneficial ownership of such entity.

   "You" (or "Your") shall mean an individual or Legal Entity exercising permissions granted by this License.

   "Source" form shall mean the preferred form for making modifications, including but not limited to software source code, documentation source, and configuration files.

   "Object" form shall mean any form resulting from mechanical transformation or translation of a Source form, including but not limited to compiled object code, generated documentation, and conversions to other media types.

   "Work" shall mean the work of authorship, whether in Source or Object form, made available under the License, as indicated by a copyright notice that is included in or attached to the work (an example is provided in the Appendix below).

"Derivative Works" shall mean any work, whether in Source or Object form, that is based on (or derived from) the Work and for which the editorial revisions, annotations, elaborations, or other modifications represent, as a whole, an original work of authorship. For the purposes of this License, Derivative Works shall not include works that remain separable from, or merely link (or bind by name) to the interfaces of, the Work and Derivative Works thereof.

"Contribution" shall mean any work of authorship, including the original version of the Work and any modifications or additions to that Work or Derivative Works thereof, that is intentionally submitted to Licensor for inclusion in the Work by the copyright owner or by an individual or Legal Entity authorized to submit on behalf of the copyright owner. For the purposes of this definition, "submitted" means any form of electronic, verbal, or written communication sent to the Licensor or its representatives, including but not limited to communication on electronic mailing lists, source code control systems, and issue tracking systems that are managed by, or on behalf of, the Licensor for the purpose of discussing and improving the Work, but excluding communication that is conspicuously marked or otherwise designated in writing by the copyright owner as "Not a Contribution."

"Contributor" shall mean Licensor and any individual or Legal Entity on behalf of whom a Contribution has been received by Licensor and subsequently incorporated within the Work.

2. **Grant of Copyright License.** Subject to the terms and conditions of this License, each Contributor hereby grants to You a perpetual, worldwide, non-exclusive, no-charge, royalty-free, irrevocable copyright license to reproduce, prepare Derivative Works of, publicly display, publicly perform, sublicense, and distribute the Work and such Derivative Works in Source or Object form.

3. **Grant of Patent License.** Subject to the terms and conditions of this License, each Contributor hereby grants to You a perpetual, worldwide, non-exclusive, no-charge, royalty-free, irrevocable (except as stated in this section) patent license to make, have made, use, offer to sell, sell, import, and otherwise transfer the Work, where such license applies only to those patent claims licensable by such Contributor that are necessarily infringed by their Contribution(s) alone or by combination of their Contribution(s) with the Work to which such Contribution(s) was submitted. If You institute patent litigation against any entity (including a cross-claim or counterclaim in a lawsuit) alleging that the Work or a Contribution incorporated within the Work constitutes direct or contributory patent infringement, then any patent licenses granted to You under this License for that Work shall terminate as of the date such litigation is filed.

4. **Redistribution.** You may reproduce and distribute copies of the Work or Derivative Works thereof in any medium, with or without modifications, and in Source or Object form, provided that You meet the following conditions:

   - You must give any other recipients of the Work or Derivative Works a copy of this License; and

   - You must cause any modified files to carry prominent notices stating that You changed the files; and

   - You must retain, in the Source form of any Derivative Works that You distribute, all copyright, patent, trademark, and attribution notices from the Source form of the Work, excluding those notices that do not pertain to any part of the Derivative Works; and

   - If the Work includes a "NOTICE" text file as part of its distribution, then any Derivative Works that You distribute must include a readable copy of the attribution notices contained within such NOTICE file, excluding those notices that do not pertain to any part of the Derivative Works, in at least one of the following places: within a NOTICE text file distributed as part of the Derivative Works; within the Source form or documentation, if provided along with the Derivative Works; or, within a display generated by the Derivative Works, if and wherever such third-party notices normally appear. The contents of the NOTICE file are for informational purposes only and do not modify the License. You may add Your own attribution notices within Derivative Works that You distribute, alongside or as an addendum to the NOTICE text from the Work, provided that such additional attribution notices cannot be construed as modifying the License.

   You may add Your own copyright statement to Your modifications and may provide additional or different license terms and conditions for use, reproduction, or distribution of Your modifications, or for any such Derivative Works as a whole, provided Your use, reproduction, and distribution of the Work otherwise complies with the conditions stated in this License.

5. **Submission of Contributions.** Unless You explicitly state otherwise, any Contribution intentionally submitted for inclusion in the Work by You to the Licensor shall be under the terms and conditions of this License, without any additional terms or conditions. Notwithstanding the above, nothing herein shall supersede or modify the terms of any separate license agreement you may have executed with Licensor regarding such Contributions.

6. **Trademarks.** This License does not grant permission to use the trade names, trademarks, service marks, or product names of the Licensor, except as required for reasonable and

customary use in describing the origin of the Work and reproducing the content of the NOTICE file.

7. **Disclaimer of Warranty.** Unless required by applicable law or agreed to in writing, Licensor provides the Work (and each Contributor provides its Contributions) on an "AS IS" BASIS, WITHOUT WARRANTIES OR CONDITIONS OF ANY KIND, either express or implied, including, without limitation, any warranties or conditions of TITLE, NON-INFRINGEMENT, MERCHANTABILITY, or FITNESS FOR A PARTICULAR PURPOSE. You are solely responsible for determining the appropriateness of using or redistributing the Work and assume any risks associated with Your exercise of permissions under this License.

8. **Limitation of Liability.** In no event and under no legal theory, whether in tort (including negligence), contract, or otherwise, unless required by applicable law (such as deliberate and grossly negligent acts) or agreed to in writing, shall any Contributor be liable to You for damages, including any direct, indirect, special, incidental, or consequential damages of any character arising as a result of this License or out of the use or inability to use the Work (including but not limited to damages for loss of goodwill, work stoppage, computer failure or malfunction, or any and all other commercial damages or losses), even if such Contributor has been advised of the possibility of such damages.

9. **Accepting Warranty or Additional Liability.** While redistributing the Work or Derivative Works thereof, You may choose to offer, and charge a fee for, acceptance of support, warranty, indemnity, or other liability obligations and/or rights consistent with this License. However, in accepting such obligations, You may act only on Your own behalf and on Your sole responsibility, not on behalf of any other Contributor, and only if You agree to indemnify, defend, and hold each Contributor harmless for any liability incurred by, or claims asserted against, such Contributor by reason of your accepting any such warranty or additional liability.

END OF TERMS AND CONDITIONS

APPENDIX: How to apply the Apache License to your work.

To apply the Apache License to your work, attach the following boilerplate notice, with the fields enclosed by brackets "[]" replaced with your own identifying information. (Don't include the brackets!) The text should be enclosed in the appropriate comment syntax for the file format. We also recommend that a file or class name and description of purpose be included on the same "printed page" as the copyright notice for easier identification within third-party archives.

# Part II.
# Using the Apache HTTP Server

# Chapter 5.

# Compiling and Installing

This document covers compilation and installation of the Apache HTTP Server on Unix and Unix-like systems only. For compiling and installation on Windows, see *Using Apache HTTPd with Microsoft Windows*. For other platforms, see the *platform* documentation.

Apache HTTPd uses `libtool` and `autoconf` to create a build environment that looks like many other Open Source projects.

If you are upgrading from one minor version to the next (for example, 2.2.50 to 2.2.51), please skip down to the *upgrading* section.

## 5.1. Overview for the impatient

| | |
|---|---|
| **Download** | `$ lynx http://httpd.apache.org/download.cgi` |
| **Extract** | `$ gzip -d httpd-`*NN*`.tar.gz` |
| | `$ tar xvf httpd-`*NN*`.tar` |
| | `$ cd httpd-`*NN* |
| **Configure** | `$ ./configure --prefix=`*PREFIX* |
| **Compile** | `$ make` |
| **Install** | `$ make install` |
| **Customize** | `$ vi `*PREFIX*`/conf/httpd.conf` |
| **Test** | `$ `*PREFIX*`/bin/apachectl -k start` |

*NN* must be replaced with the current version number, and *PREFIX* must be replaced with the filesystem path under which the server should be installed. If *PREFIX* is not specified, it defaults to `/usr/local/apache2`.

Each section of the compilation and installation process is described in more detail below, beginning with the requirements for compiling and installing Apache HTTP Server.

## 5.2. Requirements

The following requirements exist for building Apache HTTPd:

**Disk Space**

Make sure you have at least 50 MB of temporary free disk space available. After installation Apache occupies approximately 10 MB of disk space. The actual disk space requirements will vary considerably based on your chosen configuration options and any third-party modules.

**ANSI-C Compiler and Build System**

Make sure you have an ANSI-C compiler installed. The *GNU C compiler (GCC)*[1] from the *Free Software Foundation (FSF)*[2] is recommended. If you don't have GCC then at least make sure your vendor's compiler is ANSI compliant. In addition, your PATH must contain basic build tools such as make.

**Accurate time keeping**

Elements of the HTTP protocol are expressed as the time of day. So, it's time to investigate setting some time synchronization facility on your system. Usually the ntpdate or xntpd programs are used for this purpose which are based on the Network Time Protocol (NTP). See the *NTP homepage*[3] for more details about NTP software and public time servers.

**Perl 5[4] [OPTIONAL]**

For some of the support scripts like *apxs* or *dbmmanage* (which are written in Perl) the Perl 5 interpreter is required (versions 5.003 or newer are sufficient). If you have multiple Perl interpreters (for example, a systemwide install of Perl 4, and your own install of Perl 5), you are advised to use the --with-perl option (see below) to make sure the correct one is used by *configure*. If no Perl 5 interpreter is found by the *configure* script, you will not be able to use the affected support scripts. Of course, you will still be able to build and use Apache HTTPd.

**apr/apr-util >= 1.2[5]**

apr and apr-util are bundled with the Apache HTTPd source releases, and will be used without any problems in almost all circumstances. However, if apr or apr-util,

---

[1] *http://www.gnu.org/software/gcc/gcc.html*
[2] *http://www.gnu.org/*
[3] *http://www.ntp.org/*
[4] *http://www.perl.org/*
[5] *http://apr.apache.org/*

versions 1.0 or 1.1, are installed on your system, you must either upgrade your
apr/apr-util installations to 1.2, force the use of the bundled libraries or have httpd
use separate builds. To use the bundled apr/apr-util sources specify the --with-
included-apr option to configure:

 **Note**

The --with-included-apr option was added in version 2.2.3

```
# Force the use of the bundled apr/apr-util
./configure --with-included-apr
```

To build Apache HTTPd against a manually installed apr/apr-util:

```
# Build and install apr 1.2
cd srclib/apr
./configure --prefix=/usr/local/apr-httpd/
make
make install

# Build and install apr-util 1.2
cd ../apr-util
./configure --prefix=/usr/local/apr-util-httpd/ --with-apr=/usr/local/apr-httpd/
make
make install

# Configure httpd
cd ../../
./configure --with-apr=/usr/local/apr-httpd/ --with-apr-util=/usr/local/apr-
util-httpd/
```

## 5.3. Download

The Apache HTTP Server can be downloaded from the *Apache HTTP Server download site*[6],
which lists several mirrors. Most users of Apache HTTPd on unix-like systems will be better
off downloading and compiling a source version. The build process (described below) is
easy, and it allows you to customize your server to suit your needs. In addition, binary
releases are often not up to date with the latest source releases. If you do download a binary,
follow the instructions in the INSTALL.bindist file inside the distribution.

After downloading, it is important to verify that you have a complete and unmodified
version of the Apache HTTP Server. This can be accomplished by testing the downloaded
tarball against the PGP signature. Details on how to do this are available on the *download
page*[7] and an extended example is available describing the *use of PGP*[8].

[6] *http://httpd.apache.org/download.cgi*
[7] *http://httpd.apache.org/download.cgi#verify*

## 5.4. Extract

Extracting the source from the Apache HTTPd tarball is a simple matter of uncompressing, and then untarring:

```
$ gzip -d httpd-NN.tar.gz
$ tar xvf httpd-NN.tar
```

This will create a new directory under the current directory containing the source code for the distribution. You should `cd` into that directory before proceeding with compiling the server.

## 5.5. Configuring the source tree

The next step is to configure the Apache HTTPd source tree for your particular platform and personal requirements. This is done using the script `configure` included in the root directory of the distribution. (Developers downloading an unreleased version of the Apache HTTPd source tree will need to have `autoconf` and `libtool` installed and will need to run `buildconf` before proceeding with the next steps. This is not necessary for official releases.)

To configure the source tree using all the default options, simply type `./configure`. To change the default options, `configure` accepts a variety of variables and command line options.

The most important option is the location `--prefix` where the Apache HTTP Server is to be installed later, because Apache HTTPd has to be configured for this location to work correctly. More fine-tuned control of the location of files is possible with additional *configure options*.

Also at this point, you can specify which *features* you want included in Apache HTTPd by enabling and disabling *modules*. The Apache HTTP Server comes with a *Base* set of modules included by default. Other modules are enabled using the `--enable-`*module* option, where *module* is the name of the module with the `mod_` string removed and with any underscore converted to a dash. You can also choose to compile modules as *shared objects (DSOs)* -- which can be loaded or unloaded at runtime -- by using the option `--enable-`*module*`=shared`. Similarly, you can disable Base modules with the `--disable-`*module* option. Be careful when using these options, since `configure` cannot warn you if the module you specify does not exist; it will simply ignore the option.

In addition, it is sometimes necessary to provide the `configure` script with extra information about the location of your compiler, libraries, or header files. This is done by

---

[8] *http://httpd.apache.org/dev/verification.html*

---

passing either environment variables or command line options to *configure*. For more information, see the *configure* manual page.

For a short impression of what possibilities you have, here is a typical example which compiles Apache for the installation tree /sw/pkg/apache with a particular compiler and flags plus the two additional modules <u>mod_rewrite</u> and <u>mod_speling</u> for later loading through the DSO mechanism:

```
$ CC="pgcc" CFLAGS="-O2" \
./configure --prefix=/sw/pkg/apache \
--enable-rewrite=shared \
--enable-speling=shared
```

When *configure* is run it will take several minutes to test for the availability of features on your system and build Makefiles which will later be used to compile the server.

Details on all the different *configure* options are available on the *configure* manual page.

## 5.6. Build

Now you can build the various parts which form the Apache HTTPd package by simply running the command:

```
$ make
```

Please be patient here, since a base configuration takes several minutes to compile and the time will vary widely depending on your hardware and the number of modules that you have enabled.

## 5.7. Install

Now it's time to install the package under the configured installation *PREFIX* (see -- prefix option above) by running:

```
$ make install
```

If you are upgrading, the installation will not overwrite your configuration files or documents.

## 5.8. Customize

Next, you can customize your Apache HTTP Server by editing the *configuration files* under *PREFIX*/conf/.

```
$ vi PREFIX/conf/httpd.conf
```

Have a look at the Apache HTTP Server manual under *docs/manual/* or consult
*http://httpd.apache.org/docs/2.2/* for the most recent version of this manual and a complete
reference of available *configuration directives.*

## 5.9. Test

Now you can *start* your Apache HTTP Server by immediately running:

```
$ PREFIX/bin/apachectl -k start
```

and then you should be able to request your first document via URL `http://localhost/`.
The web page you see is located under the `DocumentRoot`, which will usually be
*PREFIX/*`htdocs/`. Then *stop* the server again by running:

```
$ PREFIX/bin/apachectl -k stop
```

## 5.10. Upgrading

The first step in upgrading is to read the release announcement and the file `CHANGES` in the
source distribution to find any changes that may affect your site. When changing between
major releases (for example, from 1.3 to 2.0 or from 2.0 to 2.2), there will likely be major
differences in the compile-time and run-time configuration that will require manual
adjustments. All modules will also need to be upgraded to accomodate changes in the
module API.

Upgrading from one minor version to the next (for example, from 2.2.55 to 2.2.57) is easier.
The `make install` process will not overwrite any of your existing documents, log files, or
configuration files. In addition, the developers make every effort to avoid incompatible
changes in the `configure` options, run-time configuration, or the module API between
minor versions. In most cases you should be able to use an identical `configure` command
line, an identical configuration file, and all of your modules should continue to work.

To upgrade across minor versions, start by finding the file `config.nice` in the `build`
directory of your installed server or at the root of the source tree for your old install. This
will contain the exact `configure` command line that you used to configure the source tree.
Then to upgrade from one version to the next, you need only copy the `config.nice` file to
the source tree of the new version, edit it to make any desired changes, and then run:

```
$ ./config.nice
$ make
$ make install
$ PREFIX/bin/apachectl -k graceful-stop
$ PREFIX/bin/apachectl -k start
```

You should always test any new version in your environment before putting it into production. For example, you can install and run the new version along side the old one by using a different --prefix and a different port (by adjusting the Listen directive) to test for any incompatibilities before doing the final upgrade.

# Chapter 6.
# Starting Apache

On Windows, Apache is normally run as a service on Windows NT, 2000 and XP, or as a console application on Windows 9x and ME. For details, see *Running Apache as a Service* and *Running Apache as a Console Application*.

On Unix, the *httpd* program is run as a daemon that executes continuously in the background to handle requests. This document describes how to invoke *httpd*.

## 6.1. How Apache Starts

If the Listen specified in the configuration file is default of 80 (or any other port below 1024), then it is necessary to have root privileges in order to start apache, so that it can bind to this privileged port. Once the server has started and performed a few preliminary activities such as opening its log files, it will launch several *child* processes which do the work of listening for and answering requests from clients. The main httpd process continues to run as the root user, but the child processes run as a less privileged user. This is controlled by the selected *Multi-Processing Module*.

The recommended method of invoking the *httpd* executable is to use the *apachectl* control script. This script sets certain environment variables that are necessary for *httpd* to function correctly under some operating systems, and then invokes the *httpd* binary. *apachectl* will pass through any command line arguments, so any *httpd* options may also be used with *apachectl*. You may also directly edit the *apachectl* script by changing the HTTPD variable near the top to specify the correct location of the *httpd* binary and any command-line arguments that you wish to be *always* present.

The first thing that *httpd* does when it is invoked is to locate and read the *configuration file* httpd.conf. The location of this file is set at compile-time, but it is possible to specify its location at run time using the -f command-line option as in

```
/usr/local/apache2/bin/apachectl -f /usr/local/apache2/conf/httpd.conf
```

If all goes well during startup, the server will detach from the terminal and the command prompt will return almost immediately. This indicates that the server is up and running.

You can then use your browser to connect to the server and view the test page in the `DocumentRoot` directory.

## 6.2. Errors During Start-up

If Apache suffers a fatal problem during startup, it will write a message describing the problem either to the console or to the `ErrorLog` before exiting. One of the most common error messages is "`Unable to bind to Port ...`". This message is usually caused by either:

- Trying to start the server on a privileged port when not logged in as the root user; or
- Trying to start the server when there is another instance of Apache or some other web server already bound to the same Port.

For further trouble-shooting instructions, consult the Apache *FAQ*.

## 6.3. Starting at Boot-Time

If you want your server to continue running after a system reboot, you should add a call to *apachectl* to your system startup files (typically `rc.local` or a file in an `rc.N` directory). This will start Apache as root. Before doing this ensure that your server is properly configured for security and access restrictions.

The *apachectl* script is designed to act like a standard SysV init script; it can take the arguments `start`, `restart`, and `stop` and translate them into the appropriate signals to *httpd*. So you can often simply link *apachectl* into the appropriate init directory. But be sure to check the exact requirements of your system.

## 6.4. Additional Information

Additional information about the command-line options of *httpd* and *apachectl* as well as other support programs included with the server is available on the *Server and Supporting Programs* page. There is also documentation on all the *modules* included with the Apache distribution and the *directives* that they provide.

# Chapter 7.
# Stopping and Restarting

This document covers stopping and restarting Apache on Unix-like systems. Windows NT, 2000 and XP users should see *Running Apache as a Service* and Windows 9x and ME users should see *Running Apache as a Console Application* for information on how to control Apache on those platforms.

## 7.1. Introduction

In order to stop or restart Apache, you must send a signal to the running *httpd* processes. There are two ways to send the signals. First, you can use the unix kill command to directly send signals to the processes. You will notice many *httpd* executables running on your system, but you should not send signals to any of them except the parent, whose pid is in the PidFile. That is to say you shouldn't ever need to send signals to any process except the parent. There are four signals that you can send the parent: *TERM, USR1, HUP,* and *WINCH,* which will be described in a moment.

To send a signal to the parent you should issue a command such as:

```
kill -TERM `cat /usr/local/apache2/logs/httpd.pid`
```

The second method of signaling the *httpd* processes is to use the -k command line options: stop, restart, graceful and graceful-stop, as described below. These are arguments to the *httpd* binary, but we recommend that you send them using the *apachectl* control script, which will pass them through to *httpd*.

After you have signaled *httpd*, you can read about its progress by issuing:

```
tail -f /usr/local/apache2/logs/error_log
```

Modify those examples to match your ServerRoot and PidFile settings.

## 7.2. Stop Now

**Signal: TERM**

```
apachectl -k stop
```

Sending the TERM or stop signal to the parent causes it to immediately attempt to kill off all of its children. It may take it several seconds to complete killing off its children. Then the parent itself exits. Any requests in progress are terminated, and no further requests are served.

## 7.3. Graceful Restart

**Signal: USR1**

```
apachectl -k graceful
```

The USR1 or graceful signal causes the parent process to *advise* the children to exit after their current request (or to exit immediately if they're not serving anything). The parent re-reads its configuration files and re-opens its log files. As each child dies off the parent replaces it with a child from the new *generation* of the configuration, which begins serving new requests immediately.

This code is designed to always respect the process control directive of the MPMs, so the number of processes and threads available to serve clients will be maintained at the appropriate values throughout the restart process. Furthermore, it respects StartServers in the following manner: if after one second at least StartServers new children have not been created, then create enough to pick up the slack. Hence the code tries to maintain both the number of children appropriate for the current load on the server, and respect your wishes with the StartServers parameter.

Users of mod_status will notice that the server statistics are **not** set to zero when a USR1 is sent. The code was written to both minimize the time in which the server is unable to serve new requests (they will be queued up by the operating system, so they're not lost in any event) and to respect your tuning parameters. In order to do this it has to keep the *scoreboard* used to keep track of all children across generations.

The status module will also use a G to indicate those children which are still serving requests started before the graceful restart was given.

At present there is no way for a log rotation script using USR1 to know for certain that all children writing the pre-restart log have finished. We suggest that you use a suitable delay after sending the USR1 signal before you do anything with the old log. For example if most of your hits take less than 10 minutes to complete for users on low bandwidth links then you could wait 15 minutes before doing anything with the old log.

If your configuration file has errors in it when you issue a restart then your parent will not restart, it will exit with an error. In the case of graceful restarts it will also leave children running when it exits. (These are the children which are "gracefully exiting" by handling their last request.) This will cause problems if you attempt to restart the server -- it will not be able to bind to its listening ports. Before doing a restart, you can check the syntax of the configuration files with the `-t` command line argument (see *httpd*). This still will not guarantee that the server will restart correctly. To check the semantics of the configuration files as well as the syntax, you can try starting *httpd* as a non-root user. If there are no errors it will attempt to open its sockets and logs and fail because it's not root (or because the currently running *httpd* already has those ports bound). If it fails for any other reason then it's probably a config file error and the error should be fixed before issuing the graceful restart.

## 7.4. Restart Now

**Signal: HUP**

```
apachectl -k restart
```

Sending the `HUP` or `restart` signal to the parent causes it to kill off its children like in `TERM`, but the parent doesn't exit. It re-reads its configuration files, and re-opens any log files. Then it spawns a new set of children and continues serving hits.

Users of <u>mod_status</u> will notice that the server statistics are set to zero when a `HUP` is sent.

If your configuration file has errors in it when you issue a restart then your parent will not restart, it will exit with an error. See above for a method of avoiding this.

## 7.5. Graceful Stop

**Signal: WINCH**

```
apachectl -k graceful-stop
```

The `WINCH` or `graceful-stop` signal causes the parent process to *advise* the children to exit after their current request (or to exit immediately if they're not serving anything). The parent will then remove its <u>PidFile</u> and cease listening on all ports. The parent will continue to run, and monitor children which are handling requests. Once all children have finalised and exited or the timeout specified by the <u>GracefulShutdownTimeout</u> has been reached, the parent will also exit. If the timeout is reached, any remaining children will be sent the `TERM` signal to force them to exit.

A `TERM` signal will immediately terminate the parent process and all children when in the "graceful" state. However as the <u>PidFile</u> will have been removed, you will not be able to use `apachectl` or `httpd` to send this signal.

The `graceful-stop` signal allows you to run multiple identically configured instances of *httpd* at the same time. This is a powerful feature when performing graceful upgrades of Apache, however it can also cause deadlocks and race conditions with some configurations.

Care has been taken to ensure that on-disk files such as the `Lockfile` and `ScriptSock` files contain the server PID, and should coexist without problem. However, if a configuration directive, third-party module or persistent CGI utilises any other on-disk lock or state files, care should be taken to ensure that multiple running instances of *httpd* do not clobber each others files.

You should also be wary of other potential race conditions, such as using *rotatelogs* style piped logging. Multiple running instances of *rotatelogs* attempting to rotate the same logfiles at the same time may destroy each other's logfiles.

# Chapter 8.
# Configuration Files

This document describes the files used to configure the Apache HTTP server.

## 8.1. Main Configuration Files

| Related Modules | Related Directives |
|---|---|
| mod_mime | <IfDefine><br>Include<br>TypesConfig |

Apache is configured by placing *directives* in plain text configuration files. The main configuration file is usually called httpd.conf. The location of this file is set at compile-time, but may be overridden with the -f command line flag. In addition, other configuration files may be added using the Include directive, and wildcards can be used to include many configuration files. Any directive may be placed in any of these configuration files. Changes to the main configuration files are only recognized by Apache when it is started or restarted.

The server also reads a file containing mime document types; the filename is set by the TypesConfig directive, and is mime.types by default.

## 8.2. Syntax of the Configuration Files

Apache configuration files contain one directive per line. The back-slash "\" may be used as the last character on a line to indicate that the directive continues onto the next line. There must be no other characters or white space between the back-slash and the end of the line.

Directives in the configuration files are case-insensitive, but arguments to directives are often case sensitive. Lines that begin with the hash character "#" are considered comments, and are ignored. Comments may **not** be included on a line after a configuration directive. Blank lines and white space occurring before a directive are ignored, so you may indent directives for clarity.

The values of shell environment variables can be used in configuration file lines using the syntax ${ENVVAR}. If "ENVVAR" is the name of a valid environment variable, the value of that variable is substituted into that spot in the configuration file line, and processing continues as if that text were found directly in the configuration file. (If the ENVVAR variable is not found, the characters "${ENVVAR}" are left unchanged for use by later stages in the config file processing.)

The maximum length of a line in the configuration file, after environment-variable substitution, joining any continued lines and removing leading and trailing white space, is 8192 characters.

You can check your configuration files for syntax errors without starting the server by using `apachectl configtest` or the `-t` command line option.

## 8.3. Modules

| Related Modules | Related Directives |
|---|---|
| mod_so | `<IfModule>` |
| | `LoadModule` |

Apache is a modular server. This implies that only the most basic functionality is included in the core server. Extended features are available through *modules* which can be loaded into Apache. By default, a *base* set of modules is included in the server at compile-time. If the server is compiled to use *dynamically loaded* modules, then modules can be compiled separately and added at any time using the `LoadModule` directive. Otherwise, Apache must be recompiled to add or remove modules. Configuration directives may be included conditional on a presence of a particular module by enclosing them in an `<IfModule>` block.

To see which modules are currently compiled into the server, you can use the `-l` command line option.

## 8.4. Scope of Directives

| Related Modules | Related Directives |
|---|---|
| | `<Directory>` |
| | `<DirectoryMatch>` |
| | `<Files>` |
| | `<FilesMatch>` |
| | `<Location>` |
| | `<LocationMatch>` |
| | `<VirtualHost>` |

Directives placed in the main configuration files apply to the entire server. If you wish to change the configuration for only a part of the server, you can scope your directives by placing them in `<Directory>`, `<DirectoryMatch>`, `<Files>`, `<FilesMatch>`, `<Location>`, and `<LocationMatch>` sections. These sections limit the application of the directives which they enclose to particular filesystem locations or URLs. They can also be nested, allowing for very fine grained configuration.

Apache has the capability to serve many different websites simultaneously. This is called *Virtual Hosting*. Directives can also be scoped by placing them inside `<VirtualHost>` sections, so that they will only apply to requests for a particular website.

Although most directives can be placed in any of these sections, some directives do not make sense in some contexts. For example, directives controlling process creation can only be placed in the main server context. To find which directives can be placed in which sections, check the *Context* of the directive. For further information, we provide details on *How Directory, Location and Files sections work.*

## 8.5. .htaccess Files

| Related Modules | Related Directives |
|---|---|
|  | AccessFileName |
|  | AllowOverride |

Apache allows for decentralized management of configuration via special files placed inside the web tree. The special files are usually called `.htaccess`, but any name can be specified in the `AccessFileName` directive. Directives placed in `.htaccess` files apply to the directory where you place the file, and all sub-directories. The `.htaccess` files follow the same syntax as the main configuration files. Since `.htaccess` files are read on every request, changes made in these files take immediate effect.

To find which directives can be placed in `.htaccess` files, check the *Context* of the directive. The server administrator further controls what directives may be placed in `.htaccess` files by configuring the `AllowOverride` directive in the main configuration files.

For more information on `.htaccess` files, see the *.htaccess tutorial*.

# Chapter 9.

# Configuration Sections

Directives in the *configuration files* may apply to the entire server, or they may be restricted to apply only to particular directories, files, hosts, or URLs. This document describes how to use configuration section containers or .htaccess files to change the scope of other configuration directives.

## 9.1. Types of Configuration Section Containers

| Related Modules | Related Directives |
|---|---|
| core | <Directory> |
| mod_version | <DirectoryMatch> |
| mod_proxy | <Files> |
| | <FilesMatch> |
| | <IfDefine> |
| | <IfModule> |
| | <IfVersion> |
| | <Location> |
| | <LocationMatch> |
| | <Proxy> |
| | <ProxyMatch> |
| | <VirtualHost> |

There are two basic types of containers. Most containers are evaluated for each request. The enclosed directives are applied only for those requests that match the containers. The <IfDefine>, <IfModule>, and <IfVersion> containers, on the other hand, are evaluated only at server startup and restart. If their conditions are true at startup, then the enclosed directives will apply to all requests. If the conditions are not true, the enclosed directives will be ignored.

The <IfDefine> directive encloses directives that will only be applied if an appropriate parameter is defined on the httpd command line. For example, with the following configuration, all requests will be redirected to another site only if the server is started using httpd -DClosedForNow:

```
<IfDefine ClosedForNow>
Redirect / http://otherserver.example.com/
</IfDefine>
```

The `<IfModule>` directive is very similar, except it encloses directives that will only be applied if a particular module is available in the server. The module must either be statically compiled in the server, or it must be dynamically compiled and its `LoadModule` line must be earlier in the configuration file. This directive should only be used if you need your configuration file to work whether or not certain modules are installed. It should not be used to enclose directives that you want to work all the time, because it can suppress useful error messages about missing modules.

In the following example, the `MimeMagicFiles` directive will be applied only if `mod_mime_magic` is available.

```
<IfModule mod_mime_magic.c>
MimeMagicFile conf/magic
</IfModule>
```

The `<IfVersion>` directive is very similar to `<IfDefine>` and `<IfModule>`, except it encloses directives that will only be applied if a particular version of the server is executing. This module is designed for the use in test suites and large networks which have to deal with different httpd versions and different configurations.

```
<IfVersion >= 2.1>
# this happens only in versions greater or
# equal 2.1.0.
</IfVersion>
```

`<IfDefine>`, `<IfModule>`, and the `<IfVersion>` can apply negative conditions by preceding their test with "!". Also, these sections can be nested to achieve more complex restrictions.

## 9.2. Filesystem and Webspace

The most commonly used configuration section containers are the ones that change the configuration of particular places in the filesystem or webspace. First, it is important to understand the difference between the two. The filesystem is the view of your disks as seen by your operating system. For example, in a default install, Apache resides at `/usr/local/apache2` in the Unix filesystem or `"c:/Program Files/Apache Group/Apache2"` in the Windows filesystem. (Note that forward slashes should always be used as the path separator in Apache, even for Windows.) In contrast, the webspace is the view of your site as delivered by the web server and seen by the client. So the path `/dir/` in the webspace corresponds to the path `/usr/local/apache2/htdocs/dir/` in the filesystem of a default Apache install on Unix. The webspace need not map directly to the filesystem, since webpages may be generated dynamically from databases or other locations.

## 9.2.1. Filesystem Containers

The <u><Directory></u> and <u><Files></u> directives, along with their *regex* counterparts, apply directives to parts of the filesystem. Directives enclosed in a <u><Directory></u> section apply to the named filesystem directory and all subdirectories of that directory. The same effect can be obtained using *.htaccess files*. For example, in the following configuration, directory indexes will be enabled for the `/var/web/dir1` directory and all subdirectories.

```
<Directory /var/web/dir1>
Options +Indexes
</Directory>
```

Directives enclosed in a `<Files>` section apply to any file with the specified name, regardless of what directory it lies in. So for example, the following configuration directives will, when placed in the main section of the configuration file, deny access to any file named `private.html` regardless of where it is found.

```
<Files private.html>
Order allow,deny
Deny from all
</Files>
```

To address files found in a particular part of the filesystem, the <u><Files></u> and <u><Directory></u> sections can be combined. For example, the following configuration will deny access to `/var/web/dir1/private.html`, `/var/web/dir1/subdir2/private.html`, `/var/web/dir1/subdir3/private.html`, and any other instance of `private.html` found under the `/var/web/dir1/` directory.

```
<Directory /var/web/dir1>
<Files private.html>
Order allow,deny
Deny from all
</Files>
</Directory>
```

## 9.2.2. Webspace Containers

The `<Location>` directive and its *regex* counterpart, on the other hand, change the configuration for content in the webspace. For example, the following configuration prevents access to any URL-path that begins in /private. In particular, it will apply to requests for `http://yoursite.example.com/private`, `http://yoursite.example.com/private123`, and `http://yoursite.example.com/private/dir/file.html` as well as any other requests starting with the `/private` string.

```
<Location /private>
Order Allow,Deny
Deny from all
</Location>
```

The `<Location>` directive need not have anything to do with the filesystem. For example, the following example shows how to map a particular URL to an internal Apache handler provided by `mod_status`. No file called `server-status` needs to exist in the filesystem.

```
<Location /server-status>
SetHandler server-status
</Location>
```

## 9.2.3. Wildcards and Regular Expressions

The `<Directory>`, `<Files>`, and `<Location>` directives can each use shell-style wildcard characters as in `fnmatch` from the C standard library. The character "*" matches any sequence of characters, "?" matches any single character, and "[seq]" matches any character in *seq*. The "/" character will not be matched by any wildcard; it must be specified explicitly.

If even more flexible matching is required, each container has a regular expression (regex) counterpart `<DirectoryMatch>`, `<FilesMatch>`, and `<LocationMatch>` that allow perl-compatible *regular expressions* to be used in choosing the matches. But see the section below on configuration merging to find out how using regex sections will change how directives are applied.

A non-regex wildcard section that changes the configuration of all user directories could look as follows:

```
<Directory /home/*/public_html>
Options Indexes
</Directory>
```

Using regex sections, we can deny access to many types of image files at once:

```
<FilesMatch \.(?i:gif|jpe?g|png)$>
Order allow,deny
Deny from all
</FilesMatch>
```

## 9.2.4. What to use When

Choosing between filesystem containers and webspace containers is actually quite easy. When applying directives to objects that reside in the filesystem always use `<Directory>` or `<Files>`. When applying directives to objects that do not reside in the filesystem (such as a webpage generated from a database), use `<Location>`.

It is important to never use <Location> when trying to restrict access to objects in the filesystem. This is because many different webspace locations (URLs) could map to the same filesystem location, allowing your restrictions to be circumvented. For example, consider the following configuration:

```
<Location /dir/>
Order allow,deny
Deny from all
</Location>
```

This works fine if the request is for http://yoursite.example.com/dir/. But what if you are on a case-insensitive filesystem? Then your restriction could be easily circumvented by requesting http://yoursite.example.com/DIR/. The <Directory> directive, in contrast, will apply to any content served from that location, regardless of how it is called. (An exception is filesystem links. The same directory can be placed in more than one part of the filesystem using symbolic links. The <Directory> directive will follow the symbolic link without resetting the pathname. Therefore, for the highest level of security, symbolic links should be disabled with the appropriate Options directive.)

If you are, perhaps, thinking that none of this applies to you because you use a case-sensitive filesystem, remember that there are many other ways to map multiple webspace locations to the same filesystem location. Therefore you should always use the filesystem containers when you can. There is, however, one exception to this rule. Putting configuration restrictions in a <Location /> section is perfectly safe because this section will apply to all requests regardless of the specific URL.

## 9.3. Virtual Hosts

The <VirtualHost> container encloses directives that apply to specific hosts. This is useful when serving multiple hosts from the same machine with a different configuration for each. For more information, see the *Virtual Host Documentation*.

## 9.4. Proxy

The <Proxy> and <ProxyMatch> containers apply enclosed configuration directives only to sites accessed through mod_proxy's proxy server that match the specified URL. For example, the following configuration will prevent the proxy server from being used to access the cnn.com website.

```
<Proxy http://cnn.com/*>
Order allow,deny
Deny from all
</Proxy>
```

## 9.5. What Directives are Allowed?

To find out what directives are allowed in what types of configuration sections, check the *Context* of the directive. Everything that is allowed in `<Directory>` sections is also syntactically allowed in `<DirectoryMatch>`, `<Files>`, `<FilesMatch>`, `<Location>`, `<LocationMatch>`, `<Proxy>`, and `<ProxyMatch>` sections. There are some exceptions, however:

- The AllowOverride directive works only in <Directory> sections.
- The `FollowSymLinks` and `SymLinksIfOwnerMatch` Options work only in <Directory> sections or `.htaccess` files.
- The Options directive cannot be used in <Files> and <FilesMatch> sections.

## 9.6. How the sections are merged

The configuration sections are applied in a very particular order. Since this can have important effects on how configuration directives are interpreted, it is important to understand how this works.

The order of merging is:

1. <Directory> (except regular expressions) and `.htaccess` done simultaneously (with `.htaccess`, if allowed, overriding <Directory>)
2. <DirectoryMatch> (and `<Directory ~>`)
3. <Files> and <FilesMatch> done simultaneously
4. <Location> and <LocationMatch> done simultaneously

Apart from `<Directory>`, each group is processed in the order that they appear in the configuration files. `<Directory>` (group 1 above) is processed in the order shortest directory component to longest. So for example, `<Directory /var/web/dir>` will be processed before `<Directory /var/web/dir/subdir>`. If multiple `<Directory>` sections apply to the same directory they are processed in the configuration file order. Configurations included via the `Include` directive will be treated as if they were inside the including file at the location of the `Include` directive.

Sections inside `<VirtualHost>` sections are applied *after* the corresponding sections outside the virtual host definition. This allows virtual hosts to override the main server configuration.

When the request is served by mod_proxy, the `<Proxy>` container takes the place of the `<Directory>` container in the processing order.

Later sections override earlier ones.

**Technical Note**

There is actually a <Location>/<LocationMatch> sequence performed just
before the name translation phase (where Aliases and DocumentRoots are used
to map URLs to filenames). The results of this sequence are completely thrown away
after the translation has completed.

## Some Examples

Below is an artificial example to show the order of merging. Assuming they all apply to the
request, the directives in this example will be applied in the order A > B > C > D > E.

```
<Location />
E
</Location>

<Files f.html>
D
</Files>

<VirtualHost *>
<Directory /a/b>
B
</Directory>
</VirtualHost>

<DirectoryMatch "^.*b$">
C
</DirectoryMatch>

<Directory /a/b>
A
</Directory>
```

For a more concrete example, consider the following. Regardless of any access restrictions
placed in <u>&lt;Directory&gt;</u> sections, the <u>&lt;Location&gt;</u> section will be evaluated last and will allow
unrestricted access to the server. In other words, order of merging is important, so be
careful!

```
<Location />
Order deny,allow
Allow from all
</Location>

# Woops! This <Directory> section will have no effect
<Directory />
Order allow,deny
Allow from all
Deny from badguy.example.com
</Directory>
```

# Chapter 10.
# Caching Guide

This document supplements the `mod_cache`, `mod_disk_cache`, `mod_mem_cache`, `mod_file_cache` and *htcacheclean* reference documentation. It describes how to use Apache's caching features to accelerate web and proxy serving, while avoiding common problems and misconfigurations.

## 10.1. Introduction

As of Apache HTTP server version 2.2 `mod_cache` and `mod_file_cache` are no longer marked experimental and are considered suitable for production use. These caching architectures provide a powerful means to accelerate HTTP handling, both as an origin webserver and as a proxy.

`mod_cache` and its provider modules `mod_mem_cache` and `mod_disk_cache` provide intelligent, HTTP-aware caching. The content itself is stored in the cache, and mod_cache aims to honour all of the various HTTP headers and options that control the cachability of content. It can handle both local and proxied content. `mod_cache` is aimed at both simple and complex caching configurations, where you are dealing with proxied content, dynamic local content or have a need to speed up access to local files which change with time.

`mod_file_cache` on the other hand presents a more basic, but sometimes useful, form of caching. Rather than maintain the complexity of actively ensuring the cachability of URLs, `mod_file_cache` offers file-handle and memory-mapping tricks to keep a cache of files as they were when Apache was last started. As such, `mod_file_cache` is aimed at improving the access time to local static files which do not change very often.

As `mod_file_cache` presents a relatively simple caching implementation, apart from the specific sections on `CacheFile` and `MMapFile`, the explanations in this guide cover the `mod_cache` caching architecture.

To get the most from this document, you should be familiar with the basics of HTTP, and have read the Users' Guides to *Mapping URLs to the Filesystem* and *Content negotiation*.

## 10.2. Caching Overview

| Related Modules | Related Directives |
|---|---|
| mod_cache | CacheEnable |
| mod_mem_cache | CacheDisable |
| mod_disk_cache | CacheFile |
| mod_file_cache | MMapFile |
| | UseCanonicalName |
| | CacheNegotiatedDocs |

There are two main stages in mod_cache that can occur in the lifetime of a request. First, mod_cache is a URL mapping module, which means that if a URL has been cached, and the cached version of that URL has not expired, the request will be served directly by mod_cache.

This means that any other stages that might ordinarily happen in the process of serving a request -- for example being handled by mod_proxy, or mod_rewrite -- won't happen. But then this is the point of caching content in the first place.

If the URL is not found within the cache, mod_cache will add a *filter* to the request handling. After Apache has located the content by the usual means, the filter will be run as the content is served. If the content is determined to be cacheable, the content will be saved to the cache for future serving.

If the URL is found within the cache, but also found to have expired, the filter is added anyway, but mod_cache will create a conditional request to the backend, to determine if the cached version is still current. If the cached version is still current, its meta-information will be updated and the request will be served from the cache. If the cached version is no longer current, the cached version will be deleted and the filter will save the updated content to the cache as it is served.

### 10.2.1. Improving Cache Hits

When caching locally generated content, ensuring that UseCanonicalName is set to On can dramatically improve the ratio of cache hits. This is because the hostname of the virtual-host serving the content forms a part of the cache key. With the setting set to On virtual-hosts with multiple server names or aliases will not produce differently cached entities, and instead content will be cached as per the canonical hostname.

Because caching is performed within the URL to filename translation phase, cached documents will only be served in response to URL requests. Ordinarily this is of little consequence, but there is one circumstance in which it matters: If you are using *Server Side Includes*;

```
<!-- The following include can be cached -->
<!--#include virtual="/footer.html" -->

<!-- The following include can not be cached -->
<!--#include file="/path/to/footer.html" -->
```

If you are using Server Side Includes, and want the benefit of speedy serves from the cache, you should use `virtual` include types.

## 10.2.2. Expiry Periods

The default expiry period for cached entities is one hour, however this can be easily overridden by using the `CacheDefaultExpire` directive. This default is only used when the original source of the content does not specify an expire time or time of last modification.

If a response does not include an `Expires` header but does include a `Last-Modified` header, `mod_cache` can infer an expiry period based on the use of the `CacheLastModifiedFactor` directive.

For local content, `mod_expires` may be used to fine-tune the expiry period.

The maximum expiry period may also be controlled by using the `CacheMaxExpire`.

## 10.2.3. A Brief Guide to Conditional Requests

When content expires from the cache and is re-requested from the backend or content provider, rather than pass on the original request, Apache will use a conditional request instead.

HTTP offers a number of headers which allow a client, or cache to discern between different versions of the same content. For example if a resource was served with an "Etag:" header, it is possible to make a conditional request with an "If-None-Match:" header. If a resource was served with a "Last-Modified:" header it is possible to make a conditional request with an "If-Modified-Since:" header, and so on.

When such a conditional request is made, the response differs depending on whether the content matches the conditions. If a request is made with an "If-Modified-Since:" header, and the content has not been modified since the time indicated in the request then a terse "304 Not Modified" response is issued.

If the content has changed, then it is served as if the request were not conditional to begin with.

The benefits of conditional requests in relation to caching are twofold. Firstly, when making such a request to the backend, if the content from the backend matches the content in the store, this can be determined easily and without the overhead of transferring the entire resource.

Secondly, conditional requests are usually less strenuous on the backend. For static files, typically all that is involved is a call to `stat()` or similar system call, to see if the file has changed in size or modification time. As such, even if Apache is caching local content, even expired content may still be served faster from the cache if it has not changed. As long as reading from the cache store is faster than reading from the backend (e.g. an in-memory cache compared to reading from disk).

## 10.2.4. What Can be Cached?

As mentioned already, the two styles of caching in Apache work differently, `mod_file_cache` caching maintains file contents as they were when Apache was started. When a request is made for a file that is cached by this module, it is intercepted and the cached file is served.

`mod_cache` caching on the other hand is more complex. When serving a request, if it has not been cached previously, the caching module will determine if the content is cacheable. The conditions for determining cachability of a response are;

1.  Caching must be enabled for this URL. See the `CacheEnable` and `CacheDisable` directives.
2.  The response must have a HTTP status code of 200, 203, 300, 301 or 410.
3.  The request must be a HTTP GET request.
4.  If the request contains an "Authorization:" header, the response will not be cached.
5.  If the response contains an "Authorization:" header, it must also contain an "s-maxage", "must-revalidate" or "public" option in the "Cache-Control:" header.
6.  If the URL included a query string (e.g. from a HTML form GET method) it will not be cached unless the response specifies an explicit expiration by including an "Expires:" header or the max-age or s-maxage directive of the "Cache-Control:" header, as per RFC2616 sections 13.9 and 13.2.1.
7.  If the response has a status of 200 (OK), the response must also include at least one of the "Etag", "Last-Modified" or the "Expires" headers, or the max-age or s-maxage directive of the "Cache-Control:" header, unless the `CacheIgnoreNoLastMod` directive has been used to require otherwise.
8.  If the response includes the "private" option in a "Cache-Control:" header, it will not be stored unless the `CacheStorePrivate` has been used to require otherwise.
9.  Likewise, if the response includes the "no-store" option in a "Cache-Control:" header, it will not be stored unless the `CacheStoreNoStore` has been used.
10. A response will not be stored if it includes a "Vary:" header containing the match-all "*".

## 10.2.5. What Should Not be Cached?

In short, any content which is highly time-sensitive, or which varies depending on the particulars of the request that are not covered by HTTP negotiation, should not be cached.

If you have dynamic content which changes depending on the IP address of the requester, or changes every 5 minutes, it should almost certainly not be cached.

If on the other hand, the content served differs depending on the values of various HTTP headers, it might be possible to cache it intelligently through the use of a "Vary" header.

## 10.2.6. Variable/Negotiated Content

If a response with a "Vary" header is received by mod_cache when requesting content by the backend it will attempt to handle it intelligently. If possible, mod_cache will detect the headers attributed in the "Vary" response in future requests and serve the correct cached response.

If for example, a response is received with a vary header such as;

```
Vary: negotiate,accept-language,accept-charset
```

mod_cache will only serve the cached content to requesters with accept-language and accept-charset headers matching those of the original request.

## 10.3. Security Considerations

### 10.3.1. Authorization and Access Control

Using mod_cache is very much like having a built in reverse-proxy. Requests will be served by the caching module unless it determines that the backend should be queried. When caching local resources, this drastically changes the security model of Apache.

As traversing a filesystem hierarchy to examine potential .htaccess files would be a very expensive operation, partially defeating the point of caching (to speed up requests), mod_cache makes no decision about whether a cached entity is authorised for serving. In other words; if mod_cache has cached some content, it will be served from the cache as long as that content has not expired.

If, for example, your configuration permits access to a resource by IP address you should ensure that this content is not cached. You can do this by using the CacheDisable directive, or mod_expires. Left unchecked, mod_cache - very much like a reverse proxy - would cache the content when served and then serve it to any client, on any IP address.

## 10.3.2. Local exploits

As requests to end-users can be served from the cache, the cache itself can become a target for those wishing to deface or interfere with content. It is important to bear in mind that the cache must at all times be writable by the user which Apache is running as. This is in stark contrast to the usually recommended situation of maintaining all content unwritable by the Apache user.

If the Apache user is compromised, for example through a flaw in a CGI process, it is possible that the cache may be targeted. When using `mod_disk_cache`, it is relatively easy to insert or modify a cached entity.

This presents a somewhat elevated risk in comparison to the other types of attack it is possible to make as the Apache user. If you are using `mod_disk_cache` you should bear this in mind - ensure you upgrade Apache when security upgrades are announced and run CGI processes as a non-Apache user using *suEXEC* if possible.

## 10.3.3. Cache Poisoning

When running Apache as a caching proxy server, there is also the potential for so-called cache poisoning. Cache Poisoning is a broad term for attacks in which an attacker causes the proxy server to retrieve incorrect (and usually undesirable) content from the backend.

For example if the DNS servers used by your system running Apache are vulnerable to DNS cache poisoning, an attacker may be able to control where Apache connects to when requesting content from the origin server. Another example is so-called HTTP request-smuggling attacks.

This document is not the correct place for an in-depth discussion of HTTP request smuggling (instead, try your favourite search engine) however it is important to be aware that it is possible to make a series of requests, and to exploit a vulnerability on an origin webserver such that the attacker can entirely control the content retrieved by the proxy.

## 10.4. File-Handle Caching

| Related Modules | Related Directives |
|---|---|
| mod_file_cache | CacheFile |
| mod_mem_cache | CacheEnable |
| | CacheDisable |

The act of opening a file can itself be a source of delay, particularly on network filesystems. By maintaining a cache of open file descriptors for commonly served files, Apache can avoid this delay. Currently Apache provides two different implementations of File-Handle Caching.

### 10.4.1. CacheFile

The most basic form of caching present in Apache is the file-handle caching provided by `mod_file_cache`. Rather than caching file-contents, this cache maintains a table of open file descriptors. Files to be cached in this manner are specified in the configuration file using the `CacheFile` directive.

The `CacheFile` directive instructs Apache to open the file when Apache is started and to re-use this file-handle for all subsequent access to this file.

```
CacheFile /usr/local/apache2/htdocs/index.html
```

If you intend to cache a large number of files in this manner, you must ensure that your operating system's limit for the number of open files is set appropriately.

Although using `CacheFile` does not cause the file-contents to be cached per-se, it does mean that if the file changes while Apache is running these changes will not be picked up. The file will be consistently served as it was when Apache was started.

If the file is removed while Apache is running, Apache will continue to maintain an open file descriptor and serve the file as it was when Apache was started. This usually also means that although the file will have been deleted, and not show up on the filesystem, extra free space will not be recovered until Apache is stopped and the file descriptor closed.

### 10.4.2. CacheEnable fd

`mod_mem_cache` also provides its own file-handle caching scheme, which can be enabled via the `CacheEnable` directive.

```
CacheEnable fd /
```

As with all of `mod_cache` this type of file-handle caching is intelligent, and handles will not be maintained beyond the expiry time of the cached content.

## 10.5. In-Memory Caching

| Related Modules | Related Directives |
|---|---|
| mod_mem_cache | CacheEnable |
| mod_file_cache | CacheDisable |
| | MMapFile |

Serving directly from system memory is universally the fastest method of serving content. Reading files from a disk controller or, even worse, from a remote network is orders of magnitude slower. Disk controllers usually involve physical processes, and network access is limited by your available bandwidth. Memory access on the other hand can take mere nano-seconds.

System memory isn't cheap though, byte for byte it's by far the most expensive type of storage and it's important to ensure that it is used efficiently. By caching files in memory you decrease the amount of memory available on the system. As we'll see, in the case of operating system caching, this is not so much of an issue, but when using Apache's own in-memory caching it is important to make sure that you do not allocate too much memory to a cache. Otherwise the system will be forced to swap out memory, which will likely degrade performance.

## 10.5.1. Operating System Caching

Almost all modern operating systems cache file-data in memory managed directly by the kernel. This is a powerful feature, and for the most part operating systems get it right. For example, on Linux, let's look at the difference in the time it takes to read a file for the first time and the second time;

```
colm@coroebus:~$ time cat testfile > /dev/null
real     0m0.065s
user     0m0.000s
sys      0m0.001s
colm@coroebus:~$ time cat testfile > /dev/null
real     0m0.003s
user     0m0.003s
sys      0m0.000s
```

Even for this small file, there is a huge difference in the amount of time it takes to read the file. This is because the kernel has cached the file contents in memory.

By ensuring there is "spare" memory on your system, you can ensure that more and more file-contents will be stored in this cache. This can be a very efficient means of in-memory caching, and involves no extra configuration of Apache at all.

Additionally, because the operating system knows when files are deleted or modified, it can automatically remove file contents from the cache when neccessary. This is a big advantage over Apache's in-memory caching which has no way of knowing when a file has changed.

Despite the performance and advantages of automatic operating system caching there are some circumstances in which in-memory caching may be better performed by Apache.

Firstly, an operating system can only cache files it knows about. If you are running Apache as a proxy server, the files you are caching are not locally stored but remotely served. If you still want the unbeatable speed of in-memory caching, Apache's own memory caching is needed.

## 10.5.2. MMapFile Caching

`mod_file_cache` provides the `MMapFile` directive, which allows you to have Apache map a static file's contents into memory at start time (using the mmap system call). Apache will use the in-memory contents for all subsequent accesses to this file.

```
MMapFile /usr/local/apache2/htdocs/index.html
```

As with the `CacheFile` directive, any changes in these files will not be picked up by Apache after it has started.

The `MMapFile` directive does not keep track of how much memory it allocates, so you must ensure not to over-use the directive. Each Apache child process will replicate this memory, so it is critically important to ensure that the files mapped are not so large as to cause the system to swap memory.

## 10.5.3. mod_mem_cache Caching

`mod_mem_cache` provides a HTTP-aware intelligent in-memory cache. It also uses heap memory directly, which means that even if *MMap* is not supported on your system, `mod_mem_cache` may still be able to perform caching.

Caching of this type is enabled via;

```
# Enable memory caching
CacheEnable mem /

# Limit the size of the cache to 1 Megabyte
MCacheSize 1024
```

## 10.6. Disk-based Caching

| Related Modules | Related Directives |
|-----------------|--------------------|
| mod_disk_cache | CacheEnable |
| | CacheDisable |

`mod_disk_cache` provides a disk-based caching mechanism for `mod_cache`. As with `mod_mem_cache` this cache is intelligent and content will be served from the cache only as long as it is considered valid.

Typically the module will be configured as so;

```
CacheRoot    /var/cache/apache/
CacheEnable disk /
CacheDirLevels 2
CacheDirLength 1
```

Importantly, as the cached files are locally stored, operating system in-memory caching will typically be applied to their access also. So although the files are stored on disk, if they are frequently accessed it is likely the operating system will ensure that they are actually served from memory.

### 10.6.1. Understanding the Cache-Store

To store items in the cache, `mod_disk_cache` creates a 22 character hash of the URL being requested. This hash incorporates the hostname, protocol, port, path and any CGI arguments to the URL, to ensure that multiple URLs do not collide.

Each character may be any one of 64-different characters, which mean that overall there are $64^{22}$ possible hashes. For example, a URL might be hashed to `xyTGxSMO2b68mBCykqkp1w`. This hash is used as a prefix for the naming of the files specific to that URL within the cache, however first it is split up into directories as per the `CacheDirLevels` and `CacheDirLength` directives.

`CacheDirLevels` specifies how many levels of subdirectory there should be, and `CacheDirLength` specifies how many characters should be in each directory. With the example settings given above, the hash would be turned into a filename prefix as `/var/cache/apache/x/y/TGxSMO2b68mBCykqkp1w`.

The overall aim of this technique is to reduce the number of subdirectories or files that may be in a particular directory, as most file-systems slow down as this number increases. With setting of "1" for `CacheDirLength` there can at most be 64 subdirectories at any particular level. With a setting of 2 there can be 64 * 64 subdirectories, and so on. Unless you have a good reason not to, using a setting of "1" for `CacheDirLength` is recommended.

Setting `CacheDirLevels` depends on how many files you anticipate to store in the cache. With the setting of "2" used in the above example, a grand total of 4096 subdirectories can ultimately be created. With 1 million files cached, this works out at roughly 245 cached URLs per directory.

Each URL uses at least two files in the cache-store. Typically there is a ".header" file, which includes meta-information about the URL, such as when it is due to expire and a ".data" file which is a verbatim copy of the content to be served.

In the case of a content negotiated via the "Vary" header, a ".vary" directory will be created for the URL in question. This directory will have multiple ".data" files corresponding to the differently negotiated content.

### 10.6.2. Maintaining the Disk Cache

Although `mod_disk_cache` will remove cached content as it is expired, it does not maintain any information on the total size of the cache or how little free space may be left.

Instead, provided with Apache is the *htcacheclean* tool which, as the name suggests, allows you to clean the cache periodically. Determining how frequently to run *htcacheclean* and what target size to use for the cache is somewhat complex and trial and error may be needed to select optimal values.

*htcacheclean* has two modes of operation. It can be run as persistent daemon, or periodically from cron. *htcacheclean* can take up to an hour or more to process very large (tens of gigabytes) caches and if you are running it from cron it is recommended that you determine how long a typical run takes, to avoid running more than one instance at a time.

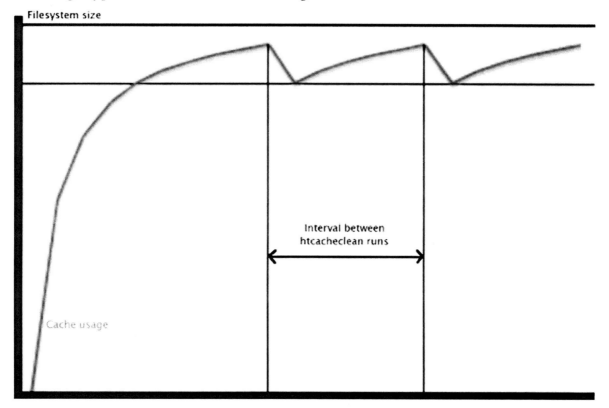

**Figure 10.1.** Typical cache growth / clean sequence

Because mod_disk_cache does not itself pay attention to how much space is used you should ensure that *htcacheclean* is configured to leave enough "grow room" following a clean.

# Chapter 11.
# Server-Wide Configuration

This document explains some of the directives provided by the core server which are used to configure the basic operations of the server.

## 11.1. Server Identification

| Related Modules | Related Directives |
|---|---|
| | ServerName |
| | ServerAdmin |
| | ServerSignature |
| | ServerTokens |
| | UseCanonicalName |
| | UseCanonicalPhysicalPort |

The ServerAdmin and ServerTokens directives control what information about the server will be presented in server-generated documents such as error messages. The ServerTokens directive sets the value of the Server HTTP response header field.

The ServerName, UseCanonicalName and UseCanonicalPhysicalPort directives are used by the server to determine how to construct self-referential URLs. For example, when a client requests a directory, but does not include the trailing slash in the directory name, Apache must redirect the client to the full name including the trailing slash so that the client will correctly resolve relative references in the document.

## 11.2. File Locations

| Related Modules | Related Directives |
|---|---|
| | CoreDumpDirectory |
| | DocumentRoot |
| | ErrorLog |
| | LockFile |
| | PidFile |

| Related Modules | Related Directives |
|---|---|
|  | `ScoreBoardFile` |
|  | `ServerRoot` |

These directives control the locations of the various files that Apache needs for proper operation. When the pathname used does not begin with a slash (/), the files are located relative to the `ServerRoot`. Be careful about locating files in paths which are writable by non-root users. See the *security tips* documentation for more details.

## 11.3. Limiting Resource Usage

| Related Modules | Related Directives |
|---|---|
|  | `LimitRequestBody` |
|  | `LimitRequestFields` |
|  | `LimitRequestFieldsize` |
|  | `LimitRequestLine` |
|  | `RLimitCPU` |
|  | `RLimitMEM` |
|  | `RLimitNPROC` |
|  | `ThreadStackSize` |

The `LimitRequest*` directives are used to place limits on the amount of resources Apache will use in reading requests from clients. By limiting these values, some kinds of denial of service attacks can be mitigated.

The `RLimit*` directives are used to limit the amount of resources which can be used by processes forked off from the Apache children. In particular, this will control resources used by CGI scripts and SSI exec commands.

The `ThreadStackSize` directive is used with some platforms to control the stack size.

# Chapter 12.
# Log Files

In order to effectively manage a web server, it is necessary to get feedback about the activity and performance of the server as well as any problems that may be occurring. The Apache HTTP Server provides very comprehensive and flexible logging capabilities. This document describes how to configure its logging capabilities, and how to understand what the logs contain.

## 12.1. Security Warning

Anyone who can write to the directory where Apache is writing a log file can almost certainly gain access to the uid that the server is started as, which is normally root. Do *NOT* give people write access to the directory the logs are stored in without being aware of the consequences; see the *security tips* document for details.

In addition, log files may contain information supplied directly by the client, without escaping. Therefore, it is possible for malicious clients to insert control-characters in the log files, so care must be taken in dealing with raw logs.

## 12.2. Error Log

| Related Modules | Related Directives |
|---|---|
| | `ErrorLog` |
| | `LogLevel` |

The server error log, whose name and location is set by the `ErrorLog` directive, is the most important log file. This is the place where Apache httpd will send diagnostic information and record any errors that it encounters in processing requests. It is the first place to look when a problem occurs with starting the server or with the operation of the server, since it will often contain details of what went wrong and how to fix it.

The error log is usually written to a file (typically `error_log` on Unix systems and `error.log` on Windows and OS/2). On Unix systems it is also possible to have the server send errors to `syslog` or *pipe them to a program*.

The format of the error log is relatively free-form and descriptive. But there is certain information that is contained in most error log entries. For example, here is a typical message.

```
[Wed Oct 11 14:32:52 2000] [error] [client 127.0.0.1] client denied by server
configuration: /export/home/live/ap/htdocs/test
```

The first item in the log entry is the date and time of the message. The second item lists the severity of the error being reported. The `LogLevel` directive is used to control the types of errors that are sent to the error log by restricting the severity level. The third item gives the IP address of the client that generated the error. Beyond that is the message itself, which in this case indicates that the server has been configured to deny the client access. The server reports the file-system path (as opposed to the web path) of the requested document.

A very wide variety of different messages can appear in the error log. Most look similar to the example above. The error log will also contain debugging output from CGI scripts. Any information written to `stderr` by a CGI script will be copied directly to the error log.

It is not possible to customize the error log by adding or removing information. However, error log entries dealing with particular requests have corresponding entries in the *access log*. For example, the above example entry corresponds to an access log entry with status code 403. Since it is possible to customize the access log, you can obtain more information about error conditions using that log file.

During testing, it is often useful to continuously monitor the error log for any problems. On Unix systems, you can accomplish this using:

```
tail -f error_log
```

## 12.3. Access Log

| Related Modules | Related Directives |
|---|---|
| mod_log_config | CustomLog |
| mod_setenvif | LogFormat |
|  | SetEnvIf |

The server access log records all requests processed by the server. The location and content of the access log are controlled by the `CustomLog` directive. The `LogFormat` directive can be used to simplify the selection of the contents of the logs. This section describes how to configure the server to record information in the access log.

Of course, storing the information in the access log is only the start of log management. The next step is to analyze this information to produce useful statistics. Log analysis in general is beyond the scope of this document, and not really part of the job of the web server itself. For more information about this topic, and for applications which perform log analysis, check the *Open Directory*[1] or *Yahoo*[2].

Various versions of Apache httpd have used other modules and directives to control access logging, including mod_log_referer, mod_log_agent, and the `TransferLog` directive. The `CustomLog` directive now subsumes the functionality of all the older directives.

The format of the access log is highly configurable. The format is specified using a format string that looks much like a C-style printf(1) format string. Some examples are presented in the next sections. For a complete list of the possible contents of the format string, see the mod_log_config *format strings*.

## 12.3.1. Common Log Format

A typical configuration for the access log might look as follows.

```
LogFormat "%h %l %u %t \"%r\" %>s %b" common
CustomLog logs/access_log common
```

This defines the *nickname* common and associates it with a particular log format string. The format string consists of percent directives, each of which tell the server to log a particular piece of information. Literal characters may also be placed in the format string and will be copied directly into the log output. The quote character (") must be escaped by placing a back-slash before it to prevent it from being interpreted as the end of the format string. The format string may also contain the special control characters "\n" for new-line and "\t" for tab.

The `CustomLog` directive sets up a new log file using the defined *nickname*. The filename for the access log is relative to the `ServerRoot` unless it begins with a slash.

The above configuration will write log entries in a format known as the Common Log Format (CLF). This standard format can be produced by many different web servers and read by many log analysis programs. The log file entries produced in CLF will look something like this:

```
127.0.0.1 - frank [10/Oct/2000:13:55:36 -0700] "GET /apache_pb.gif HTTP/1.0" 200 2326
```

Each part of this log entry is described below.

### 127.0.0.1 (%h)

This is the IP address of the client (remote host) which made the request to the server. If `HostnameLookups` is set to `On`, then the server will try to determine the hostname and

---

[1] *http://dmoz.org/Computers/Software/Internet/Site_Management/Log_analysis/*
[2] *http://dir.yahoo.com/Computers_and_Internet/Software/Internet/World_Wide_Web/Servers/Log_Analysis_Tools/*

log it in place of the IP address. However, this configuration is not recommended since it can significantly slow the server. Instead, it is best to use a log post-processor such as *logresolve* to determine the hostnames. The IP address reported here is not necessarily the address of the machine at which the user is sitting. If a proxy server exists between the user and the server, this address will be the address of the proxy, rather than the originating machine.

## - (%l)

The "hyphen" in the output indicates that the requested piece of information is not available. In this case, the information that is not available is the RFC 1413 identity of the client determined by identd on the clients machine. This information is highly unreliable and should almost never be used except on tightly controlled internal networks. Apache httpd will not even attempt to determine this information unless IdentityCheck is set to On.

## frank (%u)

This is the userid of the person requesting the document as determined by HTTP authentication. The same value is typically provided to CGI scripts in the REMOTE_USER environment variable. If the status code for the request (see below) is 401, then this value should not be trusted because the user is not yet authenticated. If the document is not password protected, this part will be "-" just like the previous one.

## [10/Oct/2000:13:55:36 -0700] (%t)

The time that the request was received. The format is:

```
[day/month/year:hour:minute:second zone]
day    = 2*digit
month  = 3*letter
year   = 4*digit
hour   = 2*digit
minute = 2*digit
second = 2*digit
zone   = (`+' | `-') 4*digit
```

It is possible to have the time displayed in another format by specifying %{format}t in the log format string, where format is as in strftime(3) from the C standard library.

## "GET /apache_pb.gif HTTP/1.0" (\"%r\")

The request line from the client is given in double quotes. The request line contains a great deal of useful information. First, the method used by the client is GET. Second, the client requested the resource /apache_pb.gif, and third, the client used the protocol HTTP/1.0. It is also possible to log one or more parts of the request line independently.

For example, the format string "%m %U%q %H" will log the method, path, query-string, and protocol, resulting in exactly the same output as "%r".

### 200 (%>s)

This is the status code that the server sends back to the client. This information is very valuable, because it reveals whether the request resulted in a successful response (codes beginning in 2), a redirection (codes beginning in 3), an error caused by the client (codes beginning in 4), or an error in the server (codes beginning in 5). The full list of possible status codes can be found in the *HTTP specification*[3] (RFC2616 section 10).

### 2326 (%b)

The last part indicates the size of the object returned to the client, not including the response headers. If no content was returned to the client, this value will be "-". To log "0" for no content, use %B instead.

## 12.3.2. Combined Log Format

Another commonly used format string is called the Combined Log Format. It can be used as follows.

```
LogFormat "%h %l %u %t \"%r\" %>s %b \"%{Referer}i\" \"%{User-agent}i\"" combined
CustomLog log/access_log combined
```

This format is exactly the same as the Common Log Format, with the addition of two more fields. Each of the additional fields uses the percent-directive %{*header*}i, where *header* can be any HTTP request header. The access log under this format will look like:

```
127.0.0.1 - frank [10/Oct/2000:13:55:36 -0700] "GET /apache_pb.gif HTTP/1.0" 200
2326 "http://www.example.com/start.html" "Mozilla/4.08 [en] (Win98; I ;Nav)"
```

The additional fields are:

### "http://www.example.com/start.html" (\"%{Referer}i\")

The "Referer" (sic) HTTP request header. This gives the site that the client reports having been referred from. (This should be the page that links to or includes /apache_pb.gif).

### "Mozilla/4.08 [en] (Win98; I ;Nav)" (\"%{User-agent}i\")

The User-Agent HTTP request header. This is the identifying information that the client browser reports about itself.

---

[3] *http://www.w3.org/Protocols/rfc2616/rfc2616.txt*

### 12.3.3. Multiple Access Logs

Multiple access logs can be created simply by specifying multiple CustomLog directives in the configuration file. For example, the following directives will create three access logs. The first contains the basic CLF information, while the second and third contain referer and browser information. The last two CustomLog lines show how to mimic the effects of the ReferLog and AgentLog directives.

```
LogFormat "%h %l %u %t \"%r\" %>s %b" common
CustomLog logs/access_log common
CustomLog logs/referer_log "%{Referer}i -> %U"
CustomLog logs/agent_log "%{User-agent}i"
```

This example also shows that it is not necessary to define a nickname with the LogFormat directive. Instead, the log format can be specified directly in the CustomLog directive.

### 12.3.4. Conditional Logs

There are times when it is convenient to exclude certain entries from the access logs based on characteristics of the client request. This is easily accomplished with the help of *environment variables*. First, an environment variable must be set to indicate that the request meets certain conditions. This is usually accomplished with SetEnvIf. Then the env= clause of the CustomLog directive is used to include or exclude requests where the environment variable is set. Some examples:

```
# Mark requests from the loop-back interface
SetEnvIf Remote_Addr "127\.0\.0\.1" dontlog
# Mark requests for the robots.txt file
SetEnvIf Request_URI "^/robots\.txt$" dontlog
# Log what remains
CustomLog logs/access_log common env=!dontlog
```

As another example, consider logging requests from english-speakers to one log file, and non-english speakers to a different log file.

```
SetEnvIf Accept-Language "en" english
CustomLog logs/english_log common env=english
CustomLog logs/non_english_log common env=!english
```

Although we have just shown that conditional logging is very powerful and flexible, it is not the only way to control the contents of the logs. Log files are more useful when they contain a complete record of server activity. It is often easier to simply post-process the log files to remove requests that you do not want to consider.

### 12.4. Log Rotation

On even a moderately busy server, the quantity of information stored in the log files is very large. The access log file typically grows 1 MB or more per 10,000 requests. It will consequently be necessary to periodically rotate the log files by moving or deleting the existing logs. This cannot be done while the server is running, because Apache will continue writing to the old log file as long as it holds the file open. Instead, the server must be *restarted* after the log files are moved or deleted so that it will open new log files.

By using a *graceful* restart, the server can be instructed to open new log files without losing any existing or pending connections from clients. However, in order to accomplish this, the server must continue to write to the old log files while it finishes serving old requests. It is therefore necessary to wait for some time after the restart before doing any processing on the log files. A typical scenario that simply rotates the logs and compresses the old logs to save space is:

```
mv access_log access_log.old
mv error_log error_log.old
apachectl graceful
sleep 600
gzip access_log.old error_log.old
```

Another way to perform log rotation is using *piped logs* as discussed in the next section.

## 12.5. Piped Logs

Apache httpd is capable of writing error and access log files through a pipe to another process, rather than directly to a file. This capability dramatically increases the flexibility of logging, without adding code to the main server. In order to write logs to a pipe, simply replace the filename with the pipe character "|", followed by the name of the executable which should accept log entries on its standard input. Apache will start the piped-log process when the server starts, and will restart it if it crashes while the server is running. (This last feature is why we can refer to this technique as "reliable piped logging".)

Piped log processes are spawned by the parent Apache httpd process, and inherit the userid of that process. This means that piped log programs usually run as root. It is therefore very important to keep the programs simple and secure.

One important use of piped logs is to allow log rotation without having to restart the server. The Apache HTTP Server includes a simple program called *rotatelogs* for this purpose. For example, to rotate the logs every 24 hours, you can use:

```
CustomLog "|/usr/local/apache/bin/rotatelogs /var/log/access_log 86400" common
```

Notice that quotes are used to enclose the entire command that will be called for the pipe. Although these examples are for the access log, the same technique can be used for the error log.

A similar but much more flexible log rotation program called *cronolog* is available at an external site.

As with conditional logging, piped logs are a very powerful tool, but they should not be used where a simpler solution like off-line post-processing is available.

## 12.6. Virtual Hosts

When running a server with many *virtual hosts*, there are several options for dealing with log files. First, it is possible to use logs exactly as in a single-host server. Simply by placing the logging directives outside the `<VirtualHost>` sections in the main server context, it is possible to log all requests in the same access log and error log. This technique does not allow for easy collection of statistics on individual virtual hosts.

If `CustomLog` or `ErrorLog` directives are placed inside a `<VirtualHost>` section, all requests or errors for that virtual host will be logged only to the specified file. Any virtual host which does not have logging directives will still have its requests sent to the main server logs. This technique is very useful for a small number of virtual hosts, but if the number of hosts is very large, it can be complicated to manage. In addition, it can often create problems with *insufficient file descriptors*.

For the access log, there is a very good compromise. By adding information on the virtual host to the log format string, it is possible to log all hosts to the same log, and later split the log into individual files. For example, consider the following directives.

```
LogFormat "%v %l %u %t \"%r\" %>s %b" comonvhost
CustomLog logs/access_log comonvhost
```

The `%v` is used to log the name of the virtual host that is serving the request. Then a program like *split-logfile* can be used to post-process the access log in order to split it into one file per virtual host.

## 12.7. Other Log Files

| Related Modules | Related Directives |
|---|---|
| mod_logio | LogFormat |
| mod_log_forensic | ForensicLog |
| mod_cgi | PidFile |
| mod_rewrite | RewriteLog |
| | RewriteLogLevel |
| | ScriptLog |
| | ScriptLogBuffer |
| | ScriptLogLength |

## Logging actual bytes sent and received

mod_logio adds in two additional `LogFormat` fields (%I and %O) that log the actual number of bytes received and sent on the network.

## Forensic Logging

`mod_log_forensic` provides for forensic logging of client requests. Logging is done before and after processing a request, so the forensic log contains two log lines for each request. The forensic logger is very strict with no customizations. It can be an invaluable debugging and security tool.

## PID File

On startup, Apache httpd saves the process id of the parent httpd process to the file `logs/httpd.pid`. This filename can be changed with the `PidFile` directive. The process-id is for use by the administrator in restarting and terminating the daemon by sending signals to the parent process; on Windows, use the -k command line option instead. For more information see the *Stopping and Restarting* page.

## Script Log

In order to aid in debugging, the `ScriptLog` directive allows you to record the input to and output from CGI scripts. This should only be used in testing - not for live servers. More information is available in the *mod_cgi* documentation.

## Rewrite Log

When using the powerful and complex features of *mod_rewrite*, it is almost always necessary to use the `RewriteLog` to help in debugging. This log file produces a detailed analysis of how the rewriting engine transforms requests. The level of detail is controlled by the `RewriteLogLevel` directive.

# Chapter 13.
# Mapping URLs to Filesystem Locations

This document explains how Apache uses the URL of a request to determine the filesystem location from which to serve a file.

## 13.1. Related Modules and Directives

| Related Modules | Related Directives |
|---|---|
| mod_alias | Alias |
| mod_proxy | AliasMatch |
| mod_rewrite | CheckSpelling |
| mod_userdir | DocumentRoot |
| mod_speling | ErrorDocument |
| mod_vhost_alias | Options |
| | ProxyPass |
| | ProxyPassReverse |
| | ProxyPassReverseCookieDomain |
| | ProxyPassReverseCookiePath |
| | Redirect |
| | RedirectMatch |
| | RewriteCond |
| | RewriteRule |
| | ScriptAlias |
| | ScriptAliasMatch |
| | UserDir |

## 13.2. DocumentRoot

In deciding what file to serve for a given request, Apache's default behavior is to take the URL-Path for the request (the part of the URL following the hostname and port) and add it to the end of the DocumentRoot specified in your configuration files. Therefore, the files and directories underneath the DocumentRoot make up the basic document tree which will be visible from the web.

For example, if `DocumentRoot` were set to `/var/www/html` then a request for `http://www.example.com/fish/guppies.html` would result in the file `/var/www/html/fish/guppies.html` being served to the requesting client.

Apache is also capable of *Virtual Hosting*, where the server receives requests for more than one host. In this case, a different `DocumentRoot` can be specified for each virtual host, or alternatively, the directives provided by the module `mod_vhost_alias` can be used to dynamically determine the appropriate place from which to serve content based on the requested IP address or hostname.

The `DocumentRoot` directive is set in your main server configuration file (`httpd.conf`) and, possibly, once per additional *Virtual Host* you create.

## 13.3. Files Outside the DocumentRoot

There are frequently circumstances where it is necessary to allow web access to parts of the filesystem that are not strictly underneath the `DocumentRoot`. Apache offers several different ways to accomplish this. On Unix systems, symbolic links can bring other parts of the filesystem under the `DocumentRoot`. For security reasons, Apache will follow symbolic links only if the `Options` setting for the relevant directory includes `FollowSymLinks` or `SymLinksIfOwnerMatch`.

Alternatively, the `Alias` directive will map any part of the filesystem into the web space. For example, with

```
Alias /docs /var/web
```

the URL `http://www.example.com/docs/dir/file.html` will be served from `/var/web/dir/file.html`. The `ScriptAlias` directive works the same way, with the additional effect that all content located at the target path is treated as *CGI* scripts.

For situations where you require additional flexibility, you can use the `AliasMatch` and `ScriptAliasMatch` directives to do powerful *regular expression* based matching and substitution. For example,

```
ScriptAliasMatch ^/~([a-zA-Z0-9]+)/cgi-bin/(.+) /home/$1/cgi-bin/$2
```

will map a request to `http://example.com/~user/cgi-bin/script.cgi` to the path `/home/user/cgi-bin/script.cgi` and will treat the resulting file as a CGI script.

## 13.4. User Directories

Traditionally on Unix systems, the home directory of a particular *user* can be referred to as ~user/. The module `mod_userdir` extends this idea to the web by allowing files under each user's home directory to be accessed using URLs such as the following.

```
http://www.example.com/~user/file.html
```

For security reasons, it is inappropriate to give direct access to a user's home directory from the web. Therefore, the `UserDir` directive specifies a directory underneath the user's home directory where web files are located. Using the default setting of `Userdir public_html`, the above URL maps to a file at a directory like `/home/user/public_html/file.html` where `/home/user/` is the user's home directory as specified in `/etc/passwd`.

There are also several other forms of the `Userdir` directive which you can use on systems where `/etc/passwd` does not contain the location of the home directory.

Some people find the "~" symbol (which is often encoded on the web as `%7e`) to be awkward and prefer to use an alternate string to represent user directories. This functionality is not supported by mod_userdir. However, if users' home directories are structured in a regular way, then it is possible to use the `AliasMatch` directive to achieve the desired effect. For example, to make `http://www.example.com/upages/user/file.html` map to `/home/user/public_html/file.html`, use the following `AliasMatch` directive:

```
AliasMatch ^/upages/([a-zA-Z0-9]+)/?(.*) /home/$1/public_html/$2
```

## 13.5. URL Redirection

The configuration directives discussed in the above sections tell Apache to get content from a specific place in the filesystem and return it to the client. Sometimes, it is desirable instead to inform the client that the requested content is located at a different URL, and instruct the client to make a new request with the new URL. This is called *redirection* and is implemented by the `Redirect` directive. For example, if the contents of the directory `/foo/` under the `DocumentRoot` are moved to the new directory `/bar/`, you can instruct clients to request the content at the new location as follows:

```
Redirect permanent /foo/ http://www.example.com/bar/
```

This will redirect any URL-Path starting in `/foo/` to the same URL path on the `www.example.com` server with `/bar/` substituted for `/foo/`. You can redirect clients to any server, not only the origin server.

Apache also provides a `RedirectMatch` directive for more complicated rewriting problems. For example, to redirect requests for the site home page to a different site, but leave all other requests alone, use the following configuration:

```
RedirectMatch permanent ^/$ http://www.example.com/startpage.html
```

Alternatively, to temporarily redirect all pages on one site to a particular page on another site, use the following:

```
RedirectMatch temp .* http://othersite.example.com/startpage.html
```

## 13.6. Reverse Proxy

Apache also allows you to bring remote documents into the URL space of the local server. This technique is called *reverse proxying* because the web server acts like a proxy server by fetching the documents from a remote server and returning them to the client. It is different from normal proxying because, to the client, it appears the documents originate at the reverse proxy server.

In the following example, when clients request documents under the /foo/ directory, the server fetches those documents from the /bar/ directory on internal.example.com and returns them to the client as if they were from the local server.

```
ProxyPass /foo/ http://internal.example.com/bar/
ProxyPassReverse /foo/ http://internal.example.com/bar/
ProxyPassReverseCookieDomain internal.example.com public.example.com
ProxyPassReverseCookiePath /foo/ /bar/
```

The ProxyPass configures the server to fetch the appropriate documents, while the ProxyPassReverse directive rewrites redirects originating at internal.example.com so that they target the appropriate directory on the local server. Similarly, the ProxyPassReverseCookieDomain and ProxyPassReverseCookiePath rewrite cookies set by the backend server.

It is important to note, however, that links inside the documents will not be rewritten. So any absolute links on internal.example.com will result in the client breaking out of the proxy server and requesting directly from internal.example.com. A third-party module *mod_proxy_html*[1] is available to rewrite links in HTML and XHTML.

## 13.7. Rewriting Engine

When even more powerful substitution is required, the rewriting engine provided by mod_rewrite can be useful. The directives provided by this module use characteristics of the request such as browser type or source IP address in deciding from where to serve content. In addition, mod_rewrite can use external database files or programs to determine how to handle a request. The rewriting engine is capable of performing all three types of mappings discussed above: internal redirects (aliases), external redirects, and proxying. Many practical examples employing mod_rewrite are discussed in the *detailed mod_rewrite documentation*.

## 13.8. File Not Found

Inevitably, URLs will be requested for which no matching file can be found in the filesystem. This can happen for several reasons. In some cases, it can be a result of moving

---

[1] *http://apache.webthing.com/mod_proxy_html/*

documents from one location to another. In this case, it is best to use *URL redirection* to inform clients of the new location of the resource. In this way, you can assure that old bookmarks and links will continue to work, even though the resource is at a new location.

Another common cause of "File Not Found" errors is accidental mistyping of URLs, either directly in the browser, or in HTML links. Apache provides the module `mod speling` (sic) to help with this problem. When this module is activated, it will intercept "File Not Found" errors and look for a resource with a similar filename. If one such file is found, mod_speling will send an HTTP redirect to the client informing it of the correct location. If several "close" files are found, a list of available alternatives will be presented to the client.

An especially useful feature of mod_speling, is that it will compare filenames without respect to case. This can help systems where users are unaware of the case-sensitive nature of URLs and the unix filesystem. But using mod_speling for anything more than the occasional URL correction can place additional load on the server, since each "incorrect" request is followed by a URL redirection and a new request from the client.

If all attempts to locate the content fail, Apache returns an error page with HTTP status code 404 (file not found). The appearance of this page is controlled with the `ErrorDocument` directive and can be customized in a flexible manner as discussed in the *Custom error responses* document.

# Chapter 14.
# Security Tips

Some hints and tips on security issues in setting up a web server. Some of the suggestions will be general, others specific to Apache.

## 14.1. Keep up to Date

The Apache HTTP Server has a good record for security and a developer community highly concerned about security issues. But it is inevitable that some problems -- small or large -- will be discovered in software after it is released. For this reason, it is crucial to keep aware of updates to the software. If you have obtained your version of the HTTP Server directly from Apache, we highly recommend you subscribe to the *Apache HTTP Server Announcements List*[1] where you can keep informed of new releases and security updates. Similar services are available from most third-party distributors of Apache software.

Of course, most times that a web server is compromised, it is not because of problems in the HTTP Server code. Rather, it comes from problems in add-on code, CGI scripts, or the underlying Operating System. You must therefore stay aware of problems and updates with all the software on your system.

## 14.2. Permissions on ServerRoot Directories

In typical operation, Apache is started by the root user, and it switches to the user defined by the User directive to serve hits. As is the case with any command that root executes, you must take care that it is protected from modification by non-root users. Not only must the files themselves be writeable only by root, but so must the directories, and parents of all directories. For example, if you choose to place ServerRoot in /usr/local/apache then it is suggested that you create that directory as root, with commands like these:

```
mkdir /usr/local/apache
cd /usr/local/apache
mkdir bin conf logs
chown 0 . bin conf logs
```

---

[1] *http://httpd.apache.org/lists.html#http-announce*

```
chgrp 0 . bin conf logs
chmod 755 . bin conf logs
```

It is assumed that /, /usr, and /usr/local are only modifiable by root. When you install the *httpd* executable, you should ensure that it is similarly protected:

```
cp httpd /usr/local/apache/bin
chown 0 /usr/local/apache/bin/httpd
chgrp 0 /usr/local/apache/bin/httpd
chmod 511 /usr/local/apache/bin/httpd
```

You can create an htdocs subdirectory which is modifiable by other users -- since root never executes any files out of there, and shouldn't be creating files in there.

If you allow non-root users to modify any files that root either executes or writes on then you open your system to root compromises. For example, someone could replace the *httpd* binary so that the next time you start it, it will execute some arbitrary code. If the logs directory is writeable (by a non-root user), someone could replace a log file with a symlink to some other system file, and then root might overwrite that file with arbitrary data. If the log files themselves are writeable (by a non-root user), then someone may be able to overwrite the log itself with bogus data.

## 14.3. Server Side Includes

Server Side Includes (SSI) present a server administrator with several potential security risks.

The first risk is the increased load on the server. All SSI-enabled files have to be parsed by Apache, whether or not there are any SSI directives included within the files. While this load increase is minor, in a shared server environment it can become significant.

SSI files also pose the same risks that are associated with CGI scripts in general. Using the exec cmd element, SSI-enabled files can execute any CGI script or program under the permissions of the user and group Apache runs as, as configured in httpd.conf.

There are ways to enhance the security of SSI files while still taking advantage of the benefits they provide.

To isolate the damage a wayward SSI file can cause, a server administrator can enable *suexec* as described in the *CGI in General* section.

Enabling SSI for files with .html or .htm extensions can be dangerous. This is especially true in a shared, or high traffic, server environment. SSI-enabled files should have a separate extension, such as the conventional .shtml. This helps keep server load at a minimum and allows for easier management of risk.

Another solution is to disable the ability to run scripts and programs from SSI pages. To do this replace `Includes` with `IncludesNOEXEC` in the `Options` directive. Note that users may still use `<--#include virtual="..." -->` to execute CGI scripts if these scripts are in directories designated by a `ScriptAlias` directive.

## 14.4. CGI in General

First of all, you always have to remember that you must trust the writers of the CGI scripts/programs or your ability to spot potential security holes in CGI, whether they were deliberate or accidental. CGI scripts can run essentially arbitrary commands on your system with the permissions of the web server user and can therefore be extremely dangerous if they are not carefully checked.

All the CGI scripts will run as the same user, so they have potential to conflict (accidentally or deliberately) with other scripts e.g. User A hates User B, so he writes a script to trash User B's CGI database. One program which can be used to allow scripts to run as different users is *suEXEC* which is included with Apache as of 1.2 and is called from special hooks in the Apache server code. Another popular way of doing this is with *CGIWrap*[2].

## 14.5. Non Script Aliased CGI

Allowing users to execute CGI scripts in any directory should only be considered if:

- You trust your users not to write scripts which will deliberately or accidentally expose your system to an attack.
- You consider security at your site to be so feeble in other areas, as to make one more potential hole irrelevant.
- You have no users, and nobody ever visits your server.

## 14.6. Script Aliased CGI

Limiting CGI to special directories gives the admin control over what goes into those directories. This is inevitably more secure than non script aliased CGI, but only if users with write access to the directories are trusted or the admin is willing to test each new CGI script/program for potential security holes.

Most sites choose this option over the non script aliased CGI approach.

## 14.7. Other sources of dynamic content

Embedded scripting options which run as part of the server itself, such as mod_php, mod_perl, mod_tcl, and mod_python, run under the identity of the server itself (see the

---

[2] *http://cgiwrap.sourceforge.net/*

User directive), and therefore scripts executed by these engines potentially can access anything the server user can. Some scripting engines may provide restrictions, but it is better to be safe and assume not.

## 14.8. Protecting System Settings

To run a really tight ship, you'll want to stop users from setting up .htaccess files which can override security features you've configured. Here's one way to do it.

In the server configuration file, put

```
<Directory />
AllowOverride None
</Directory>
```

This prevents the use of .htaccess files in all directories apart from those specifically enabled.

## 14.9. Protect Server Files by Default

One aspect of Apache which is occasionally misunderstood is the feature of default access. That is, unless you take steps to change it, if the server can find its way to a file through normal URL mapping rules, it can serve it to clients.

For instance, consider the following example:

```
# cd /; ln -s / public_html
Accessing http://localhost/~root/
```

This would allow clients to walk through the entire filesystem. To work around this, add the following block to your server's configuration:

```
<Directory />
Order Deny,Allow
Deny from all
</Directory>
```

This will forbid default access to filesystem locations. Add appropriate Directory blocks to allow access only in those areas you wish. For example,

```
<Directory /usr/users/*/public_html>
Order Deny,Allow
Allow from all
</Directory>
<Directory /usr/local/httpd>
Order Deny,Allow
Allow from all
</Directory>
```

Pay particular attention to the interactions of <u>Location</u> and <u>Directory</u> directives; for instance, even if <Directory /> denies access, a <Location /> directive might overturn it.

Also be wary of playing games with the UserDir directive; setting it to something like ./ would have the same effect, for root, as the first example above. If you are using Apache 1.3 or above, we strongly recommend that you include the following line in your server configuration files:

```
UserDir disabled root
```

## 14.10. Watching Your Logs

To keep up-to-date with what is actually going on against your server you have to check the *Log Files*. Even though the log files only reports what has already happened, they will give you some understanding of what attacks is thrown against the server and allow you to check if the necessary level of security is present.

A couple of examples:

```
grep -c "/jsp/source.jsp?/jsp/ /jsp/source.jsp??" access_log
grep "client denied" error_log | tail -n 10
```

The first example will list the number of attacks trying to exploit the *Apache Tomcat Source.JSP Malformed Request Information Disclosure Vulnerability*[3], the second example will list the ten last denied clients, for example:

```
[Thu Jul 11 17:18:39 2002] [error] [client foo.example.com] client denied by server
configuration: /usr/local/apache/htdocs/.htpasswd
```

As you can see, the log files only report what already has happened, so if the client had been able to access the .htpasswd file you would have seen something similar to:

```
foo.example.com - - [12/Jul/2002:01:59:13 +0200] "GET /.htpasswd HTTP/1.1"
```

in your *Access Log*. This means you probably commented out the following in your server configuration file:

```
<Files ~ "^\.ht">
Order allow,deny
Deny from all
</Files>
```

---

[3] *http://online.securityfocus.com/bid/4876/info/*

# Chapter 15.
# Dynamic Shared Object (DSO) Support

The Apache HTTP Server is a modular program where the administrator can choose the functionality to include in the server by selecting a set of modules. The modules can be statically compiled into the *httpd* binary when the server is built. Alternatively, modules can be compiled as Dynamic Shared Objects (DSOs) that exist separately from the main *httpd* binary file. DSO modules may be compiled at the time the server is built, or they may be compiled and added at a later time using the Apache Extension Tool (*apxs*).

This document describes how to use DSO modules as well as the theory behind their use.

## 15.1. Implementation

| Related Modules | Related Directives |
|---|---|
| mod_so | LoadModule |

The DSO support for loading individual Apache modules is based on a module named mod_so which must be statically compiled into the Apache core. It is the only module besides core which cannot be put into a DSO itself. Practically all other distributed Apache modules can then be placed into a DSO by individually enabling the DSO build for them via *configure*'s --enable-*module*=shared option as discussed in the *install documentation*. After a module is compiled into a DSO named mod_foo.so you can use mod_so's LoadModule command in your httpd.conf file to load this module at server startup or restart.

To simplify this creation of DSO files for Apache modules (especially for third-party modules) a new support program named *apxs* (*APache eXtenSion*) is available. It can be used to build DSO based modules *outside of* the Apache source tree. The idea is simple: When installing Apache the *configure*'s make install procedure installs the Apache C header files and puts the platform-dependent compiler and linker flags for building DSO files into the *apxs* program. This way the user can use *apxs* to compile his Apache module sources without the Apache distribution source tree and without having to fiddle with the platform-dependent compiler and linker flags for DSO support.

## 15.2. Usage Summary

To give you an overview of the DSO features of Apache 2.x, here is a short and concise summary:

1. Build and install a *distributed* Apache module, say mod_foo.c, into its own DSO mod_foo.so:

```
$ ./configure --prefix=/path/to/install --enable-foo=shared
$ make install
```

2. Build and install a *third-party* Apache module, say mod_foo.c, into its own DSO mod_foo.so:

```
$ ./configure --add-module=module_type:/path/to/3rdparty/mod_foo.c \
--enable-foo=shared
$ make install
```

3. Configure Apache for *later installation* of shared modules:

```
$ ./configure --enable-so
$ make install
```

4. Build and install a *third-party* Apache module, say mod_foo.c, into its own DSO mod_foo.so *outside of* the Apache source tree using *apxs*:

```
$ cd /path/to/3rdparty
$ apxs -c mod_foo.c
$ apxs -i -a -n foo mod_foo.la
```

In all cases, once the shared module is compiled, you must use a LoadModule directive in httpd.conf to tell Apache to activate the module.

## 15.3. Background

On modern Unix derivatives there exists a nifty mechanism usually called dynamic linking/loading of *Dynamic Shared Objects* (DSO) which provides a way to build a piece of program code in a special format for loading it at run-time into the address space of an executable program.

This loading can usually be done in two ways: Automatically by a system program called ld.so when an executable program is started or manually from within the executing program via a programmatic system interface to the Unix loader through the system calls dlopen()/dlsym().

In the first way the DSO's are usually called *shared libraries* or *DSO libraries* and named libfoo.so or libfoo.so.1.2. They reside in a system directory (usually /usr/lib) and the link to the executable program is established at build-time by specifying -lfoo to the linker command. This hard-codes library references into the executable program file so that at start-time the Unix loader is able to locate `libfoo.so` in /usr/lib, in paths hard-coded via linker-options like `-R` or in paths configured via the environment variable `LD_LIBRARY_PATH`. It then resolves any (yet unresolved) symbols in the executable program which are available in the DSO.

Symbols in the executable program are usually not referenced by the DSO (because it's a reusable library of general code) and hence no further resolving has to be done. The executable program has no need to do anything on its own to use the symbols from the DSO because the complete resolving is done by the Unix loader. (In fact, the code to invoke `ld.so` is part of the run-time startup code which is linked into every executable program which has been bound non-static). The advantage of dynamic loading of common library code is obvious: the library code needs to be stored only once, in a system library like `libc.so`, saving disk space for every program.

In the second way the DSO's are usually called *shared objects* or *DSO files* and can be named with an arbitrary extension (although the canonical name is `foo.so`). These files usually stay inside a program-specific directory and there is no automatically established link to the executable program where they are used. Instead the executable program manually loads the DSO at run-time into its address space via `dlopen()`. At this time no resolving of symbols from the DSO for the executable program is done. But instead the Unix loader automatically resolves any (yet unresolved) symbols in the DSO from the set of symbols exported by the executable program and its already loaded DSO libraries (especially all symbols from the ubiquitous `libc.so`). This way the DSO gets knowledge of the executable program's symbol set as if it had been statically linked with it in the first place.

Finally, to take advantage of the DSO's API the executable program has to resolve particular symbols from the DSO via `dlsym()` for later use inside dispatch tables *etc*. In other words: The executable program has to manually resolve every symbol it needs to be able to use it. The advantage of such a mechanism is that optional program parts need not be loaded (and thus do not spend memory) until they are needed by the program in question. When required, these program parts can be loaded dynamically to extend the base program's functionality.

Although this DSO mechanism sounds straightforward there is at least one difficult step here: The resolving of symbols from the executable program for the DSO when using a DSO to extend a program (the second way). Why? Because "reverse resolving" DSO symbols from the executable program's symbol set is against the library design (where the library has no knowledge about the programs it is used by) and is neither available under all platforms nor standardized. In practice the executable program's global symbols are often not re-exported and thus not available for use in a DSO. Finding a way to force the linker to export all global symbols is the main problem one has to solve when using DSO for extending a program at run-time.

The shared library approach is the typical one, because it is what the DSO mechanism was designed for, hence it is used for nearly all types of libraries the operating system provides. On the other hand using shared objects for extending a program is not used by a lot of programs.

As of 1998 there are only a few software packages available which use the DSO mechanism to actually extend their functionality at run-time: Perl 5 (via its XS mechanism and the DynaLoader module), Netscape Server, *etc.* Starting with version 1.3, Apache joined the crew, because Apache already uses a module concept to extend its functionality and internally uses a dispatch-list-based approach to link external modules into the Apache core functionality. So, Apache is really predestined for using DSO to load its modules at run-time.

## 15.4. Advantages and Disadvantages

The above DSO based features have the following advantages:

- The server package is more flexible at run-time because the actual server process can be assembled at run-time via `LoadModule` `httpd.conf` configuration commands instead of *configure* options at build-time. For instance this way one is able to run different server instances (standard & SSL version, minimalistic & powered up version [mod_perl, PHP3], *etc.*) with only one Apache installation.
- The server package can be easily extended with third-party modules even after installation. This is at least a great benefit for vendor package maintainers who can create a Apache core package and additional packages containing extensions like PHP3, mod_perl, mod_fastcgi, *etc.*
- Easier Apache module prototyping because with the DSO/*apxs* pair you can both work outside the Apache source tree and only need an `apxs` `-i` command followed by an `apachectl` `restart` to bring a new version of your currently developed module into the running Apache server.

DSO has the following disadvantages:

- The DSO mechanism cannot be used on every platform because not all operating systems support dynamic loading of code into the address space of a program.
- The server is approximately 20% slower at startup time because of the symbol resolving overhead the Unix loader now has to do.
- The server is approximately 5% slower at execution time under some platforms because position independent code (PIC) sometimes needs complicated assembler tricks for relative addressing which are not necessarily as fast as absolute addressing.
- Because DSO modules cannot be linked against other DSO-based libraries (`ld` `-lfoo`) on all platforms (for instance a.out-based platforms usually don't provide this

functionality while ELF-based platforms do) you cannot use the DSO mechanism for all types of modules. Or in other words, modules compiled as DSO files are restricted to only use symbols from the Apache core, from the C library (`libc`) and all other dynamic or static libraries used by the Apache core, or from static library archives (`libfoo.a`) containing position independent code. The only chances to use other code is to either make sure the Apache core itself already contains a reference to it or loading the code yourself via `dlopen()`.

# Chapter 16.
# Content Negotiation

Apache supports content negotiation as described in the HTTP/1.1 specification. It can choose the best representation of a resource based on the browser-supplied preferences for media type, languages, character set and encoding. It also implements a couple of features to give more intelligent handling of requests from browsers that send incomplete negotiation information.

Content negotiation is provided by the <u>mod_negotiation</u> module, which is compiled in by default.

## 16.1. About Content Negotiation

A resource may be available in several different representations. For example, it might be available in different languages or different media types, or a combination. One way of selecting the most appropriate choice is to give the user an index page, and let them select. However it is often possible for the server to choose automatically. This works because browsers can send, as part of each request, information about what representations they prefer. For example, a browser could indicate that it would like to see information in French, if possible, else English will do. Browsers indicate their preferences by headers in the request. To request only French representations, the browser would send

```
Accept-Language: fr
```

Note that this preference will only be applied when there is a choice of representations and they vary by language.

As an example of a more complex request, this browser has been configured to accept French and English, but prefer French, and to accept various media types, preferring HTML over plain text or other text types, and preferring GIF or JPEG over other media types, but also allowing any other media type as a last resort:

```
Accept-Language: fr; q=1.0, en; q=0.5
Accept: text/html; q=1.0, text/*; q=0.8, image/gif; q=0.6, image/jpeg; q=0.6,
image/*; q=0.5, */*; q=0.1
```

Apache supports 'server driven' content negotiation, as defined in the HTTP/1.1 specification. It fully supports the `Accept`, `Accept-Language`, `Accept-Charset` and `Accept-Encoding` request headers. Apache also supports 'transparent' content negotiation, which is an experimental negotiation protocol defined in RFC 2295 and RFC 2296. It does not offer support for 'feature negotiation' as defined in these RFCs.

A **resource** is a conceptual entity identified by a URI (RFC 2396). An HTTP server like Apache provides access to **representations** of the resource(s) within its namespace, with each representation in the form of a sequence of bytes with a defined media type, character set, encoding, etc. Each resource may be associated with zero, one, or more than one representation at any given time. If multiple representations are available, the resource is referred to as **negotiable** and each of its representations is termed a **variant**. The ways in which the variants for a negotiable resource vary are called the **dimensions** of negotiation.

## 16.2. Negotiation in Apache

In order to negotiate a resource, the server needs to be given information about each of the variants. This is done in one of two ways:

- Using a type map (*i.e.*, a `*.var` file) which names the files containing the variants explicitly, or
- Using a 'MultiViews' search, where the server does an implicit filename pattern match and chooses from among the results.

### 16.2.1. Using a type-map file

A type map is a document which is associated with the handler named `type-map` (or, for backwards-compatibility with older Apache configurations, the *MIME-type* `application/x-type-map`). Note that to use this feature, you must have a handler set in the configuration that defines a file suffix as `type-map`; this is best done with

```
AddHandler type-map .var
```

in the server configuration file.

Type map files should have the same name as the resource which they are describing, and have an entry for each available variant; these entries consist of contiguous HTTP-format header lines. Entries for different variants are separated by blank lines. Blank lines are illegal within an entry. It is conventional to begin a map file with an entry for the combined entity as a whole (although this is not required, and if present will be ignored). An example map file is shown below. This file would be named `foo.var`, as it describes a resource named `foo`.

```
URI: foo

URI: foo.en.html
Content-type: text/html
Content-language: en

URI: foo.fr.de.html
Content-type: text/html;charset=iso-8859-2
Content-language: fr, de
```

Note also that a typemap file will take precedence over the filename's extension, even when Multiviews is on. If the variants have different source qualities, that may be indicated by the "qs" parameter to the media type, as in this picture (available as JPEG, GIF, or ASCII-art):

```
URI: foo

URI: foo.jpeg
Content-type: image/jpeg; qs=0.8

URI: foo.gif
Content-type: image/gif; qs=0.5

URI: foo.txt
Content-type: text/plain; qs=0.01
```

qs values can vary in the range 0.000 to 1.000. Note that any variant with a qs value of 0.000 will never be chosen. Variants with no 'qs' parameter value are given a qs factor of 1.0. The qs parameter indicates the relative 'quality' of this variant compared to the other available variants, independent of the client's capabilities. For example, a JPEG file is usually of higher source quality than an ASCII file if it is attempting to represent a photograph. However, if the resource being represented is an original ASCII art, then an ASCII representation would have a higher source quality than a JPEG representation. A qs value is therefore specific to a given variant depending on the nature of the resource it represents.

The full list of headers recognized is available in the *mod_negotation typemap* documentation.

## 16.2.2. Multiviews

MultiViews is a per-directory option, meaning it can be set with an Options directive within a <Directory>, <Location> or <Files> section in httpd.conf, or (if AllowOverride is properly set) in .htaccess files. Note that Options All does not set MultiViews; you have to ask for it by name.

The effect of MultiViews is as follows: if the server receives a request for /some/dir/foo, if /some/dir has MultiViews enabled, and /some/dir/foo does *not* exist, then the server reads the directory looking for files named foo.*, and effectively fakes up a type map which names all those files, assigning them the same media types and content-encodings it would have if the client had asked for one of them by name. It then chooses the best match to the client's requirements.

`MultiViews` may also apply to searches for the file named by the `DirectoryIndex` directive, if the server is trying to index a directory. If the configuration files specify

```
DirectoryIndex index
```

then the server will arbitrate between `index.html` and `index.html3` if both are present. If neither are present, and `index.cgi` is there, the server will run it.

If one of the files found when reading the directory does not have an extension recognized by mod_mime to designate its Charset, Content-Type, Language, or Encoding, then the result depends on the setting of the `MultiViewsMatch` directive. This directive determines whether handlers, filters, and other extension types can participate in MultiViews negotiation.

## 16.3. The Negotiation Methods

After Apache has obtained a list of the variants for a given resource, either from a type-map file or from the filenames in the directory, it invokes one of two methods to decide on the 'best' variant to return, if any. It is not necessary to know any of the details of how negotiation actually takes place in order to use Apache's content negotiation features. However the rest of this document explains the methods used for those interested.

There are two negotiation methods:

1.  **Server driven negotiation with the Apache algorithm** is used in the normal case. The Apache algorithm is explained in more detail below. When this algorithm is used, Apache can sometimes 'fiddle' the quality factor of a particular dimension to achieve a better result. The ways Apache can fiddle quality factors is explained in more detail below.

2.  **Transparent content negotiation** is used when the browser specifically requests this through the mechanism defined in RFC 2295. This negotiation method gives the browser full control over deciding on the 'best' variant, the result is therefore dependent on the specific algorithms used by the browser. As part of the transparent negotiation process, the browser can ask Apache to run the 'remote variant selection algorithm' defined in RFC 2296.

### 16.3.1. Dimensions of Negotiation

| Dimension | Notes |
|---|---|
| Media Type | Browser indicates preferences with the `Accept` header field. Each item |

| Dimension | Notes |
|-----------|-------|
|           | can have an associated quality factor. Variant description can also have a quality factor (the "qs" parameter). |
| Language  | Browser indicates preferences with the Accept-Language header field. Each item can have a quality factor. Variants can be associated with none, one or more than one language. |
| Encoding  | Browser indicates preference with the Accept-Encoding header field. Each item can have a quality factor. |
| Charset   | Browser indicates preference with the Accept-Charset header field. Each item can have a quality factor. Variants can indicate a charset as a parameter of the media type. |

## 16.3.2. Apache Negotiation Algorithm

Apache can use the following algorithm to select the 'best' variant (if any) to return to the browser. This algorithm is not further configurable. It operates as follows:

1. First, for each dimension of the negotiation, check the appropriate *Accept\** header field and assign a quality to each variant. If the *Accept\** header for any dimension implies that this variant is not acceptable, eliminate it. If no variants remain, go to step 4.

2. Select the 'best' variant by a process of elimination. Each of the following tests is applied in order. Any variants not selected at each test are eliminated. After each test, if only one variant remains, select it as the best match and proceed to step 3. If more than one variant remains, move on to the next test.

   1. Multiply the quality factor from the Accept header with the quality-of-source factor for this variants media type, and select the variants with the highest value.

   2. Select the variants with the highest language quality factor.

   3. Select the variants with the best language match, using either the order of languages in the Accept-Language header (if present), or else the order of languages in the LanguagePriority directive (if present).

   4. Select the variants with the highest 'level' media parameter (used to give the version of text/html media types).

   5. Select variants with the best charset media parameters, as given on the Accept-Charset header line. Charset ISO-8859-1 is acceptable unless explicitly excluded. Variants with a text/* media type but not explicitly associated with a particular charset are assumed to be in ISO-8859-1.

6. Select those variants which have associated charset media parameters that are *not* ISO-8859-1. If there are no such variants, select all variants instead.

7. Select the variants with the best encoding. If there are variants with an encoding that is acceptable to the user-agent, select only these variants. Otherwise if there is a mix of encoded and non-encoded variants, select only the unencoded variants. If either all variants are encoded or all variants are not encoded, select all variants.

8. Select the variants with the smallest content length.

9. Select the first variant of those remaining. This will be either the first listed in the type-map file, or when variants are read from the directory, the one whose file name comes first when sorted using ASCII code order.

3. The algorithm has now selected one 'best' variant, so return it as the response. The HTTP response header `Vary` is set to indicate the dimensions of negotiation (browsers and caches can use this information when caching the resource). End.

4. To get here means no variant was selected (because none are acceptable to the browser). Return a 406 status (meaning "No acceptable representation") with a response body consisting of an HTML document listing the available variants. Also set the HTTP `Vary` header to indicate the dimensions of variance.

## 16.4. Fiddling with Quality Values

Apache sometimes changes the quality values from what would be expected by a strict interpretation of the Apache negotiation algorithm above. This is to get a better result from the algorithm for browsers which do not send full or accurate information. Some of the most popular browsers send `Accept` header information which would otherwise result in the selection of the wrong variant in many cases. If a browser sends full and correct information these fiddles will not be applied.

### 16.4.1. Media Types and Wildcards

The `Accept:` request header indicates preferences for media types. It can also include 'wildcard' media types, such as "image/*" or "*/*" where the * matches any string. So a request including:

```
Accept: image/*, */*
```

would indicate that any type starting "image/" is acceptable, as is any other type. Some browsers routinely send wildcards in addition to explicit types they can handle. For example:

```
Accept: text/html, text/plain, image/gif, image/jpeg, */*
```

The intention of this is to indicate that the explicitly listed types are preferred, but if a different representation is available, that is ok too. Using explicit quality values, what the browser really wants is something like:

```
Accept: text/html, text/plain, image/gif, image/jpeg, */*; q=0.01
```

The explicit types have no quality factor, so they default to a preference of 1.0 (the highest). The wildcard */* is given a low preference of 0.01, so other types will only be returned if no variant matches an explicitly listed type.

If the Accept: header contains *no* q factors at all, Apache sets the q value of "*/*", if present, to 0.01 to emulate the desired behavior. It also sets the q value of wildcards of the format "type/*" to 0.02 (so these are preferred over matches against "*/*". If any media type on the Accept: header contains a q factor, these special values are *not* applied, so requests from browsers which send the explicit information to start with work as expected.

### 16.4.2. Language Negotiation Exceptions

New in Apache 2.0, some exceptions have been added to the negotiation algorithm to allow graceful fallback when language negotiation fails to find a match.

When a client requests a page on your server, but the server cannot find a single page that matches the Accept-language sent by the browser, the server will return either a "No Acceptable Variant" or "Multiple Choices" response to the client. To avoid these error messages, it is possible to configure Apache to ignore the Accept-language in these cases and provide a document that does not explicitly match the client's request. The ForceLanguagePriority directive can be used to override one or both of these error messages and substitute the servers judgement in the form of the LanguagePriority directive.

The server will also attempt to match language-subsets when no other match can be found. For example, if a client requests documents with the language en-GB for British English, the server is not normally allowed by the HTTP/1.1 standard to match that against a document that is marked as simply en. (Note that it is almost surely a configuration error to include en-GB and not en in the Accept-Language header, since it is very unlikely that a reader understands British English, but doesn't understand English in general. Unfortunately, many current clients have default configurations that resemble this.) However, if no other language match is possible and the server is about to return a "No Acceptable Variants" error or fallback to the LanguagePriority, the server will ignore the subset specification and match en-GB against en documents. Implicitly, Apache will add the parent language to the client's acceptable language list with a very low quality value. But note that if the client requests "en-GB; q=0.9, fr; q=0.8", and the server has documents designated "en" and "fr", then the "fr" document will be returned. This is necessary to maintain compliance with the HTTP/1.1 specification and to work effectively with properly configured clients.

In order to support advanced techniques (such as cookies or special URL-paths) to determine the user's preferred language, since Apache 2.0.47 mod_negotiation recognizes the *environment variable* prefer-language. If it exists and contains an appropriate language tag, mod_negotiation will try to select a matching variant. If there's no such variant, the normal negotiation process applies.

**Example**

```
SetEnvIf Cookie "language=(.+)" prefer-language=$1
Header append Vary cookie
```

## 16.5. Extensions to Transparent Content Negotiation

Apache extends the transparent content negotiation protocol (RFC 2295) as follows. A new {encoding ..} element is used in variant lists to label variants which are available with a specific content-encoding only. The implementation of the RVSA/1.0 algorithm (RFC 2296) is extended to recognize encoded variants in the list, and to use them as candidate variants whenever their encodings are acceptable according to the Accept-Encoding request header. The RVSA/1.0 implementation does not round computed quality factors to 5 decimal places before choosing the best variant.

## 16.6. Note on hyperlinks and naming conventions

If you are using language negotiation you can choose between different naming conventions, because files can have more than one extension, and the order of the extensions is normally irrelevant (see the *mod_mime* documentation for details).

A typical file has a MIME-type extension (*e.g.*, html), maybe an encoding extension (*e.g.*, gz), and of course a language extension (*e.g.*, en) when we have different language variants of this file.

Examples:

- foo.en.html
- foo.html.en
- foo.en.html.gz

Here some more examples of filenames together with valid and invalid hyperlinks:

| Filename | Valid hyperlink | Invalid hyperlink |
|---|---|---|
| *foo.html.en* | foo<br>foo.html | - |
| *foo.en.html* | foo | foo.html |

| Filename | Valid hyperlink | Invalid hyperlink |
|---|---|---|
| *foo.html.en.gz* | foo<br>foo.html | foo.gz<br>foo.html.gz |
| *foo.en.html.gz* | foo | foo.html<br>foo.html.gz<br>foo.gz |
| *foo.gz.html.en* | foo<br>foo.gz<br>foo.gz.html | foo.html |
| *foo.html.gz.en* | foo<br>foo.html<br>foo.html.gz | foo.gz |

Looking at the table above, you will notice that it is always possible to use the name without any extensions in a hyperlink (*e.g.*, foo). The advantage is that you can hide the actual type of a document rsp. file and can change it later, *e.g.*, from html to shtml or cgi without changing any hyperlink references.

If you want to continue to use a MIME-type in your hyperlinks (*e.g.* foo.html) the language extension (including an encoding extension if there is one) must be on the right hand side of the MIME-type extension (*e.g.*, foo.html.en).

## 16.7. Note on Caching

When a cache stores a representation, it associates it with the request URL. The next time that URL is requested, the cache can use the stored representation. But, if the resource is negotiable at the server, this might result in only the first requested variant being cached and subsequent cache hits might return the wrong response. To prevent this, Apache normally marks all responses that are returned after content negotiation as non-cacheable by HTTP/1.0 clients. Apache also supports the HTTP/1.1 protocol features to allow caching of negotiated responses.

For requests which come from a HTTP/1.0 compliant client (either a browser or a cache), the directive CacheNegotiatedDocs can be used to allow caching of responses which were subject to negotiation. This directive can be given in the server config or virtual host, and takes no arguments. It has no effect on requests from HTTP/1.1 clients.

For HTTP/1.1 clients, Apache sends a Vary HTTP response header to indicate the negotiation dimensions for the response. Caches can use this information to determine whether a subsequent request can be served from the local copy. To encourage a cache to use the local copy regardless of the negotiation dimensions, set the force-no-vary *environment variable*.

# Chapter 17.

# Custom Error Responses

Additional functionality allows webmasters to configure the response of Apache to some error or problem.

Customizable responses can be defined to be activated in the event of a server detected error or problem.

If a script crashes and produces a "500 Server Error" response, then this response can be replaced with either some friendlier text or by a redirection to another URL (local or external).

## 17.1. Behavior

### Old Behavior

NCSA httpd 1.3 would return some boring old error/problem message which would often be meaningless to the user, and would provide no means of logging the symptoms which caused it.

### New Behavior

The server can be asked to:

1.  Display some other text, instead of the NCSA hard coded messages, or
2.  redirect to a local URL, or
3.  redirect to an external URL.

Redirecting to another URL can be useful, but only if some information can be passed which can then be used to explain and/or log the error/problem more clearly.

To achieve this, Apache will define new CGI-like environment variables:

```
REDIRECT_HTTP_ACCEPT=*/*, image/gif, image/x-xbitmap, image/jpeg
REDIRECT_HTTP_USER_AGENT=Mozilla/1.1b2 (X11; I; HP-UX A.09.05 9000/712)
REDIRECT_PATH=.:/bin:/usr/local/bin:/etc
REDIRECT_QUERY_STRING=
```

```
REDIRECT_REMOTE_ADDR=121.345.78.123
REDIRECT_REMOTE_HOST=ooh.ahhh.com
REDIRECT_SERVER_NAME=crash.bang.edu
REDIRECT_SERVER_PORT=80
REDIRECT_SERVER_SOFTWARE=Apache/0.8.15
REDIRECT_URL=/cgi-bin/buggy.pl
```

Note the `REDIRECT_` prefix.

At least `REDIRECT_URL` and `REDIRECT_QUERY_STRING` will be passed to the new URL (assuming it's a cgi-script or a cgi-include). The other variables will exist only if they existed prior to the error/problem. **None** of these will be set if your `ErrorDocument` is an *external* redirect (anything starting with a scheme name like `http:`, even if it refers to the same host as the server).

## 17.2. Configuration

Use of `ErrorDocument` is enabled for .htaccess files when the `AllowOverride` is set accordingly.

Here are some examples...

```
ErrorDocument 500 /cgi-bin/crash-recover
ErrorDocument 500 "Sorry, our script crashed. Oh dear"
ErrorDocument 500 http://xxx/
ErrorDocument 404 /Lame_excuses/not_found.html
ErrorDocument 401 /Subscription/how_to_subscribe.html
```

The syntax is,

```
ErrorDocument <3-digit-code> <action>
```

where the action can be,

1. Text to be displayed. Wrap the text with quotes (").
2. An external URL to redirect to.
3. A local URL to redirect to.

## 17.3. Custom Error Responses and Redirects

Apache's behavior to redirected URLs has been modified so that additional environment variables are available to a script/server-include.

### Old behavior

Standard CGI vars were made available to a script which has been redirected to. No indication of where the redirection came from was provided.

## New behavior

A new batch of environment variables will be initialized for use by a script which has been redirected to. Each new variable will have the prefix REDIRECT_. REDIRECT_ environment variables are created from the CGI environment variables which existed prior to the redirect, they are renamed with a REDIRECT_ prefix, *i.e.*, HTTP_USER_AGENT becomes REDIRECT_HTTP_USER_AGENT. In addition to these new variables, Apache will define REDIRECT_URL and REDIRECT_STATUS to help the script trace its origin. Both the original URL and the URL being redirected to can be logged in the access log.

If the ErrorDocument specifies a local redirect to a CGI script, the script should include a "Status:" header field in its output in order to ensure the propagation all the way back to the client of the error condition that caused it to be invoked. For instance, a Perl ErrorDocument script might include the following:

```
...
print "Content-type: text/html\n";
printf "Status: %s Condition Intercepted\n", $ENV{"REDIRECT_STATUS"};
...
```

If the script is dedicated to handling a particular error condition, such as 404 Not Found, it can use the specific code and error text instead.

Note that the script *must* emit an appropriate Status: header (such as 302 Found), if the response contains a Location: header (in order to issue a client side redirect). Otherwise the Location: header may have no effect.

# Chapter 18.
# Binding

Configuring Apache to listen on specific addresses and ports.

## 18.1. Overview

| Related Modules | Related Directives |
|-----------------|--------------------|
| core | <VirtualHost> |
| mpm_common | Listen |

When Apache starts, it binds to some port and address on the local machine and waits for incoming requests. By default, it listens to all addresses on the machine. However, it may need to be told to listen on specific ports, or only on selected addresses, or a combination of both. This is often combined with the Virtual Host feature, which determines how Apache responds to different IP addresses, hostnames and ports.

The `Listen` directive tells the server to accept incoming requests only on the specified ports or address-and-port combinations. If only a port number is specified in the `Listen` directive, the server listens to the given port on all interfaces. If an IP address is given as well as a port, the server will listen on the given port and interface. Multiple `Listen` directives may be used to specify a number of addresses and ports to listen on. The server will respond to requests from any of the listed addresses and ports.

For example, to make the server accept connections on both port 80 and port 8000, on all interfaces, use:

```
Listen 80
Listen 8000
```

To make the server accept connections on port 80 for one interface, and port 8000 on another, use

```
Listen 192.0.2.1:80
Listen 192.0.2.5:8000
```

IPv6 addresses must be enclosed in square brackets, as in the following example:

```
Listen [2001:db8::a00:20ff:fea7:ccea]:80
```

## 18.2. Special IPv6 Considerations

A growing number of platforms implement IPv6, and *APR* supports IPv6 on most of these platforms, allowing Apache to allocate IPv6 sockets, and to handle requests sent over IPv6.

One complicating factor for Apache administrators is whether or not an IPv6 socket can handle both IPv4 connections and IPv6 connections. Handling IPv4 connections with an IPv6 socket uses IPv4-mapped IPv6 addresses, which are allowed by default on most platforms, but are disallowed by default on FreeBSD, NetBSD, and OpenBSD, in order to match the system-wide policy on those platforms. On systems where it is disallowed by default, a special `configure` parameter can change this behavior for Apache.

On the other hand, on some platforms, such as Linux and Tru64, the **only** way to handle both IPv6 and IPv4 is to use mapped addresses. If you want Apache to handle IPv4 and IPv6 connections with a minimum of sockets, which requires using IPv4-mapped IPv6 addresses, specify the `--enable-v4-mapped` `configure` option.

`--enable-v4-mapped` is the default on all platforms except FreeBSD, NetBSD, and OpenBSD, so this is probably how your Apache was built.

If you want Apache to handle IPv4 connections only, regardless of what your platform and APR will support, specify an IPv4 address on all `Listen` directives, as in the following examples:

```
Listen 0.0.0.0:80
Listen 192.0.2.1:80
```

If your platform supports it and you want Apache to handle IPv4 and IPv6 connections on separate sockets (i.e., to disable IPv4-mapped addresses), specify the `--disable-v4-mapped` `configure` option. `--disable-v4-mapped` is the default on FreeBSD, NetBSD, and OpenBSD.

## 18.3. How This Works With Virtual Hosts

The Listen directive does not implement Virtual Hosts - it only tells the main server what addresses and ports to listen on. If no <VirtualHost> directives are used, the server will behave in the same way for all accepted requests. However, <VirtualHost> can be used to specify a different behavior for one or more of the addresses or ports. To implement a VirtualHost, the server must first be told to listen to the address and port to be used. Then a <VirtualHost> section should be created for the specified address and port to set the behavior of this virtual host. Note that if the <VirtualHost> is set for an address and port that the server is not listening to, it cannot be accessed.

# Chapter 19.

# Multi-Processing Modules (MPMs)

This document describes what a Multi-Processing Module is and how they are used by the Apache HTTP Server.

## 19.1. Introduction

The Apache HTTP Server is designed to be a powerful and flexible web server that can work on a very wide variety of platforms in a range of different environments. Different platforms and different environments often require different features, or may have different ways of implementing the same feature most efficiently. Apache has always accommodated a wide variety of environments through its modular design. This design allows the webmaster to choose which features will be included in the server by selecting which modules to load either at compile-time or at run-time.

Apache 2.0 extends this modular design to the most basic functions of a web server. The server ships with a selection of Multi-Processing Modules (MPMs) which are responsible for binding to network ports on the machine, accepting requests, and dispatching children to handle the requests.

Extending the modular design to this level of the server allows two important benefits:

- Apache can more cleanly and efficiently support a wide variety of operating systems. In particular, the Windows version of Apache is now much more efficient, since `mpm_winnt` can use native networking features in place of the POSIX layer used in Apache 1.3. This benefit also extends to other operating systems that implement specialized MPMs.

- The server can be better customized for the needs of the particular site. For example, sites that need a great deal of scalability can choose to use a threaded MPM like `worker` or `event`, while sites requiring stability or compatibility with older software can use a `prefork`.

At the user level, MPMs appear much like other Apache modules. The main difference is that one and only one MPM must be loaded into the server at any time. The list of available MPMs appears on the *module index page*.

## 19.2. Choosing an MPM

MPMs must be chosen during configuration, and compiled into the server. Compilers are capable of optimizing a lot of functions if threads are used, but only if they know that threads are being used.

To actually choose the desired MPM, use the argument `--with-mpm=`*NAME* with the `configure` script. *NAME* is the name of the desired MPM.

Once the server has been compiled, it is possible to determine which MPM was chosen by using `./httpd -l`. This command will list every module that is compiled into the server, including the MPM.

## 19.3. MPM Defaults

The following table lists the default MPMs for various operating systems. This will be the MPM selected if you do not make another choice at compile-time.

| | |
|---|---|
| BeOS | `beos` |
| Netware | `mpm netware` |
| OS/2 | `mpmt os2` |
| Unix | `prefork` |
| Windows | `mpm winnt` |

# Chapter 20.

# Environment Variables in Apache

The Apache HTTP Server provides a mechanism for storing information in named variables that are called *environment variables*. This information can be used to control various operations such as logging or access control. The variables are also used as a mechanism to communicate with external programs such as CGI scripts. This document discusses different ways to manipulate and use these variables.

Although these variables are referred to as *environment variables*, they are not the same as the environment variables controlled by the underlying operating system. Instead, these variables are stored and manipulated in an internal Apache structure. They only become actual operating system environment variables when they are provided to CGI scripts and Server Side Include scripts. If you wish to manipulate the operating system environment under which the server itself runs, you must use the standard environment manipulation mechanisms provided by your operating system shell.

## 20.1. Setting Environment Variables

| Related Modules | Related Directives |
|---|---|
| mod_env | BrowserMatch |
| mod_rewrite | BrowserMatchNoCase |
| mod_setenvif | PassEnv |
| mod_unique_id | RewriteRule |
| | SetEnv |
| | SetEnvIf |
| | SetEnvIfNoCase |
| | UnsetEnv |

## Basic Environment Manipulation

The most basic way to set an environment variable in Apache is using the unconditional SetEnv directive. Variables may also be passed from the environment of the shell which started the server using the PassEnv directive.

## Conditional Per-Request Settings

For additional flexibility, the directives provided by `mod_setenvif` allow environment variables to be set on a per-request basis, conditional on characteristics of particular requests. For example, a variable could be set only when a specific browser (User-Agent) is making a request, or only when a specific Referer [sic] header is found. Even more flexibility is available through the `mod_rewrite`'s `RewriteRule` which uses the `[E=...]` option to set environment variables.

## Unique Identifiers

Finally, `mod_unique_id` sets the environment variable `UNIQUE_ID` for each request to a value which is guaranteed to be unique across "all" requests under very specific conditions.

## Standard CGI Variables

In addition to all environment variables set within the Apache configuration and passed from the shell, CGI scripts and SSI pages are provided with a set of environment variables containing meta-information about the request as required by the *CGI specification*[1].

## Some Caveats

- It is not possible to override or change the standard CGI variables using the environment manipulation directives.
- When *suexec* is used to launch CGI scripts, the environment will be cleaned down to a set of *safe* variables before CGI scripts are launched. The list of *safe* variables is defined at compile-time in `suexec.c`.
- For portability reasons, the names of environment variables may contain only letters, numbers, and the underscore character. In addition, the first character may not be a number. Characters which do not match this restriction will be replaced by an underscore when passed to CGI scripts and SSI pages.
- The `SetEnv` directive runs late during request processing meaning that directives such as `SetEnvIf` and `RewriteCond` will not see the variables set with it.

## 20.2. Using Environment Variables

| Related Modules | Related Directives |
| --- | --- |
| mod_authz_host | Allow |
| mod_cgi | CustomLog |

---

[1] *http://www.w3.org/CGI/*

| Related Modules | Related Directives |
|---|---|
| mod_ext_filter | Deny |
| mod_headers | ExtFilterDefine |
| mod_include | Header |
| mod_log_config | LogFormat |
| mod_rewrite | RewriteCond |
| | RewriteRule |

## CGI Scripts

One of the primary uses of environment variables is to communicate information to CGI scripts. As discussed above, the environment passed to CGI scripts includes standard meta-information about the request in addition to any variables set within the Apache configuration. For more details, see the *CGI tutorial*.

## SSI Pages

Server-parsed (SSI) documents processed by mod_include's INCLUDES filter can print environment variables using the echo element, and can use environment variables in flow control elements to makes parts of a page conditional on characteristics of a request. Apache also provides SSI pages with the standard CGI environment variables as discussed above. For more details, see the *SSI tutorial*.

## Access Control

Access to the server can be controlled based on the value of environment variables using the allow from env= and deny from env= directives. In combination with SetEnvIf, this allows for flexible control of access to the server based on characteristics of the client. For example, you can use these directives to deny access to a particular browser (User-Agent).

## Conditional Logging

Environment variables can be logged in the access log using the LogFormat option %e. In addition, the decision on whether or not to log requests can be made based on the status of environment variables using the conditional form of the CustomLog directive. In combination with SetEnvIf this allows for flexible control of which requests are logged. For example, you can choose not to log requests for filenames ending in gif, or you can choose to only log requests from clients which are outside your subnet.

## Conditional Response Headers

The `Header` directive can use the presence or absence of an environment variable to determine whether or not a certain HTTP header will be placed in the response to the client. This allows, for example, a certain response header to be sent only if a corresponding header is received in the request from the client.

## External Filter Activation

External filters configured by `mod_ext_filter` using the ExtFilterDefine directive can by activated conditional on an environment variable using the `disableenv=` and `enableenv=` options.

## URL Rewriting

The `%{ENV:`*variable*`}` form of *TestString* in the RewriteCond allows `mod_rewrite`'s rewrite engine to make decisions conditional on environment variables. Note that the variables accessible in `mod_rewrite` without the `ENV:` prefix are not actually environment variables. Rather, they are variables special to `mod_rewrite` which cannot be accessed from other modules.

# 20.3. Special Purpose Environment Variables

Interoperability problems have led to the introduction of mechanisms to modify the way Apache behaves when talking to particular clients. To make these mechanisms as flexible as possible, they are invoked by defining environment variables, typically with `BrowserMatch`, though `SetEnv` and `PassEnv` could also be used, for example.

## downgrade-1.0

This forces the request to be treated as a HTTP/1.0 request even if it was in a later dialect.

## force-gzip

If you have the `DEFLATE` filter activated, this environment variable will ignore the accept-encoding setting of your browser and will send compressed output unconditionally.

## force-no-vary

This causes any `Vary` fields to be removed from the response header before it is sent back to the client. Some clients don't interpret this field correctly; setting this variable can work around this problem. Setting this variable also implies **force-response-1.0**.

## force-response-1.0

This forces an HTTP/1.0 response to clients making an HTTP/1.0 request. It was originally implemented as a result of a problem with AOL's proxies. Some HTTP/1.0 clients may not behave correctly when given an HTTP/1.1 response, and this can be used to interoperate with them.

## gzip-only-text/html

When set to a value of "1", this variable disables the DEFLATE output filter provided by mod_deflate for content-types other than text/html. If you'd rather use statically compressed files, mod_negotiation evaluates the variable as well (not only for gzip, but for all encodings that differ from "identity").

## no-gzip

When set, the DEFLATE filter of mod_deflate will be turned off and mod_negotiation will refuse to deliver encoded resources.

## no-cache

*Available in versions 2.2.12 and later*

When set, mod_cache will not save an otherwise cacheable response. This environment variable does not influence whether a response already in the cache will be served for the current request.

## nokeepalive

This disables KeepAlive when set.

## prefer-language

This influences mod_negotiation's behaviour. If it contains a language tag (such as en, ja or x-klingon), mod_negotiation tries to deliver a variant with that language. If there's no such variant, the normal *negotiation* process applies.

## redirect-carefully

This forces the server to be more careful when sending a redirect to the client. This is typically used when a client has a known problem handling redirects. This was originally implemented as a result of a problem with Microsoft's WebFolders software which has a problem handling redirects on directory resources via DAV methods.

## suppress-error-charset

*Available in versions after 2.0.54*

When Apache issues a redirect in response to a client request, the response includes some actual text to be displayed in case the client can't (or doesn't) automatically follow the redirection. Apache ordinarily labels this text according to the character set which it uses, which is ISO-8859-1.

However, if the redirection is to a page that uses a different character set, some broken browser versions will try to use the character set from the redirection text rather than the actual page. This can result in Greek, for instance, being incorrectly rendered.

Setting this environment variable causes Apache to omit the character set for the redirection text, and these broken browsers will then correctly use that of the destination page.

 **Security Note**

Sending error pages without a specified character set may allow a cross-site-scripting attack for existing browsers (MSIE) which do not follow the HTTP/1.1 specification and attempt to "guess" the character set from the content. Such browsers can be easily fooled into using the UTF-7 character set, and UTF-7 content from input data (such as the request-URI) will not be escaped by the usual escaping mechanisms designed to prevent cross-site-scripting attacks.

## force-proxy-request-1.0, proxy-nokeepalive, proxy-sendchunked, proxy-sendcl, proxy-chain-auth, proxy-interim-response, proxy-initial-not-pooled

These directives alter the protocol behavior of `mod_proxy`. See the `mod_proxy` and `mod_proxy_http` documentation for more details.

## 20.4. Examples

### Changing protocol behavior with misbehaving clients

Earlier versions recommended that the following lines be included in httpd.conf to deal with known client problems. Since the affected clients are no longer seen in the wild, this configuration is likely no-longer necessary.

```
# The following directives modify normal HTTP response behavior.
# The first directive disables keepalive for Netscape 2.x and browsers that
# spoof it. There are known problems with these browser implementations.
# The second directive is for Microsoft Internet Explorer 4.0b2
# which has a broken HTTP/1.1 implementation and does not properly
# support keepalive when it is used on 301 or 302 (redirect) responses.
#
BrowserMatch "Mozilla/2" nokeepalive
```

```
BrowserMatch "MSIE 4\.0b2;" nokeepalive downgrade-1.0 force-response-1.0

#
# The following directive disables HTTP/1.1 responses to browsers which
# are in violation of the HTTP/1.0 spec by not being able to grok a
# basic 1.1 response.
#
BrowserMatch "RealPlayer 4\.0" force-response-1.0
BrowserMatch "Java/1\.0" force-response-1.0
BrowserMatch "JDK/1\.0" force-response-1.0
```

## Do not log requests for images in the access log

This example keeps requests for images from appearing in the access log. It can be easily modified to prevent logging of particular directories, or to prevent logging of requests coming from particular hosts.

```
SetEnvIf Request_URI \.gif image-request
SetEnvIf Request_URI \.jpg image-request
SetEnvIf Request_URI \.png image-request
CustomLog logs/access_log common env=!image-request
```

## Prevent "Image Theft"

This example shows how to keep people not on your server from using images on your server as inline-images on their pages. This is not a recommended configuration, but it can work in limited circumstances. We assume that all your images are in a directory called /web/images.

```
SetEnvIf Referer "^http://www\.example\.com/" local_referal # Allow browsers that
do not send Referer info SetEnvIf Referer "^$" local_referal <Directory
/web/images> Order Deny,Allow
Deny from all
Allow from env=local_referal </Directory>
```

For more information about this technique, see the "*Keeping Your Images from Adorning Other Sites*"[2] tutorial on ServerWatch.

---

[2] *http://www.serverwatch.com/tutorials/article.php/1132731*

# Chapter 21.
# Apache's Handler Use

This document describes the use of Apache's Handlers.

## 21.1.What is a Handler

| Related Modules | Related Directives |
|---|---|
| mod_actions | Action |
| mod_asis | AddHandler |
| mod_cgi | RemoveHandler |
| mod_imagemap | SetHandler |
| mod_info | |
| mod_mime | |
| mod_negotiation | |
| mod_status | |

A "handler" is an internal Apache representation of the action to be performed when a file is called. Generally, files have implicit handlers, based on the file type. Normally, all files are simply served by the server, but certain file types are "handled" separately.

Handlers may also be configured explicitly, based on either filename extensions or on location, without relation to file type. This is advantageous both because it is a more elegant solution, and because it also allows for both a type **and** a handler to be associated with a file. (See also *Files with Multiple Extensions*.)

Handlers can either be built into the server or included in a module, or they can be added with the Action directive. The built-in handlers in the standard distribution are as follows:

- **default-handler**: Send the file using the default_handler(), which is the handler used by default to handle static content. (core)
- **send-as-is**: Send file with HTTP headers as is. (mod_asis)
- **cgi-script**: Treat the file as a CGI script. (mod_cgi)
- **imap-file**: Parse as an imagemap rule file. (mod_imagemap)
- **server-info**: Get the server's configuration information. (mod_info)

- **server-status**: Get the server's status report. (mod_status)
- **type-map**: Parse as a type map file for content negotiation. (mod_negotiation)

## 21.2. Examples

### Modifying static content using a CGI script

The following directives will cause requests for files with the html extension to trigger the launch of the footer.pl CGI script.

```
Action add-footer /cgi-bin/footer.pl
AddHandler add-footer .html
```

Then the CGI script is responsible for sending the originally requested document (pointed to by the PATH_TRANSLATED environment variable) and making whatever modifications or additions are desired.

### Files with HTTP headers

The following directives will enable the send-as-is handler, which is used for files which contain their own HTTP headers. All files in the /web/htdocs/asis/ directory will be processed by the send-as-is handler, regardless of their filename extensions.

```
<Directory /web/htdocs/asis>
SetHandler send-as-is
</Directory>
```

## 21.3. Programmer's Note

In order to implement the handler features, an addition has been made to the *Apache API* that you may wish to make use of. Specifically, a new record has been added to the request_rec structure:

```
char *handler
```

If you wish to have your module engage a handler, you need only to set r->handler to the name of the handler at any time prior to the invoke_handler stage of the request. Handlers are implemented as they were before, albeit using the handler name instead of a content type. While it is not necessary, the naming convention for handlers is to use a dash-separated word, with no slashes, so as to not invade the media type name-space.

# Chapter 22.

# Filters

This document describes the use of filters in Apache.

## 22.1. Filtering in Apache 2

| Related Modules | Related Directives |
|---|---|
| mod_filter | FilterChain |
| mod_deflate | FilterDeclare |
| mod_ext_filter | FilterProtocol |
| mod_include | FilterProvider |
| mod_charset_lite | AddInputFilter |
| | AddOutputFilter |
| | RemoveInputFilter |
| | RemoveOutputFilter |
| | ExtFilterDefine |
| | ExtFilterOptions |
| | SetInputFilter |
| | SetOutputFilter |

The Filter Chain is available in Apache 2.0 and higher, and enables applications to process incoming and outgoing data in a highly flexible and configurable manner, regardless of where the data comes from. We can pre-process incoming data, and post-process outgoing data, at will. This is basically independent of the traditional request processing phases.

Some examples of filtering in the standard Apache distribution are:

- mod_include, implements server-side includes.
- mod_ssl, implements SSL encryption (https).
- mod_deflate, implements compression/decompression on the fly.
- mod_charset_lite, transcodes between different character sets.
- mod_ext_filter, runs an external program as a filter.

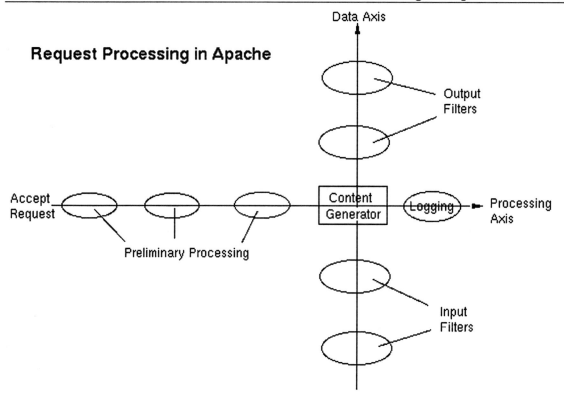

Apache also uses a number of filters internally to perform functions like chunking and byte-range handling.

A wider range of applications are implemented by third-party filter modules available from *modules.apache.org* and elsewhere. A few of these are:

- HTML and XML processing and rewriting
- XSLT transforms and XIncludes
- XML Namespace support
- File Upload handling and decoding of HTML Forms
- Image processing
- Protection of vulnerable applications such as PHP scripts
- Text search-and-replace editing

## 22.2. Smart Filtering

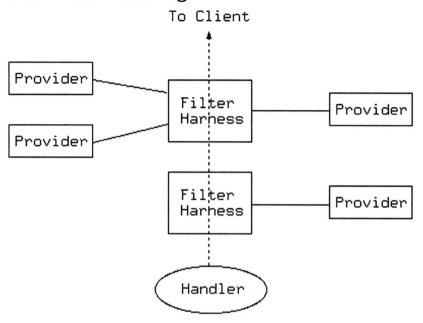

mod_filter, included in Apache 2.1 and later, enables the filter chain to be configured dynamically at run time. So for example you can set up a proxy to rewrite HTML with an HTML filter and JPEG images with a completely separate filter, despite the proxy having no prior information about what the origin server will send. This works by using a filter harness, that dispatches to different providers according to the actual contents at runtime. Any filter may be either inserted directly in the chain and run unconditionally, or used as a provider and inserted dynamically. For example,

- an HTML processing filter will only run if the content is text/html or application/xhtml+xml
- A compression filter will only run if the input is a compressible type and not already compressed
- A charset conversion filter will be inserted if a text document is not already in the desired charset

## 22.3. Using Filters

There are two ways to use filtering: Simple and Dynamic. In general, you should use one or the other; mixing them can have unexpected consequences (although simple Input filtering can be mixed freely with either simple or dynamic Output filtering).

The Simple Way is the only way to configure input filters, and is sufficient for output filters where you need a static filter chain. Relevant directives are SetInputFilter,

SetOutputFilter, AddInputFilter, AddOutputFilter, RemoveInputFilter, and RemoveOutputFilter.

The Dynamic Way enables both static and flexible, dynamic configuration of output filters, as discussed in the mod_filter page. Relevant directives are FilterChain, FilterDeclare, and FilterProvider.

One further directive AddOutputFilterByType is still supported, but may be problematic and is now deprecated. Use dynamic configuration instead.

# Chapter 23.
# suEXEC Support

The **suEXEC** feature provides Apache users the ability to run **CGI** and **SSI** programs under user IDs different from the user ID of the calling web server. Normally, when a CGI or SSI program executes, it runs as the same user who is running the web server.

Used properly, this feature can reduce considerably the security risks involved with allowing users to develop and run private CGI or SSI programs. However, if suEXEC is improperly configured, it can cause any number of problems and possibly create new holes in your computer's security. If you aren't familiar with managing *setuid root* programs and the security issues they present, we highly recommend that you not consider using suEXEC.

## 23.1. Before we begin

Before jumping head-first into this document, you should be aware of the assumptions made on the part of the Apache Group and this document.

First, it is assumed that you are using a UNIX derivative operating system that is capable of **setuid** and **setgid** operations. All command examples are given in this regard. Other platforms, if they are capable of supporting suEXEC, may differ in their configuration.

Second, it is assumed you are familiar with some basic concepts of your computer's security and its administration. This involves an understanding of **setuid/setgid** operations and the various effects they may have on your system and its level of security.

Third, it is assumed that you are using an **unmodified** version of suEXEC code. All code for suEXEC has been carefully scrutinized and tested by the developers as well as numerous beta testers. Every precaution has been taken to ensure a simple yet solidly safe base of code. Altering this code can cause unexpected problems and new security risks. It is **highly** recommended you not alter the suEXEC code unless you are well versed in the particulars of security programming and are willing to share your work with the Apache Group for consideration.

Fourth, and last, it has been the decision of the Apache Group to **NOT** make suEXEC part of the default installation of Apache. To this end, suEXEC configuration requires of the administrator careful attention to details. After due consideration has been given to the various settings for suEXEC, the administrator may install suEXEC through normal installation methods. The values for these settings need to be carefully determined and specified by the administrator to properly maintain system security during the use of suEXEC functionality. It is through this detailed process that the Apache Group hopes to limit suEXEC installation only to those who are careful and determined enough to use it.

Still with us? Yes? Good. Let's move on!

## 23.2. suEXEC Security Model

Before we begin configuring and installing suEXEC, we will first discuss the security model you are about to implement. By doing so, you may better understand what exactly is going on inside suEXEC and what precautions are taken to ensure your system's security.

**suEXEC** is based on a setuid "wrapper" program that is called by the main Apache web server. This wrapper is called when an HTTP request is made for a CGI or SSI program that the administrator has designated to run as a userid other than that of the main server. When such a request is made, Apache provides the suEXEC wrapper with the program's name and the user and group IDs under which the program is to execute.

The wrapper then employs the following process to determine success or failure -- if any one of these conditions fail, the program logs the failure and exits with an error, otherwise it will continue:

1. **Is the user executing this wrapper a valid user of this system?**

    This is to ensure that the user executing the wrapper is truly a user of the system.

2. **Was the wrapper called with the proper number of arguments?**

    The wrapper will only execute if it is given the proper number of arguments. The proper argument format is known to the Apache web server. If the wrapper is not receiving the proper number of arguments, it is either being hacked, or there is something wrong with the suEXEC portion of your Apache binary.

3. **Is this valid user allowed to run the wrapper?**

    Is this user the user allowed to run this wrapper? Only one user (the Apache user) is allowed to execute this program.

4. **Does the target CGI or SSI program have an unsafe hierarchical reference?**

    Does the target CGI or SSI program's path contain a leading '/' or have a '..' backreference? These are not allowed; the target CGI/SSI program must reside within suEXEC's document root (see --with-suexec-docroot=*DIR* below).

5. **Is the target user name valid?**

    Does the target user exist?

6. **Is the target group name valid?**

   Does the target group exist?

7. **Is the target user *NOT* superuser?**

   Presently, suEXEC does not allow *root* to execute CGI/SSI programs.

8. **Is the target userid *ABOVE* the minimum ID number?**

   The minimum user ID number is specified during configuration. This allows you to set the lowest possible userid that will be allowed to execute CGI/SSI programs. This is useful to block out "system" accounts.

9. **Is the target group *NOT* the superuser group?**

   Presently, suEXEC does not allow the *root* group to execute CGI/SSI programs.

10. **Is the target groupid *ABOVE* the minimum ID number?**

    The minimum group ID number is specified during configuration. This allows you to set the lowest possible groupid that will be allowed to execute CGI/SSI programs. This is useful to block out "system" groups.

11. **Can the wrapper successfully become the target user and group?**

    Here is where the program becomes the target user and group via setuid and setgid calls. The group access list is also initialized with all of the groups of which the user is a member.

12. **Can we change directory to the one in which the target CGI/SSI program resides?**

    If it doesn't exist, it can't very well contain files. If we can't change directory to it, it might aswell not exist.

13. **Is the directory within the Apache webspace?**

    If the request is for a regular portion of the server, is the requested directory within suEXEC's document root? If the request is for a `UserDir`, is the requested directory within the directory configured as suEXEC's userdir (see *suEXEC's configuration options*)?

14. **Is the directory *NOT* writable by anyone else?**

    We don't want to open up the directory to others; only the owner user may be able to alter this directories contents.

15. **Does the target CGI/SSI program exist?**

    If it doesn't exists, it can't very well be executed.

16. **Is the target CGI/SSI program *NOT* writable by anyone else?**

    We don't want to give anyone other than the owner the ability to change the CGI/SSI program.

17. **Is the target CGI/SSI program *NOT* setuid or setgid?**

    We do not want to execute programs that will then change our UID/GID again.

18. **Is the target user/group the same as the program's user/group?**

    Is the user the owner of the file?

19. **Can we successfully clean the process environment to ensure safe operations?**

    suEXEC cleans the process' environment by establishing a safe execution PATH (defined during configuration), as well as only passing through those variables whose names are listed in the safe environment list (also created during configuration).

20. **Can we successfully become the target CGI/SSI program and execute?**

    Here is where suEXEC ends and the target CGI/SSI program begins.

This is the standard operation of the suEXEC wrapper's security model. It is somewhat stringent and can impose new limitations and guidelines for CGI/SSI design, but it was developed carefully step-by-step with security in mind.

For more information as to how this security model can limit your possibilities in regards to server configuration, as well as what security risks can be avoided with a proper suEXEC setup, see the *"Beware the Jabberwock"* section of this document.

## 23.3. Configuring & Installing suEXEC

Here's where we begin the fun.

**suEXEC configuration options**

**`--enable-suexec`**

This option enables the suEXEC feature which is never installed or activated by default. At least one `--with-suexec-xxxxx` option has to be provided together with the `--enable-suexec` option to let APACI accept your request for using the suEXEC feature.

**`--with-suexec-bin=`*PATH*`**

The path to the `suexec` binary must be hard-coded in the server for security reasons. Use this option to override the default path. *e.g.* `--with-suexec-bin=/usr/sbin/suexec`

**`--with-suexec-caller=`*UID*`**

The *username* under which Apache normally runs. This is the only user allowed to execute this program.

**`--with-suexec-userdir=`*DIR*`**

Define to be the subdirectory under users' home directories where suEXEC access should be allowed. All executables under this directory will be executable by suEXEC as the user so they should be "safe" programs. If you are using a "simple" `UserDir` directive (ie. one without a "*" in it) this should be set to the same value. suEXEC will not work properly in cases where the `UserDir` directive points to a location that is not the same as the user's home directory as referenced in the `passwd` file. Default value is "`public_html`".

If you have virtual hosts with a different `UserDir` for each, you will need to define them to all reside in one parent directory; then name that parent directory here. **If this is not defined properly, "~userdir" cgi requests will not work!**

**--with-suexec-docroot=***DIR*

Define as the DocumentRoot set for Apache. This will be the only hierarchy (aside from `UserDirs`) that can be used for suEXEC behavior. The default directory is the `--datadir` value with the suffix "`/htdocs`", *e.g.* if you configure with "`--datadir=/home/apache`" the directory "`/home/apache/htdocs`" is used as document root for the suEXEC wrapper.

**--with-suexec-uidmin=***UID*

Define this as the lowest UID allowed to be a target user for suEXEC. For most systems, 500 or 100 is common. Default value is 100.

**--with-suexec-gidmin=***GID*

Define this as the lowest GID allowed to be a target group for suEXEC. For most systems, 100 is common and therefore used as default value.

**--with-suexec-logfile=***FILE*

This defines the filename to which all suEXEC transactions and errors are logged (useful for auditing and debugging purposes). By default the logfile is named "`suexec_log`" and located in your standard logfile directory (`--logfiledir`).

**--with-suexec-safepath=***PATH*

Define a safe PATH environment to pass to CGI executables. Default value is "`/usr/local/bin:/usr/bin:/bin`".

## Compiling and installing the suEXEC wrapper

If you have enabled the suEXEC feature with the `--enable-suexec` option the `suexec` binary (together with Apache itself) is automatically built if you execute the `make` command.

After all components have been built you can execute the command `make install` to install them. The binary image `suexec` is installed in the directory defined by the `--sbindir` option. The default location is "/usr/local/apache2/bin/suexec".

Please note that you need *root privileges* for the installation step. In order for the wrapper to set the user ID, it must be installed as owner *root* and must have the setuserid execution bit set for file modes.

### Setting paranoid permissions

Although the suEXEC wrapper will check to ensure that its caller is the correct user as specified with the `--with-suexec-caller` *configure* option, there is always the possibility that a system or library call suEXEC uses before this check may be exploitable on your system. To counter this, and because it is best-practise in general, you should use filesystem permissions to ensure that only the group Apache runs as may execute suEXEC.

If for example, your web server is configured to run as:

```
User www
Group webgroup
```

and *suexec* is installed at "/usr/local/apache2/bin/suexec", you should run:

```
chgrp webgroup /usr/local/apache2/bin/suexec
chmod 4750 /usr/local/apache2/bin/suexec
```

This will ensure that only the group Apache runs as can even execute the suEXEC wrapper.

## 23.4. Enabling & Disabling suEXEC

Upon startup of Apache, it looks for the file *suexec* in the directory defined by the `--sbindir` option (default is "/usr/local/apache/sbin/suexec"). If Apache finds a properly configured suEXEC wrapper, it will print the following message to the error log:

```
[notice] suEXEC mechanism enabled (wrapper: /path/to/suexec)
```

If you don't see this message at server startup, the server is most likely not finding the wrapper program where it expects it, or the executable is not installed *setuid root*.

If you want to enable the suEXEC mechanism for the first time and an Apache server is already running you must kill and restart Apache. Restarting it with a simple HUP or USR1 signal will not be enough.

If you want to disable suEXEC you should kill and restart Apache after you have removed the *suexec* file.

## 23.5. Using suEXEC

Requests for CGI programs will call the suEXEC wrapper only if they are for a virtual host containing a SuexecUserGroup directive or if they are processed by mod_userdir.

**Virtual Hosts:**

One way to use the suEXEC wrapper is through the `SuexecUserGroup` directive in `VirtualHost` definitions. By setting this directive to values different from the main server user ID, all requests for CGI resources will be executed as the *User* and *Group* defined for that `<VirtualHost>`. If this directive is not specified for a `<VirtualHost>` then the main server userid is assumed.

**User directories:**

Requests that are processed by `mod_userdir` will call the suEXEC wrapper to execute CGI programs under the userid of the requested user directory. The only requirement needed for this feature to work is for CGI execution to be enabled for the user and that the script must meet the scrutiny of the *security checks* above. See also the `--with-suexec-userdir` *compile time option*.

## 23.6. Debugging suEXEC

The suEXEC wrapper will write log information to the file defined with the `--with-suexec-logfile` option as indicated above. If you feel you have configured and installed the wrapper properly, have a look at this log and the error_log for the server to see where you may have gone astray.

## 23.7. Beware the Jabberwock: Warnings & Examples

There are a few points of interest regarding the wrapper that can cause limitations on server setup. Please review these before submitting any "bugs" regarding suEXEC.

- **suEXEC Points Of Interest**
- Hierarchy limitations

  For security and efficiency reasons, all suEXEC requests must remain within either a top-level document root for virtual host requests, or one top-level personal document root for userdir requests. For example, if you have four VirtualHosts configured, you would need to structure all of your VHosts' document roots off of one main Apache document hierarchy to take advantage of suEXEC for VirtualHosts. (Example forthcoming.)
- suEXEC's PATH environment variable

  This can be a dangerous thing to change. Make certain every path you include in this define is a **trusted** directory. You don't want to open people up to having someone from across the world running a trojan horse on them.
- Altering the suEXEC code

  Again, this can cause **Big Trouble** if you try this without knowing what you are doing. Stay away from it if at all possible.

# Chapter 24.

# Apache Performance Tuning

Apache 2.x is a general-purpose webserver, designed to provide a balance of flexibility, portability, and performance. Although it has not been designed specifically to set benchmark records, Apache 2.x is capable of high performance in many real-world situations.

Compared to Apache 1.3, release 2.x contains many additional optimizations to increase throughput and scalability. Most of these improvements are enabled by default. However, there are compile-time and run-time configuration choices that can significantly affect performance. This document describes the options that a server administrator can configure to tune the performance of an Apache 2.x installation. Some of these configuration options enable the httpd to better take advantage of the capabilities of the hardware and OS, while others allow the administrator to trade functionality for speed.

## 24.1. Hardware and Operating System Issues

The single biggest hardware issue affecting webserver performance is RAM. A webserver should never ever have to swap, as swapping increases the latency of each request beyond a point that users consider "fast enough". This causes users to hit stop and reload, further increasing the load. You can, and should, control the `MaxClients` setting so that your server does not spawn so many children it starts swapping. This procedure for doing this is simple: determine the size of your average Apache process, by looking at your process list via a tool such as `top`, and divide this into your total available memory, leaving some room for other processes.

Beyond that the rest is mundane: get a fast enough CPU, a fast enough network card, and fast enough disks, where "fast enough" is something that needs to be determined by experimentation.

Operating system choice is largely a matter of local concerns. But some guidelines that have proven generally useful are:

- Run the latest stable release and patchlevel of the operating system that you choose. Many OS suppliers have introduced significant performance improvements to their TCP stacks and thread libraries in recent years.

- If your OS supports a sendfile(2) system call, make sure you install the release and/or patches needed to enable it. (With Linux, for example, this means using Linux 2.4 or later. For early releases of Solaris 8, you may need to apply a patch.) On systems where it is available, sendfile enables Apache 2 to deliver static content faster and with lower CPU utilization.

## 24.2. Run-Time Configuration Issues

| Related Modules | Related Directives |
|---|---|
| mod_dir | AllowOverride |
| mpm_common | DirectoryIndex |
| mod_status | HostnameLookups |
| | EnableMMAP |
| | EnableSendfile |
| | KeepAliveTimeout |
| | MaxSpareServers |
| | MinSpareServers |
| | Options |
| | StartServers |

### 24.2.1. HostnameLookups and other DNS considerations

Prior to Apache 1.3, HostnameLookups defaulted to On. This adds latency to every request because it requires a DNS lookup to complete before the request is finished. In Apache 1.3 this setting defaults to Off. If you need to have addresses in your log files resolved to hostnames, use the *logresolve* program that comes with Apache, or one of the numerous log reporting packages which are available.

It is recommended that you do this sort of postprocessing of your log files on some machine other than the production web server machine, in order that this activity not adversely affect server performance.

If you use any Allow from domain or Deny from domain directives (i.e., using a hostname, or a domain name, rather than an IP address) then you will pay for two DNS lookups (a reverse, followed by a forward lookup to make sure that the reverse is not being spoofed). For best performance, therefore, use IP addresses, rather than names, when using these directives, if possible.

Note that it's possible to scope the directives, such as within a <Location /server-status> section. In this case the DNS lookups are only performed on requests matching the criteria. Here's an example which disables lookups except for .html and .cgi files:

```
HostnameLookups off
<Files ~ "\.(html|cgi)$">
HostnameLookups on
</Files>
```

But even still, if you just need DNS names in some CGIs you could consider doing the `gethostbyname` call in the specific CGIs that need it.

### 24.2.2. FollowSymLinks and SymLinksIfOwnerMatch

Wherever in your URL-space you do not have an `Options FollowSymLinks`, or you do have an `Options SymLinksIfOwnerMatch` Apache will have to issue extra system calls to check up on symlinks. One extra call per filename component. For example, if you had:

```
DocumentRoot /www/htdocs
<Directory />
Options SymLinksIfOwnerMatch
</Directory>
```

and a request is made for the URI `/index.html`. Then Apache will perform `lstat(2)` on `/www`, `/www/htdocs`, and `/www/htdocs/index.html`. The results of these `lstats` are never cached, so they will occur on every single request. If you really desire the symlinks security checking you can do something like this:

```
DocumentRoot /www/htdocs
<Directory />
Options FollowSymLinks
</Directory>

<Directory /www/htdocs>
Options -FollowSymLinks +SymLinksIfOwnerMatch
</Directory>
```

This at least avoids the extra checks for the `DocumentRoot` path. Note that you'll need to add similar sections if you have any `Alias` or `RewriteRule` paths outside of your document root. For highest performance, and no symlink protection, set `FollowSymLinks` everywhere, and never set `SymLinksIfOwnerMatch`.

### 24.2.3. AllowOverride

Wherever in your URL-space you allow overrides (typically `.htaccess` files) Apache will attempt to open `.htaccess` for each filename component. For example,

```
DocumentRoot /www/htdocs
<Directory />
AllowOverride all
</Directory>
```

and a request is made for the URI /index.html. Then Apache will attempt to open /.htaccess, /www/.htaccess, and /www/htdocs/.htaccess. The solutions are similar to the previous case of Options FollowSymLinks. For highest performance use AllowOverride None everywhere in your filesystem.

## 24.2.4. Negotiation

If at all possible, avoid content-negotiation if you're really interested in every last ounce of performance. In practice the benefits of negotiation outweigh the performance penalties. There's one case where you can speed up the server. Instead of using a wildcard such as:

```
DirectoryIndex index
```

Use a complete list of options:

```
DirectoryIndex index.cgi index.pl index.shtml index.html
```

where you list the most common choice first.

Also note that explicitly creating a type-map file provides better performance than using MultiViews, as the necessary information can be determined by reading this single file, rather than having to scan the directory for files.

If your site needs content negotiation consider using type-map files, rather than the Options MultiViews directive to accomplish the negotiation. See the *Content Negotiation* documentation for a full discussion of the methods of negotiation, and instructions for creating type-map files.

## 24.2.5. Memory-mapping

In situations where Apache 2.x needs to look at the contents of a file being delivered--for example, when doing server-side-include processing--it normally memory-maps the file if the OS supports some form of mmap(2).

On some platforms, this memory-mapping improves performance. However, there are cases where memory-mapping can hurt the performance or even the stability of the httpd:

- On some operating systems, mmap does not scale as well as read(2) when the number of CPUs increases. On multiprocessor Solaris servers, for example, Apache 2.x sometimes delivers server-parsed files faster when mmap is disabled.

- If you memory-map a file located on an NFS-mounted filesystem and a process on another NFS client machine deletes or truncates the file, your process may get a bus error the next time it tries to access the mapped file content.

For installations where either of these factors applies, you should use EnableMMAP off to disable the memory-mapping of delivered files. (Note: This directive can be overridden on a per-directory basis.)

## 24.2.6. Sendfile

In situations where Apache 2.x can ignore the contents of the file to be delivered -- for example, when serving static file content -- it normally uses the kernel sendfile support the file if the OS supports the `sendfile(2)` operation.

On most platforms, using sendfile improves performance by eliminating separate read and send mechanics. However, there are cases where using sendfile can harm the stability of the httpd:

- Some platforms may have broken sendfile support that the build system did not detect, especially if the binaries were built on another box and moved to such a machine with broken sendfile support.
- With an NFS-mounted files, the kernel may be unable to reliably serve the network file through it's own cache.

For installations where either of these factors applies, you should use `EnableSendfile off` to disable sendfile delivery of file contents. (Note: This directive can be overridden on a per-directory basis.)

## 24.2.7. Process Creation

Prior to Apache 1.3 the `MinSpareServers`, `MaxSpareServers`, and `StartServers` settings all had drastic effects on benchmark results. In particular, Apache required a "ramp-up" period in order to reach a number of children sufficient to serve the load being applied. After the initial spawning of `StartServers` children, only one child per second would be created to satisfy the `MinSpareServers` setting. So a server being accessed by 100 simultaneous clients, using the default `StartServers` of 5 would take on the order 95 seconds to spawn enough children to handle the load. This works fine in practice on real-life servers, because they aren't restarted frequently. But does really poorly on benchmarks which might only run for ten minutes.

The one-per-second rule was implemented in an effort to avoid swamping the machine with the startup of new children. If the machine is busy spawning children it can't service requests. But it has such a drastic effect on the perceived performance of Apache that it had to be replaced. As of Apache 1.3, the code will relax the one-per-second rule. It will spawn one, wait a second, then spawn two, wait a second, then spawn four, and it will continue exponentially until it is spawning 32 children per second. It will stop whenever it satisfies the `MinSpareServers` setting.

This appears to be responsive enough that it's almost unnecessary to twiddle the `MinSpareServers`, `MaxSpareServers` and `StartServers` knobs. When more than 4 children are spawned per second, a message will be emitted to the `ErrorLog`. If you see a lot of these errors then consider tuning these settings. Use the mod_status output as a guide.

Related to process creation is process death induced by the MaxRequestsPerChild setting. By default this is 0, which means that there is no limit to the number of requests handled per child. If your configuration currently has this set to some very low number, such as 30, you may want to bump this up significantly. If you are running SunOS or an old version of Solaris, limit this to 10000 or so because of memory leaks.

When keep-alives are in use, children will be kept busy doing nothing waiting for more requests on the already open connection. The default KeepAliveTimeout of 5 seconds attempts to minimize this effect. The tradeoff here is between network bandwidth and server resources. In no event should you raise this above about 60 seconds, as *most of the benefits are lost*[1].

## 24.3. Compile-Time Configuration Issues

### 24.3.1. Choosing an MPM

Apache 2.x supports pluggable concurrency models, called *Multi-Processing Modules* (MPMs). When building Apache, you must choose an MPM to use. There are platform-specific MPMs for some platforms: beos, mpm_netware, mpmt_os2, and mpm_winnt. For general Unix-type systems, there are several MPMs from which to choose. The choice of MPM can affect the speed and scalability of the httpd:

- The worker MPM uses multiple child processes with many threads each. Each thread handles one connection at a time. Worker generally is a good choice for high-traffic servers because it has a smaller memory footprint than the prefork MPM.

- The prefork MPM uses multiple child processes with one thread each. Each process handles one connection at a time. On many systems, prefork is comparable in speed to worker, but it uses more memory. Prefork's threadless design has advantages over worker in some situations: it can be used with non-thread-safe third-party modules, and it is easier to debug on platforms with poor thread debugging support.

For more information on these and other MPMs, please see the MPM *documentation*.

### 24.3.2. Modules

Since memory usage is such an important consideration in performance, you should attempt to eliminate modules that you are not actually using. If you have built the modules as *DSOs*,

[1] *http://www.hpl.hp.com/techreports/Compaq-DEC/WRL-95-4.html*

eliminating modules is a simple matter of commenting out the associated `LoadModule` directive for that module. This allows you to experiment with removing modules, and seeing if your site still functions in their absense.

If, on the other hand, you have modules statically linked into your Apache binary, you will need to recompile Apache in order to remove unwanted modules.

An associated question that arises here is, of course, what modules you need, and which ones you don't. The answer here will, of course, vary from one web site to another. However, the *minimal* list of modules which you can get by with tends to include `mod_mime`, `mod_dir`, and `mod_log_config`. `mod_log_config` is, of course, optional, as you can run a web site without log files. This is, however, not recommended.

### 24.3.3. Atomic Operations

Some modules, such as `mod_cache` and recent development builds of the worker MPM, use APR's atomic API. This API provides atomic operations that can be used for lightweight thread synchronization.

By default, APR implements these operations using the most efficient mechanism available on each target OS/CPU platform. Many modern CPUs, for example, have an instruction that does an atomic compare-and-swap (CAS) operation in hardware. On some platforms, however, APR defaults to a slower, mutex-based implementation of the atomic API in order to ensure compatibility with older CPU models that lack such instructions. If you are building Apache for one of these platforms, and you plan to run only on newer CPUs, you can select a faster atomic implementation at build time by configuring Apache with the `--enable-nonportable-atomics` option:

```
./buildconf
./configure --with-mpm=worker --enable-nonportable-atomics=yes
```

The `--enable-nonportable-atomics` option is relevant for the following platforms:

- Solaris on SPARC
  By default, APR uses mutex-based atomics on Solaris/SPARC. If you configure with `--enable-nonportable-atomics`, however, APR generates code that uses a SPARC v8plus opcode for fast hardware compare-and-swap. If you configure Apache with this option, the atomic operations will be more efficient (allowing for lower CPU utilization and higher concurrency), but the resulting executable will run only on UltraSPARC chips.

- Linux on x86
  By default, APR uses mutex-based atomics on Linux. If you configure with `--enable-nonportable-atomics`, however, APR generates code that uses a 486 opcode for fast hardware compare-and-swap. This will result in more efficient

atomic operations, but the resulting executable will run only on 486 and later chips (and not on 386).

### 24.3.4. mod_status and ExtendedStatus On

If you include mod status and you also set ExtendedStatus On when building and running Apache, then on every request Apache will perform two calls to gettimeofday(2) (or times(2) depending on your operating system), and (pre-1.3) several extra calls to time(2). This is all done so that the status report contains timing indications. For highest performance, set ExtendedStatus off (which is the default).

### 24.3.5. accept Serialization - multiple sockets

**Warning**

This section has not been fully updated to take into account changes made in the 2.x version of the Apache HTTP Server. Some of the information may still be relevant, but please use it with care.

This discusses a shortcoming in the Unix socket API. Suppose your web server uses multiple Listen statements to listen on either multiple ports or multiple addresses. In order to test each socket to see if a connection is ready Apache uses select(2). select(2) indicates that a socket has *zero* or *at least one* connection waiting on it. Apache's model includes multiple children, and all the idle ones test for new connections at the same time. A naive implementation looks something like this (these examples do not match the code, they're contrived for pedagogical purposes):

```
for (;;) {
for (;;) {
fd_set accept_fds;

FD_ZERO (&accept_fds);
for (i = first_socket; i <= last_socket; ++i) {
FD_SET (i, &accept_fds);
}
rc = select (last_socket+1, &accept_fds, NULL, NULL, NULL);
if (rc < 1) continue;
new_connection = -1;
for (i = first_socket; i <= last_socket; ++i) {
if (FD_ISSET (i, &accept_fds)) {
new_connection = accept (i, NULL, NULL);
if (new_connection != -1) break;
}
}
if (new_connection != -1) break;
}
```

```
process the new_connection;
}
```

But this naive implementation has a serious starvation problem. Recall that multiple children execute this loop at the same time, and so multiple children will block at `select` when they are in between requests. All those blocked children will awaken and return from `select` when a single request appears on any socket (the number of children which awaken varies depending on the operating system and timing issues). They will all then fall down into the loop and try to `accept` the connection. But only one will succeed (assuming there's still only one connection ready), the rest will be *blocked* in `accept`. This effectively locks those children into serving requests from that one socket and no other sockets, and they'll be stuck there until enough new requests appear on that socket to wake them all up. This starvation problem was first documented in *PR#467*[2]. There are at least two solutions.

One solution is to make the sockets non-blocking. In this case the `accept` won't block the children, and they will be allowed to continue immediately. But this wastes CPU time. Suppose you have ten idle children in `select`, and one connection arrives. Then nine of those children will wake up, try to `accept` the connection, fail, and loop back into `select`, accomplishing nothing. Meanwhile none of those children are servicing requests that occurred on other sockets until they get back up to the `select` again. Overall this solution does not seem very fruitful unless you have as many idle CPUs (in a multiprocessor box) as you have idle children, not a very likely situation.

Another solution, the one used by Apache, is to serialize entry into the inner loop. The loop looks like this (differences highlighted):

```
for (;;) {
accept_mutex_on ();
for (;;) {
fd_set accept_fds;

FD_ZERO (&accept_fds);
for (i = first_socket; i <= last_socket; ++i) {
FD_SET (i, &accept_fds);
}
rc = select (last_socket+1, &accept_fds, NULL, NULL, NULL);
if (rc < 1) continue;
new_connection = -1;
for (i = first_socket; i <= last_socket; ++i) {
if (FD_ISSET (i, &accept_fds)) {
new_connection = accept (i, NULL, NULL);
if (new_connection != -1) break;
}
```

---

[2] *http://bugs.apache.org/index/full/467*

---

```
}
if (new_connection != -1) break;
}
accept_mutex_off ();
process the new_connection;
}
```

The functions `accept_mutex_on` and `accept_mutex_off` implement a mutual exclusion semaphore. Only one child can have the mutex at any time. There are several choices for implementing these mutexes. The choice is defined in `src/conf.h` (pre-1.3) or `src/include/ap_config.h` (1.3 or later). Some architectures do not have any locking choice made, on these architectures it is unsafe to use multiple `Listen` directives.

The directive `AcceptMutex` can be used to change the selected mutex implementation at run-time.

**AcceptMutex flock**

This method uses the `flock(2)` system call to lock a lock file (located by the `LockFile` directive).

**AcceptMutex fcntl**

This method uses the `fcntl(2)` system call to lock a lock file (located by the `LockFile` directive).

**AcceptMutex sysvsem**

(1.3 or later) This method uses SysV-style semaphores to implement the mutex. Unfortunately SysV-style semaphores have some bad side-effects. One is that it's possible Apache will die without cleaning up the semaphore (see the `ipcs(8)` man page). The other is that the semaphore API allows for a denial of service attack by any CGIs running under the same uid as the webserver (*i.e.*, all CGIs, unless you use something like *suexec* or `cgiwrapper`). For these reasons this method is not used on any architecture except IRIX (where the previous two are prohibitively expensive on most IRIX boxes).

**AcceptMutex pthread**

(1.3 or later) This method uses POSIX mutexes and should work on any architecture implementing the full POSIX threads specification, however appears to only work on Solaris (2.5 or later), and even then only in certain configurations. If you experiment with this you should watch out for your server hanging and not responding. Static content only servers may work just fine.

**AcceptMutex posixsem**

(2.0 or later) This method uses POSIX semaphores. The semaphore ownership is not recovered if a thread in the process holding the mutex segfaults, resulting in a hang of the web server.

If your system has another method of serialization which isn't in the above list then it may be worthwhile adding code for it to APR.

Another solution that has been considered but never implemented is to partially serialize the loop -- that is, let in a certain number of processes. This would only be of interest on multiprocessor boxes where it's possible multiple children could run simultaneously, and the serialization actually doesn't take advantage of the full bandwidth. This is a possible area of future investigation, but priority remains low because highly parallel web servers are not the norm.

Ideally you should run servers without multiple `Listen` statements if you want the highest performance. But read on.

### 24.3.6. accept Serialization - single socket

The above is fine and dandy for multiple socket servers, but what about single socket servers? In theory they shouldn't experience any of these same problems because all children can just block in `accept(2)` until a connection arrives, and no starvation results. In practice this hides almost the same "spinning" behaviour discussed above in the non-blocking solution. The way that most TCP stacks are implemented, the kernel actually wakes up all processes blocked in `accept` when a single connection arrives. One of those processes gets the connection and returns to user-space, the rest spin in the kernel and go back to sleep when they discover there's no connection for them. This spinning is hidden from the user-land code, but it's there nonetheless. This can result in the same load-spiking wasteful behaviour that a non-blocking solution to the multiple sockets case can.

For this reason we have found that many architectures behave more "nicely" if we serialize even the single socket case. So this is actually the default in almost all cases. Crude experiments under Linux (2.0.30 on a dual Pentium pro 166 w/128Mb RAM) have shown that the serialization of the single socket case causes less than a 3% decrease in requests per second over unserialized single-socket. But unserialized single-socket showed an extra 100ms latency on each request. This latency is probably a wash on long haul lines, and only an issue on LANs. If you want to override the single socket serialization you can define `SINGLE_LISTEN_UNSERIALIZED_ACCEPT` and then single-socket servers will not serialize at all.

### 24.3.7. Lingering Close

As discussed in *draft-ietf-http-connection-00.txt*[3] section 8, in order for an HTTP server to **reliably** implement the protocol it needs to shutdown each direction of the communication

---

[3] *http://www.ics.uci.edu/pub/ietf/http/draft-ietf-http-connection-00.txt*

independently (recall that a TCP connection is bi-directional, each half is independent of the other). This fact is often overlooked by other servers, but is correctly implemented in Apache as of 1.2.

When this feature was added to Apache it caused a flurry of problems on various versions of Unix because of a shortsightedness. The TCP specification does not state that the FIN_WAIT_2 state has a timeout, but it doesn't prohibit it. On systems without the timeout, Apache 1.2 induces many sockets stuck forever in the FIN_WAIT_2 state. In many cases this can be avoided by simply upgrading to the latest TCP/IP patches supplied by the vendor. In cases where the vendor has never released patches (*i.e.*, SunOS4 -- although folks with a source license can patch it themselves) we have decided to disable this feature.

There are two ways of accomplishing this. One is the socket option SO_LINGER. But as fate would have it, this has never been implemented properly in most TCP/IP stacks. Even on those stacks with a proper implementation (*i.e.*, Linux 2.0.31) this method proves to be more expensive (cputime) than the next solution.

For the most part, Apache implements this in a function called lingering_close (in http_main.c). The function looks roughly like this:

```
void lingering_close (int s)
{
char junk_buffer[2048];

/* shutdown the sending side */
shutdown (s, 1);

signal (SIGALRM, lingering_death);
alarm (30);

for (;;) {
select (s for reading, 2 second timeout);
if (error) break;
if (s is ready for reading) {
if (read (s, junk_buffer, sizeof (junk_buffer)) <= 0) {
break;
}
/* just toss away whatever is here */
}
}

close (s);
}
```

This naturally adds some expense at the end of a connection, but it is required for a reliable implementation. As HTTP/1.1 becomes more prevalent, and all connections are persistent, this expense will be amortized over more requests. If you want to play with fire and disable this feature you can define NO_LINGCLOSE, but this is not recommended at all. In particular, as HTTP/1.1 pipelined persistent connections come into use lingering_close is an absolute necessity (and *pipelined connections are faster*[4], so you want to support them).

### 24.3.8. Scoreboard File

Apache's parent and children communicate with each other through something called the scoreboard. Ideally this should be implemented in shared memory. For those operating systems that we either have access to, or have been given detailed ports for, it typically is implemented using shared memory. The rest default to using an on-disk file. The on-disk file is not only slow, but it is unreliable (and less featured). Peruse the `src/main/conf.h` file for your architecture and look for either `USE_MMAP_SCOREBOARD` or `USE_SHMGET_SCOREBOARD`. Defining one of those two (as well as their companions `HAVE_MMAP` and `HAVE_SHMGET` respectively) enables the supplied shared memory code. If your system has another type of shared memory, edit the file `src/main/http_main.c` and add the hooks necessary to use it in Apache. (Send us back a patch too please.)

> Historical note: The Linux port of Apache didn't start to use shared memory until version 1.2 of Apache. This oversight resulted in really poor and unreliable behaviour of earlier versions of Apache on Linux.

### 24.3.9. DYNAMIC_MODULE_LIMIT

If you have no intention of using dynamically loaded modules (you probably don't if you're reading this and tuning your server for every last ounce of performance) then you should add `-DDYNAMIC_MODULE_LIMIT=0` when building your server. This will save RAM that's allocated only for supporting dynamically loaded modules.

## 24.4. Appendix: Detailed Analysis of a Trace

Here is a system call trace of Apache 2.0.38 with the worker MPM on Solaris 8. This trace was collected using:

```
truss -l -p httpd_child_pid.
```

The `-l` option tells truss to log the ID of the LWP (lightweight process--Solaris's form of kernel-level thread) that invokes each system call.

Other systems may have different system call tracing utilities such as `strace`, `ktrace`, or `par`. They all produce similar output.

---

[4] *http://www.w3.org/Protocols/HTTP/Performance/Pipeline.html*

In this trace, a client has requested a 10KB static file from the httpd. Traces of non-static requests or requests with content negotiation look wildly different (and quite ugly in some cases).

```
/67:      accept(3, 0x00200BEC, 0x00200C0C, 1) (sleeping...)
/67:      accept(3, 0x00200BEC, 0x00200C0C, 1)              = 9
```

In this trace, the listener thread is running within LWP #67.

> Note the lack of accept(2) serialization. On this particular platform, the worker MPM uses an unserialized accept by default unless it is listening on multiple ports.

```
/65:      lwp_park(0x00000000, 0)                           = 0
/67:      lwp_unpark(65, 1)                                 = 0
```

Upon accepting the connection, the listener thread wakes up a worker thread to do the request processing. In this trace, the worker thread that handles the request is mapped to LWP #65.

```
/65:      getsockname(9, 0x00200BA4, 0x00200BC4, 1)         = 0
```

In order to implement virtual hosts, Apache needs to know the local socket address used to accept the connection. It is possible to eliminate this call in many situations (such as when there are no virtual hosts, or when Listen directives are used which do not have wildcard addresses). But no effort has yet been made to do these optimizations.

```
/65:      brk(0x002170E8)                                   = 0
/65:      brk(0x002190E8)                                   = 0
```

The brk(2) calls allocate memory from the heap. It is rare to see these in a system call trace, because the httpd uses custom memory allocators (apr_pool and apr_bucket_alloc) for most request processing. In this trace, the httpd has just been started, so it must call malloc(3) to get the blocks of raw memory with which to create the custom memory allocators.

```
/65:      fcntl(9, F_GETFL, 0x00000000)                     = 2
/65:      fstat64(9, 0xFAF7B818)                            = 0
/65:      getsockopt(9, 65535, 8192, 0xFAF7B918, 0xFAF7B910, 2190656) = 0
/65:      fstat64(9, 0xFAF7B818)                            = 0
/65:      getsockopt(9, 65535, 8192, 0xFAF7B918, 0xFAF7B914, 2190656) = 0
/65:      setsockopt(9, 65535, 8192, 0xFAF7B918, 4, 2190656) = 0
/65:      fcntl(9, F_SETFL, 0x00000082)                     = 0
```

Next, the worker thread puts the connection to the client (file descriptor 9) in non-blocking mode. The setsockopt(2) and getsockopt(2) calls are a side-effect of how Solaris's libc handles fcntl(2) on sockets.

```
/65:      read(9, " G E T   / 1 0 k . h t m".., 8000)       = 97
```

The worker thread reads the request from the client.

```
/65:      stat("/var/httpd/apache/httpd-8999/htdocs/10k.html", 0xFAF7B978) = 0
/65:      open("/var/httpd/apache/httpd-8999/htdocs/10k.html", O_RDONLY) = 10
```

This httpd has been configured with `Options FollowSymLinks` and `AllowOverride None`. Thus it doesn't need to `lstat(2)` each directory in the path leading up to the requested file, nor check for `.htaccess` files. It simply calls `stat(2)` to verify that the file: 1) exists, and 2) is a regular file, not a directory.

```
/65:      sendfilev(0, 9, 0x00200F90, 2, 0xFAF7B53C)          = 10269
```

In this example, the httpd is able to send the HTTP response header and the requested file with a single `sendfilev(2)` system call. Sendfile semantics vary among operating systems. On some other systems, it is necessary to do a `write(2)` or `writev(2)` call to send the headers before calling `sendfile(2)`.

```
/65:      write(4, " 1 2 7 . 0 . 0 . 1   -   ".., 78)        = 78
```

This `write(2)` call records the request in the access log. Note that one thing missing from this trace is a `time(2)` call. Unlike Apache 1.3, Apache 2.x uses `gettimeofday(3)` to look up the time. On some operating systems, like Linux or Solaris, `gettimeofday` has an optimized implementation that doesn't require as much overhead as a typical system call.

```
/65:      shutdown(9, 1, 1)                                  = 0
/65:      poll(0xFAF7B980, 1, 2000)                          = 1
/65:      read(9, 0xFAF7BC20, 512)                           = 0
/65:      close(9)                                           = 0
```

The worker thread does a lingering close of the connection.

```
/65:      close(10)                                          = 0
/65:      lwp_park(0x00000000, 0)          (sleeping...)
```

Finally the worker thread closes the file that it has just delivered and blocks until the listener assigns it another connection.

```
/67:      accept(3, 0x001FEB74, 0x001FEB94, 1) (sleeping...)
```

Meanwhile, the listener thread is able to accept another connection as soon as it has dispatched this connection to a worker thread (subject to some flow-control logic in the worker MPM that throttles the listener if all the available workers are busy). Though it isn't apparent from this trace, the next `accept(2)` can (and usually does, under high load conditions) occur in parallel with the worker thread's handling of the just-accepted connection.

# Chapter 25.

# Frequently Asked Questions

This document is not a traditional FAQ, but rather a quick guide showing you what to do when you run into problems with the Apache HTTP Server.

A more traditional but quite outdated document is the *Apache 1.3 FAQ*[1].

## "Why can't I ...? Why won't ... work?" What to do in case of problems

If you are having trouble with your Apache server software, you should take the following steps:

### Check the ErrorLog!

Apache tries to be helpful when it encounters a problem. In many cases, it will provide some details by writing one or more messages to the server error log. Sometimes this is enough for you to diagnose and fix the problem yourself (such as file permissions or the like). The default location of the error log is `/usr/local/apache2/logs/error_log`, but see the ErrorLog directive in your config files for the location on your server.

If you end up in any of the support forums this is quite likely to be the first place they will ask you retrieve information from. Please ensure you know where to find your errorlog. If you are unsure, the wiki page *http://wiki.apache.org/httpd/DistrosDefaultLayout* can give you some ideas where to look.

### Consult the wiki

The *Apache HTTP Server Wiki*[2] contains guides to solving many common problems.

### Check the Apache bug database

Most problems that get reported to The Apache Group are recorded in the *bug database*[3]. **Do not** submit a new bug report until you have checked existing reports (open *and*

---

[1] *http://httpd.apache.org/docs/misc/FAQ.html*
[2] *http://wiki.apache.org/httpd/*
[3] *http://httpd.apache.org/bug_report.html*

closed) and asked about your problem in a user-support forum (see below). If you find that your issue has already been reported, please *don't* add a "me, too" report.

### Ask in a user support forum

Apache has an active community of users who are willing to share their knowledge. Participating in this community is usually the best and fastest way to get answers to your questions and problems.

*Users mailing list*[4]

*#httpd*[5] on *Freenode IRC*[6] is also available for user support issues.

### Please use the bug database for bugs!

If you've gone through those steps above that are appropriate and have obtained no relief, then please *do* let the httpd developers know about the problem by *logging a bug report*[7].

If your problem involves the server crashing and generating a core dump, please *include a backtrace*[8] (if possible).

## Whom do I contact for support?

With millions of users and fewer than sixty volunteer developers, we cannot provide personal support for Apache. For free support, we suggest participating in a user forum (see above).

Professional, commercial support for Apache is available from a number of companies.

---

[4] *http://httpd.apache.org/userslist.html*
[5] *irc://irc.freenode.net/#httpd*
[6] *http://freenode.net/*
[7] *http://httpd.apache.org/bug_report.html*
[8] *http://httpd.apache.org/dev/debugging.html*

# Part III.
# Apache Virtual Host documentation

The term *Virtual Host* refers to the practice of running more than one web site (such as www.company1.com and www.company2.com) on a single machine. Virtual hosts can be "*IP-based*", meaning that you have a different IP address for every web site, or "*name-based*", meaning that you have multiple names running on each IP address. The fact that they are running on the same physical server is not apparent to the end user.

Apache was one of the first servers to support IP-based virtual hosts right out of the box. Versions 1.1 and later of Apache support both IP-based and name-based virtual hosts (vhosts). The latter variant of virtual hosts is sometimes also called *host-based* or *non-IP virtual hosts*.

Below is a list of documentation pages which explain all details of virtual host support in Apache version 1.3 and later.

## Virtual Host Support

- *Name-based Virtual Hosts* (More than one web site per IP address)
- *IP-based Virtual Hosts* (An IP address for each web site)
- *Virtual Host examples for common setups*
- *File Descriptor Limits* (or, *Too many log files*)
- *Dynamically Configured Mass Virtual Hosting*
- *In-Depth Discussion of Virtual Host Matching*

## Configuration directives

- `<VirtualHost>`
- `NameVirtualHost`
- `ServerName`
- `ServerAlias`
- `ServerPath`

If you are trying to debug your virtual host configuration, you may find the Apache -S command line switch useful. That is, type the following command:

```
/usr/local/apache2/bin/httpd -S
```

This command will dump out a description of how Apache parsed the configuration file. Careful examination of the IP addresses and server names may help uncover configuration mistakes. (See the docs for the *httpd* program for other command line options)

# Chapter 26.
# Name-based Virtual Host Support

This document describes when and how to use name-based virtual hosts.

## 26.1. Name-based vs. IP-based Virtual Hosts

IP-based virtual hosts use the IP address of the connection to determine the correct virtual host to serve. Therefore you need to have a separate IP address for each host. With name-based virtual hosting, the server relies on the client to report the hostname as part of the HTTP headers. Using this technique, many different hosts can share the same IP address.

Name-based virtual hosting is usually simpler, since you need only configure your DNS server to map each hostname to the correct IP address and then configure the Apache HTTP Server to recognize the different hostnames. Name-based virtual hosting also eases the demand for scarce IP addresses. Therefore you should use name-based virtual hosting unless there is a specific reason to choose IP-based virtual hosting. Some reasons why you might consider using IP-based virtual hosting:

- Some ancient clients are not compatible with name-based virtual hosting. For name-based virtual hosting to work, the client must send the HTTP Host header. This is required by HTTP/1.1, and is implemented by all modern HTTP/1.0 browsers as an extension. If you need to support obsolete clients and still use name-based virtual hosting, a possible technique is discussed at the end of this document.
- Name-based virtual hosting cannot be used with SSL secure servers because of the nature of the SSL protocol.
- Some operating systems and network equipment implement bandwidth management techniques that cannot differentiate between hosts unless they are on separate IP addresses.

## 26.2. Using Name-based Virtual Hosts

| Related Modules | Related Directives |
|---|---|
| core | DocumentRoot |
| | NameVirtualHost |

| Related Modules | Related Directives |
|---|---|
| | ServerAlias |
| | ServerName |
| | ServerPath |
| | <VirtualHost> |

To use name-based virtual hosting, you must designate the IP address (and possibly port) on the server that will be accepting requests for the hosts. This is configured using the NameVirtualHost directive. In the normal case where any and all IP addresses on the server should be used, you can use * as the argument to NameVirtualHost. If you're planning to use multiple ports (e.g. running SSL) you should add a Port to the argument, such as *:80. Note that mentioning an IP address in a NameVirtualHost directive does not automatically make the server listen to that IP address. See *Setting which addresses and ports Apache uses* for more details. In addition, any IP address specified here must be associated with a network interface on the server.

The next step is to create a <VirtualHost> block for each different host that you would like to serve. The argument to the <VirtualHost> directive must match a defined NameVirtualHost directive. (In this usual case, this will be "*:80"). Inside each <VirtualHost> block, you will need at minimum a ServerName directive to designate which host is served and a DocumentRoot directive to show where in the filesystem the content for that host lives.

---

**Main host goes away**

If you are adding virtual hosts to an existing web server, you must also create a <VirtualHost> block for the existing host. The ServerName and DocumentRoot included in this virtual host should be the same as the global ServerName and DocumentRoot. List this virtual host first in the configuration file so that it will act as the default host.

---

For example, suppose that you are serving the domain www.domain.tld and you wish to add the virtual host www.otherdomain.tld, which points at the same IP address. Then you simply add the following to httpd.conf:

```
NameVirtualHost *:80

<VirtualHost *:80>
ServerName www.domain.tld
ServerAlias domain.tld *.domain.tld
DocumentRoot /www/domain
</VirtualHost>
```

```
<VirtualHost *:80>
ServerName www.otherdomain.tld
DocumentRoot /www/otherdomain
</VirtualHost>
```

You can alternatively specify an explicit IP address in place of the `*` in both the `NameVirtualHost` and `<VirtualHost>` directives. For example, you might want to do this in order to run some name-based virtual hosts on one IP address, and either IP-based, or another set of name-based virtual hosts on another address.

Many servers want to be accessible by more than one name. This is possible with the `ServerAlias` directive, placed inside the `<VirtualHost>` section. For example in the first `<VirtualHost>` block above, the `ServerAlias` directive indicates that the listed names are other names which people can use to see that same web site:

```
ServerAlias domain.tld *.domain.tld
```

then requests for all hosts in the `domain.tld` domain will be served by the `www.domain.tld` virtual host. The wildcard characters `*` and `?` can be used to match names. Of course, you can't just make up names and place them in `ServerName` or `ServerAlias`. You must first have your DNS server properly configured to map those names to an IP address associated with your server.

Finally, you can fine-tune the configuration of the virtual hosts by placing other directives inside the `<VirtualHost>` containers. Most directives can be placed in these containers and will then change the configuration only of the relevant virtual host. To find out if a particular directive is allowed, check the *Context* of the directive. Configuration directives set in the *main server context* (outside any `<VirtualHost>` container) will be used only if they are not overridden by the virtual host settings.

Now when a request arrives, the server will first check if it is using an IP address that matches the `NameVirtualHost`. If it is, then it will look at each `<VirtualHost>` section with a matching IP address and try to find one where the `ServerName` or `ServerAlias` matches the requested hostname. If it finds one, then it uses the configuration for that server. If no matching virtual host is found, then **the first listed virtual host** that matches the IP address will be used.

As a consequence, the first listed virtual host is the *default* virtual host. The `DocumentRoot` from the *main server* will **never** be used when an IP address matches the `NameVirtualHost` directive. If you would like to have a special configuration for requests that do not match any particular virtual host, simply put that configuration in a `<VirtualHost>` container and list it first in the configuration file.

## 26.3. Compatibility with Older Browsers

As mentioned earlier, there are some clients who do not send the required data for the name-based virtual hosts to work properly. These clients will always be sent the pages from the first virtual host listed for that IP address (the *primary* name-based virtual host).

---

**How much older?**

Please note that when we say older, we really do mean older. You are very unlikely to encounter one of these browsers in use today. All current versions of any browser send the `Host` header as required for name-based virtual hosts.

---

There is a possible workaround with the `ServerPath` directive, albeit a slightly cumbersome one:

Example configuration:

```
NameVirtualHost 111.22.33.44

<VirtualHost 111.22.33.44>
ServerName www.domain.tld
ServerPath /domain
DocumentRoot /web/domain
</VirtualHost>
```

What does this mean? It means that a request for any URI beginning with "/domain" will be served from the virtual host `www.domain.tld`. This means that the pages can be accessed as `http://www.domain.tld/domain/` for all clients, although clients sending a `Host:` header can also access it as `http://www.domain.tld/`.

In order to make this work, put a link on your primary virtual host's page to `http://www.domain.tld/domain/`. Then, in the virtual host's pages, be sure to use either purely relative links (*e.g.*, `"file.html"` or `"../icons/image.gif"`) or links containing the prefacing /domain/ (*e.g.*, `"http://www.domain.tld/domain/misc/file.html"` or `"/domain/misc/file.html"`).

This requires a bit of discipline, but adherence to these guidelines will, for the most part, ensure that your pages will work with all browsers, new and old.

# Chapter 27.
# Apache IP-based Virtual Host Support

## 27.1. System requirements

As the term *IP-based* indicates, the server **must have a different IP address for each IP-based virtual host**. This can be achieved by the machine having several physical network connections, or by use of virtual interfaces which are supported by most modern operating systems (see system documentation for details, these are frequently called "ip aliases", and the "ifconfig" command is most commonly used to set them up).

## 27.2. How to set up Apache

There are two ways of configuring apache to support multiple hosts. Either by running a separate `httpd` daemon for each hostname, or by running a single daemon which supports all the virtual hosts.

Use multiple daemons when:

- There are security partitioning issues, such as company1 does not want anyone at company2 to be able to read their data except via the web. In this case you would need two daemons, each running with different `User`, `Group`, `Listen`, and `ServerRoot` settings.
- You can afford the memory and file descriptor requirements of listening to every IP alias on the machine. It's only possible to `Listen` to the "wildcard" address, or to specific addresses. So if you have a need to listen to a specific address for whatever reason, then you will need to listen to all specific addresses. (Although one `httpd` could listen to N-1 of the addresses, and another could listen to the remaining address.)

Use a single daemon when:

- Sharing of the httpd configuration between virtual hosts is acceptable.
- The machine services a large number of requests, and so the performance loss in running separate daemons may be significant.

## 27.3. Setting up multiple daemons

Create a separate *httpd* installation for each virtual host. For each installation, use the Listen directive in the configuration file to select which IP address (or virtual host) that daemon services. e.g.

```
Listen www.smallco.com:80
```

It is recommended that you use an IP address instead of a hostname (see *DNS caveats*).

## 27.4. Setting up a single daemon with virtual hosts

For this case, a single *httpd* will service requests for the main server and all the virtual hosts. The VirtualHost directive in the configuration file is used to set the values of ServerAdmin, ServerName, DocumentRoot, ErrorLog and TransferLog or CustomLog configuration directives to different values for each virtual host. e.g.

```
<VirtualHost www.smallco.com>
ServerAdmin webmaster@mail.smallco.com
DocumentRoot /groups/smallco/www
ServerName www.smallco.com
ErrorLog /groups/smallco/logs/error_log
TransferLog /groups/smallco/logs/access_log
</VirtualHost>

<VirtualHost www.baygroup.org>
ServerAdmin webmaster@mail.baygroup.org
DocumentRoot /groups/baygroup/www
ServerName www.baygroup.org
ErrorLog /groups/baygroup/logs/error_log
TransferLog /groups/baygroup/logs/access_log
</VirtualHost>
```

It is recommended that you use an IP address instead of a hostname (see *DNS caveats*).

Almost **any** configuration directive can be put in the VirtualHost directive, with the exception of directives that control process creation and a few other directives. To find out if a directive can be used in the VirtualHost directive, check the *Context* using the *directive index*.

SuexecUserGroup may be used inside a VirtualHost directive if the *suEXEC wrapper* is used.

*SECURITY:* When specifying where to write log files, be aware of some security risks which are present if anyone other than the user that starts Apache has write access to the directory where they are written. See the *security tips* document for details.

# Chapter 28.

# Dynamically configured mass virtual hosting

This document describes how to efficiently serve an arbitrary number of virtual hosts with Apache.

## 28.1. Motivation

The techniques described here are of interest if your `httpd.conf` contains many `<VirtualHost>` sections that are substantially the same, for example:

```
NameVirtualHost 111.22.33.44
<VirtualHost 111.22.33.44>
ServerName www.customer-1.com
DocumentRoot /www/hosts/www.customer-1.com/docs
ScriptAlias /cgi-bin/ /www/hosts/www.customer-1.com/cgi-bin
</VirtualHost>
<VirtualHost 111.22.33.44>
ServerName www.customer-2.com
DocumentRoot /www/hosts/www.customer-2.com/docs
ScriptAlias /cgi-bin/ /www/hosts/www.customer-2.com/cgi-bin
</VirtualHost>
# blah blah blah
<VirtualHost 111.22.33.44>
ServerName www.customer-N.com
DocumentRoot /www/hosts/www.customer-N.com/docs
ScriptAlias /cgi-bin/ /www/hosts/www.customer-N.com/cgi-bin
</VirtualHost>
```

The basic idea is to replace all of the static `<VirtualHost>` configuration with a mechanism that works it out dynamically. This has a number of advantages:

1. Your configuration file is smaller so Apache starts faster and uses less memory.
2. Adding virtual hosts is simply a matter of creating the appropriate directories in the filesystem and entries in the DNS - you don't need to reconfigure or restart Apache.

The main disadvantage is that you cannot have a different log file for each virtual host; however if you have very many virtual hosts then doing this is dubious anyway because it eats file descriptors. It is better to log to a pipe or a fifo and arrange for the process at the other end to distribute the logs to the customers (it can also accumulate statistics, etc.).

## 28.2. Overview

A virtual host is defined by two pieces of information: its IP address, and the contents of the `Host:` header in the HTTP request. The dynamic mass virtual hosting technique is based on automatically inserting this information into the pathname of the file that is used to satisfy the request. This is done most easily using `mod_vhost_alias`, but if you are using a version of Apache up to 1.3.6 then you must use `mod_rewrite`. Both of these modules are disabled by default; you must enable one of them when configuring and building Apache if you want to use this technique.

A couple of things need to be `faked' to make the dynamic virtual host look like a normal one. The most important is the server name which is used by Apache to generate self-referential URLs, etc. It is configured with the `ServerName` directive, and it is available to CGIs via the `SERVER_NAME` environment variable. The actual value used at run time is controlled by the `UseCanonicalName` setting. With `UseCanonicalName Off` the server name comes from the contents of the `Host:` header in the request. With `UseCanonicalName DNS` it comes from a reverse DNS lookup of the virtual host's IP address. The former setting is used for name-based dynamic virtual hosting, and the latter is used for IP-based hosting. If Apache cannot work out the server name because there is no `Host:` header or the DNS lookup fails then the value configured with `ServerName` is used instead.

The other thing to `fake' is the document root (configured with `DocumentRoot` and available to CGIs via the `DOCUMENT_ROOT` environment variable). In a normal configuration this setting is used by the core module when mapping URIs to filenames, but when the server is configured to do dynamic virtual hosting that job is taken over by another module (either `mod_vhost_alias` or `mod_rewrite`) which has a different way of doing the mapping. Neither of these modules is responsible for setting the `DOCUMENT_ROOT` environment variable so if any CGIs or SSI documents make use of it they will get a misleading value.

## 28.3. Simple dynamic virtual hosts

This extract from `httpd.conf` implements the virtual host arrangement outlined in the *Motivation* section above, but in a generic fashion using `mod_vhost_alias`.

```
# get the server name from the Host: header
UseCanonicalName Off

# this log format can be split per-virtual-host based on the first field
LogFormat "%V %h %l %u %t \"%r\" %s %b" vcommon
CustomLog logs/access_log vcommon
```

```
# include the server name in the filenames used to satisfy requests
VirtualDocumentRoot /www/hosts/%0/docs
VirtualScriptAlias /www/hosts/%0/cgi-bin
```

This configuration can be changed into an IP-based virtual hosting solution by just turning
`UseCanonicalName Off` into `UseCanonicalName DNS`. The server name that is inserted
into the filename is then derived from the IP address of the virtual host.

## 28.4. A virtually hosted homepages system

This is an adjustment of the above system tailored for an ISP's homepages server. Using a
slightly more complicated configuration we can select substrings of the server name to use
in the filename so that e.g. the documents for `www.user.isp.com` are found in
`/home/user/`. It uses a single `cgi-bin` directory instead of one per virtual host.

```
# all the preliminary stuff is the same as above, then

# include part of the server name in the filenames
VirtualDocumentRoot /www/hosts/%2/docs

# single cgi-bin directory
ScriptAlias /cgi-bin/ /www/std-cgi/
```

There are examples of more complicated `VirtualDocumentRoot` settings in the
mod_vhost_alias documentation.

## 28.5. Using more than one virtual hosting system on the same server

With more complicated setups you can use Apache's normal `<VirtualHost>` directives to
control the scope of the various virtual hosting configurations. For example, you could have
one IP address for homepages customers and another for commercial customers with the
following setup. This can of course be combined with conventional `<VirtualHost>`
configuration sections.

```
UseCanonicalName Off

LogFormat "%V %h %l %u %t \"%r\" %s %b" vcommon

<Directory /www/commercial>
Options FollowSymLinks
AllowOverride All
</Directory>

<Directory /www/homepages>
Options FollowSymLinks
AllowOverride None
</Directory>
```

```
<VirtualHost 111.22.33.44>
ServerName www.commercial.isp.com

CustomLog logs/access_log.commercial vcommon

VirtualDocumentRoot /www/commercial/%0/docs
VirtualScriptAlias /www/commercial/%0/cgi-bin
</VirtualHost>

<VirtualHost 111.22.33.45>
ServerName www.homepages.isp.com

CustomLog logs/access_log.homepages vcommon

VirtualDocumentRoot /www/homepages/%0/docs
ScriptAlias /cgi-bin/ /www/std-cgi/
</VirtualHost>
```

 **Note**

If the first VirtualHost block does *not* include a `ServerName` directive, the reverse DNS of the relevant IP will be used instead. If this is not the server name you wish to use, a bogus entry (`ServerName none.example.com`) can be added to get around this behaviour.

## 28.6. More efficient IP-based virtual hosting

After *the first example* I noted that it is easy to turn it into an IP-based virtual hosting setup. Unfortunately that configuration is not very efficient because it requires a DNS lookup for every request. This can be avoided by laying out the filesystem according to the IP addresses themselves rather than the corresponding names and changing the logging similarly. Apache will then usually not need to work out the server name and so incur a DNS lookup.

```
# get the server name from the reverse DNS of the IP address
UseCanonicalName DNS

# include the IP address in the logs so they may be split
LogFormat "%A %h %l %u %t \"%r\" %s %b" vcommon
CustomLog logs/access_log vcommon

# include the IP address in the filenames
VirtualDocumentRootIP /www/hosts/%0/docs
VirtualScriptAliasIP /www/hosts/%0/cgi-bin
```

## 28.7. Using older versions of Apache

The examples above rely on `mod_vhost_alias` which appeared after version 1.3.6. If you are using a version of Apache without `mod_vhost_alias` then you can implement this technique with `mod_rewrite` as illustrated below, but only for Host:-header-based virtual hosts.

In addition there are some things to beware of with logging. Apache 1.3.6 is the first version to include the `%V` log format directive; in versions 1.3.0 - 1.3.3 the `%v` option did what `%V` does; version 1.3.4 has no equivalent. In all these versions of Apache the `UseCanonicalName` directive can appear in `.htaccess` files which means that customers can cause the wrong thing to be logged. Therefore the best thing to do is use the `%{Host}i` directive which logs the `Host:` header directly; note that this may include `:port` on the end which is not the case for `%V`.

## 28.8. Simple dynamic virtual hosts using

This extract from `httpd.conf` does the same thing as *the first example*. The first half is very similar to the corresponding part above but with some changes for backward compatibility and to make the `mod_rewrite` part work properly; the second half configures `mod_rewrite` to do the actual work.

There are a couple of especially tricky bits: By default, `mod_rewrite` runs before the other URI translation modules (`mod_alias` etc.) so if they are used then `mod_rewrite` must be configured to accommodate them. Also, some magic must be performed to do a per-dynamic-virtual-host equivalent of `ScriptAlias`.

```
# get the server name from the Host: header
UseCanonicalName Off

# splittable logs
LogFormat "%{Host}i %h %l %u %t \"%r\" %s %b" vcommon
CustomLog logs/access_log vcommon

<Directory /www/hosts>
# ExecCGI is needed here because we can't force
# CGI execution in the way that ScriptAlias does
Options FollowSymLinks ExecCGI
</Directory>

# now for the hard bit

RewriteEngine On

# a ServerName derived from a Host: header may be any case at all
RewriteMap lowercase int:tolower

## deal with normal documents first:
# allow Alias /icons/ to work - repeat for other aliases
RewriteCond %{REQUEST_URI} !^/icons/
# allow CGIs to work
```

```
RewriteCond %{REQUEST_URI} !^/cgi-bin/
# do the magic
RewriteRule ^/(.*)$ /www/hosts/${lowercase:%{SERVER_NAME}}/docs/$1

## and now deal with CGIs - we have to force a MIME type
RewriteCond %{REQUEST_URI} ^/cgi-bin/
RewriteRule ^/(.*)$ /www/hosts/${lowercase:%{SERVER_NAME}}/cgi-bin/$1
[T=application/x-httpd-cgi]

# that's it!
```

## 28.9. A homepages system using

This does the same thing as *the second example*.

```
RewriteEngine on

RewriteMap lowercase int:tolower

# allow CGIs to work
RewriteCond %{REQUEST_URI} !^/cgi-bin/

# check the hostname is right so that the RewriteRule works
RewriteCond ${lowercase:%{SERVER_NAME}} ^www\.[a-z-]+\.isp\.com$

# concatenate the virtual host name onto the start of the URI
# the [C] means do the next rewrite on the result of this one
RewriteRule ^(.+) ${lowercase:%{SERVER_NAME}}$1 [C]

# now create the real file name
RewriteRule ^www\.([a-z-]+)\.isp\.com/(.*) /home/$1/$2

# define the global CGI directory
ScriptAlias /cgi-bin/ /www/std-cgi/
```

## 28.10. Using a separate virtual host configuration file

This arrangement uses more advanced mod_rewrite features to get the translation from virtual host to document root from a separate configuration file. This provides more flexibility but requires more complicated configuration.

The vhost.map file contains something like this:

```
www.customer-1.com /www/customers/1
www.customer-2.com /www/customers/2
# ...
www.customer-N.com /www/customers/N
```

The http.conf contains this:

```
RewriteEngine on

RewriteMap lowercase int:tolower

# define the map file
RewriteMap vhost txt:/www/conf/vhost.map

# deal with aliases as above
RewriteCond %{REQUEST_URI} !^/icons/
RewriteCond %{REQUEST_URI} !^/cgi-bin/
RewriteCond ${lowercase:%{SERVER_NAME}} ^(.+)$
# this does the file-based remap
RewriteCond ${vhost:%1} ^(/.*)$
RewriteRule ^/(.*)$ %1/docs/$1

RewriteCond %{REQUEST_URI} ^/cgi-bin/
RewriteCond ${lowercase:%{SERVER_NAME}} ^(.+)$
RewriteCond ${vhost:%1} ^(/.*)$
RewriteRule ^/(.*)$ %1/cgi-bin/$1
```

# Chapter 29.

# VirtualHost Examples

This document attempts to answer the commonly-asked questions about setting up virtual hosts. These scenarios are those involving multiple web sites running on a single server, via *name-based* or *IP-based* virtual hosts.

### 29.1. Running several name-based web sites on a single IP address.

Your server has a single IP address, and multiple aliases (CNAMES) point to this machine in DNS. You want to run a web server for www.example.com and www.example.org on this machine.

 **Note**

Creating virtual host configurations on your Apache server does not magically cause DNS entries to be created for those host names. You *must* have the names in DNS, resolving to your IP address, or nobody else will be able to see your web site. You can put entries in your hosts file for local testing, but that will work only from the machine with those hosts entries.

**Server configuration**

```
# Ensure that Apache listens on port 80
Listen 80

# Listen for virtual host requests on all IP addresses
NameVirtualHost *:80

<VirtualHost *:80>
DocumentRoot /www/example1
ServerName www.example.com

# Other directives here

</VirtualHost>

<VirtualHost *:80>
DocumentRoot /www/example2
ServerName www.example.org
```

```
# Other directives here

</VirtualHost>
```

The asterisks match all addresses, so the main server serves no requests. Due to the fact that www.example.com is first in the configuration file, it has the highest priority and can be seen as the *default* or *primary* server. That means that if a request is received that does not match one of the specified ServerName directives, it will be served by this first VirtualHost.

 **Note**

You can, if you wish, replace * with the actual IP address of the system. In that case, the argument to VirtualHost *must* match the argument to NameVirtualHost:

```
NameVirtualHost 172.20.30.40

<VirtualHost 172.20.30.40>
# etc ...
```

However, it is additionally useful to use * on systems where the IP address is not predictable - for example if you have a dynamic IP address with your ISP, and you are using some variety of dynamic DNS solution. Since * matches any IP address, this configuration would work without changes whenever your IP address changes.

The above configuration is what you will want to use in almost all name-based virtual hosting situations. The only thing that this configuration will not work for, in fact, is when you are serving different content based on differing IP addresses or ports.

## 29.2. Name-based hosts on more than one IP address.

 **Note**

Any of the techniques discussed here can be extended to any number of IP addresses.

The server has two IP addresses. On one (172.20.30.40), we will serve the "main" server, server.domain.com and on the other (172.20.30.50), we will serve two or more virtual hosts.

**Server configuration**

```
Listen 80

# This is the "main" server running on 172.20.30.40
ServerName server.domain.com
DocumentRoot /www/mainserver
```

```
# This is the other address
NameVirtualHost 172.20.30.50

<VirtualHost 172.20.30.50>
DocumentRoot /www/example1
ServerName www.example.com

# Other directives here ...

</VirtualHost>

<VirtualHost 172.20.30.50>
DocumentRoot /www/example2
ServerName www.example.org

# Other directives here ...

</VirtualHost>
```

Any request to an address other than 172.20.30.50 will be served from the main server. A request to 172.20.30.50 with an unknown hostname, or no Host: header, will be served from www.example.com.

## 29.3. Serving the same content on different IP addresses (such as an internal and external address).

The server machine has two IP addresses (192.168.1.1 and 172.20.30.40). The machine is sitting between an internal (intranet) network and an external (internet) network. Outside of the network, the name server.example.com resolves to the external address (172.20.30.40), but inside the network, that same name resolves to the internal address (192.168.1.1).

The server can be made to respond to internal and external requests with the same content, with just one VirtualHost section.

**Server configuration**

```
NameVirtualHost 192.168.1.1
NameVirtualHost 172.20.30.40

<VirtualHost 192.168.1.1 172.20.30.40>
DocumentRoot /www/server1
ServerName server.example.com
ServerAlias server
</VirtualHost>
```

Now requests from both networks will be served from the same VirtualHost.

**Note**

On the internal network, one can just use the name `server` rather than the fully qualified host name `server.example.com`.

Note also that, in the above example, you can replace the list of IP addresses with `*`, which will cause the server to respond the same on all addresses.

## 29.4. Running different sites on different ports.

You have multiple domains going to the same IP and also want to serve multiple ports. By defining the ports in the "NameVirtualHost" tag, you can allow this to work. If you try using <VirtualHost name:port> without the NameVirtualHost name:port or you try to use the Listen directive, your configuration will not work.

**Server configuration**

```
Listen 80
Listen 8080

NameVirtualHost 172.20.30.40:80
NameVirtualHost 172.20.30.40:8080

<VirtualHost 172.20.30.40:80>
ServerName www.example.com
DocumentRoot /www/domain-80
</VirtualHost>

<VirtualHost 172.20.30.40:8080>
ServerName www.example.com
DocumentRoot /www/domain-8080
</VirtualHost>

<VirtualHost 172.20.30.40:80>
ServerName www.example.org
DocumentRoot /www/otherdomain-80
</VirtualHost>

<VirtualHost 172.20.30.40:8080>
ServerName www.example.org
DocumentRoot /www/otherdomain-8080
</VirtualHost>
```

## 29.5. IP-based virtual hosting

The server has two IP addresses (172.20.30.40 and 172.20.30.50) which resolve to the names www.example.com and www.example.org respectively.

**Server configuration**

```
Listen 80

<VirtualHost 172.20.30.40>
DocumentRoot /www/example1
ServerName www.example.com
</VirtualHost>

<VirtualHost 172.20.30.50>
DocumentRoot /www/example2
ServerName www.example.org
</VirtualHost>
```

Requests for any address not specified in one of the `<VirtualHost>` directives (such as `localhost`, for example) will go to the main server, if there is one.

## 29.6. Mixed port-based and ip-based virtual hosts

The server machine has two IP addresses (`172.20.30.40` and `172.20.30.50`) which resolve to the names `www.example.com` and `www.example.org` respectively. In each case, we want to run hosts on ports 80 and 8080.

**Server configuration**

```
Listen 172.20.30.40:80
Listen 172.20.30.40:8080
Listen 172.20.30.50:80
Listen 172.20.30.50:8080

<VirtualHost 172.20.30.40:80>
DocumentRoot /www/example1-80
ServerName www.example.com
</VirtualHost>

<VirtualHost 172.20.30.40:8080>
DocumentRoot /www/example1-8080
ServerName www.example.com
</VirtualHost>

<VirtualHost 172.20.30.50:80>
DocumentRoot /www/example2-80
ServerName www.example.org
</VirtualHost>

<VirtualHost 172.20.30.50:8080>
DocumentRoot /www/example2-8080
ServerName www.example.org
</VirtualHost>
```

## 29.7. Mixed name-based and IP-based vhosts

On some of my addresses, I want to do name-based virtual hosts, and on others, IP-based hosts.

### Server configuration

```
Listen 80

NameVirtualHost 172.20.30.40

<VirtualHost 172.20.30.40>
DocumentRoot /www/example1
ServerName www.example.com
</VirtualHost>

<VirtualHost 172.20.30.40>
DocumentRoot /www/example2
ServerName www.example.org
</VirtualHost>

<VirtualHost 172.20.30.40>
DocumentRoot /www/example3
ServerName www.example3.net
</VirtualHost>

# IP-based
<VirtualHost 172.20.30.50>
DocumentRoot /www/example4
ServerName www.example4.edu
</VirtualHost>

<VirtualHost 172.20.30.60>
DocumentRoot /www/example5
ServerName www.example5.gov
</VirtualHost>
```

## 29.8. Using `Virtual_host` and `mod_proxy` together

The following example allows a front-end machine to proxy a virtual host through to a server running on another machine. In the example, a virtual host of the same name is configured on a machine at 192.168.111.2. The ProxyPreserveHost On directive is used so that the desired hostname is passed through, in case we are proxying multiple hostnames to a single machine.

```
<VirtualHost *:*>
ProxyPreserveHost On
ProxyPass / http://192.168.111.2/
ProxyPassReverse / http://192.168.111.2/
ServerName hostname.example.com
</VirtualHost>
```

## 29.9. Using `_default_` vhosts

### `_default_` vhosts for all ports

Catching *every* request to any unspecified IP address and port, *i.e.*, an address/port combination that is not used for any other virtual host.

#### Server configuration

```
<VirtualHost _default_:*>
DocumentRoot /www/default
</VirtualHost>
```

Using such a default vhost with a wildcard port effectively prevents any request going to the main server.

A default vhost never serves a request that was sent to an address/port that is used for name-based vhosts. If the request contained an unknown or no `Host:` header it is always served from the primary name-based vhost (the vhost for that address/port appearing first in the configuration file).

You can use `AliasMatch` or `RewriteRule` to rewrite any request to a single information page (or script).

### `_default_` vhosts for different ports

Same as setup 1, but the server listens on several ports and we want to use a second `_default_` vhost for port 80.

#### Server configuration

```
<VirtualHost _default_:80>
DocumentRoot /www/default80
# ...
</VirtualHost>

<VirtualHost _default_:*>
DocumentRoot /www/default
# ...
</VirtualHost>
```

The default vhost for port 80 (which *must* appear before any default vhost with a wildcard port) catches all requests that were sent to an unspecified IP address. The main server is never used to serve a request.

### `_default_` vhosts for one port

We want to have a default vhost for port 80, but no other default vhosts.

**Server configuration**

```
<VirtualHost _default_:80>
DocumentRoot /www/default
...
</VirtualHost>
```

A request to an unspecified address on port 80 is served from the default vhost. Any other request to an unspecified address and port is served from the main server.

## 29.10. Migrating a name-based vhost to an IP-based vhost

The name-based vhost with the hostname www.example.org (from our *name-based* example, setup 2) should get its own IP address. To avoid problems with name servers or proxies who cached the old IP address for the name-based vhost we want to provide both variants during a migration phase.

The solution is easy, because we can simply add the new IP address (172.20.30.50) to the VirtualHost directive.

**Server configuration**

```
Listen 80
ServerName www.example.com
DocumentRoot /www/example1

NameVirtualHost 172.20.30.40

<VirtualHost 172.20.30.40 172.20.30.50>
DocumentRoot /www/example2
ServerName www.example.org
# ...
</VirtualHost>

<VirtualHost 172.20.30.40>
DocumentRoot /www/example3
ServerName www.example.net
ServerAlias *.example.net
# ...
</VirtualHost>
```

The vhost can now be accessed through the new address (as an IP-based vhost) and through the old address (as a name-based vhost).

## 29.11. Using the ServerPath directive

We have a server with two name-based vhosts. In order to match the correct virtual host a client must send the correct Host: header. Old HTTP/1.0 clients do not send such a header and Apache has no clue what vhost the client tried to reach (and serves the request from the primary vhost). To provide as much backward compatibility as possible we create a primary vhost which returns a single page containing links with an URL prefix to the name-based virtual hosts.

### Server configuration

```
NameVirtualHost 172.20.30.40

<VirtualHost 172.20.30.40>
# primary vhost
DocumentRoot /www/subdomain
RewriteEngine On
RewriteRule ^/.* /www/subdomain/index.html
# ...
</VirtualHost>

<VirtualHost 172.20.30.40>
DocumentRoot /www/subdomain/sub1
ServerName www.sub1.domain.tld
ServerPath /sub1/
RewriteEngine On
RewriteRule ^(/sub1/.*) /www/subdomain$1
# ...
</VirtualHost>

<VirtualHost 172.20.30.40>
DocumentRoot /www/subdomain/sub2
ServerName www.sub2.domain.tld
ServerPath /sub2/
RewriteEngine On
RewriteRule ^(/sub2/.*) /www/subdomain$1
# ...
</VirtualHost>
```

Due to the `ServerPath` directive a request to the URL
`http://www.sub1.domain.tld/sub1/` is *always* served from the sub1-vhost.
A request to the URL `http://www.sub1.domain.tld/` is only served from the sub1-vhost if the client sent a correct `Host:` header. If no `Host:` header is sent the client gets the information page from the primary host.

Please note that there is one oddity: A request to `http://www.sub2.domain.tld/sub1/` is also served from the sub1-vhost if the client sent no `Host:` header.

The `RewriteRule` directives are used to make sure that a client which sent a correct `Host:` header can use both URL variants, *i.e.*, with or without URL prefix.

# Chapter 30.

# An In-Depth Discussion of Virtual Host Matching

The virtual host code was completely rewritten in **Apache 1.3**. This document attempts to explain exactly what Apache does when deciding what virtual host to serve a hit from. With the help of the new `NameVirtualHost` directive virtual host configuration should be a lot easier and safer than with versions prior to 1.3.

If you just want to *make it work* without understanding how, here are *some examples*.

## 30.1. Config File Parsing

There is a *main_server* which consists of all the definitions appearing outside of `<VirtualHost>` sections. There are virtual servers, called *vhosts*, which are defined by `<VirtualHost>` sections.

The directives `ServerName` and `ServerPath` can appear anywhere within the definition of a server. However, each appearance overrides the previous appearance (within that server).

The main_server has no default `ServerPath`, or `ServerAlias`. The default `ServerName` is deduced from the server's IP address.

Port numbers specified in the `VirtualHost` directive do not influence what port numbers Apache will listen on, they only discriminate between which `VirtualHost` will be selected to handle a request.

Each address appearing in the `VirtualHost` directive can have an optional port. If the port is unspecified it is treated as a wildcard port. The special port * indicates a wildcard that matches any port. Collectively the entire set of addresses (including multiple A record results from DNS lookups) are called the vhost's *address set*.

Unless a `NameVirtualHost` directive is used for the exact IP address and port pair in the `VirtualHost` directive, Apache selects the best match only on the basis of the IP address (or wildcard) and port number. If there are multiple identical best matches, the first `VirtualHost` appearing in the configuration file will be selected.

If you want Apache to *further* discriminate on the basis of the HTTP Host header supplied by the client, the NameVirtualHost directive *must* appear with the exact IP address (or wildcard) and port pair used in a correspnding set of VirtualHost directives.

The name-based virtual host selection occurs only after a single IP-based virtual host has been selected, and only considers the set of virtual hosts that carry an identical IP address and port pair.

Hostnames can be used in place of IP addresses in a virtual host definition, but it is resolved at startup and is not recommended.

Multiple NameVirtualHost directives can be used each with a set of VirtualHost directives but only one NameVirtualHost directive should be used for each specific IP:port pair.

The ordering of NameVirtualHost and VirtualHost directives is not important which makes the following two examples identical (only the order of the VirtualHost directives for *one* address set is important, see below):

```
NameVirtualHost 111.22.33.44          <VirtualHost 111.22.33.44>
<VirtualHost 111.22.33.44>            # server A
# server A                            </VirtualHost>
...                                   <VirtualHost 111.22.33.55>
</VirtualHost>                         # server C
<VirtualHost 111.22.33.44>            ...
# server B                            </VirtualHost>
...                                   <VirtualHost 111.22.33.44>
</VirtualHost>                         # server B
                                       ...
NameVirtualHost 111.22.33.55          </VirtualHost>
<VirtualHost 111.22.33.55>            <VirtualHost 111.22.33.55>
# server C                             # server D
...                                    ...
</VirtualHost>                         </VirtualHost>
<VirtualHost 111.22.33.55>
# server D                            NameVirtualHost 111.22.33.44
...                                   NameVirtualHost 111.22.33.55
</VirtualHost>
```

(To aid the readability of your configuration you should prefer the left variant.)

During initialization a list for each IP address is generated and inserted into an hash table. If the IP address is used in a NameVirtualHost directive the list contains all name-based vhosts for the given IP address. If there are no vhosts defined for that address the NameVirtualHost directive is ignored and an error is logged. For an IP-based vhost the list in the hash table is empty.

Due to a fast hashing function the overhead of hashing an IP address during a request is minimal and almost not existent. Additionally the table is optimized for IP addresses which vary in the last octet.

For every vhost various default values are set. In particular:

1.  If a vhost has no `ServerAdmin`, `Timeout`, `KeepAliveTimeout`, `KeepAlive`, `MaxKeepAliveRequests`, `ReceiveBufferSize`, or `SendBufferSize` directive then the respective value is inherited from the main_server. (That is, inherited from whatever the final setting of that value is in the main_server.)

2.  The "lookup defaults" that define the default directory permissions for a vhost are merged with those of the main_server. This includes any per-directory configuration information for any module.

3.  The per-server configs for each module from the main_server are merged into the vhost server.

Essentially, the main_server is treated as "defaults" or a "base" on which to build each vhost. But the positioning of these main_server definitions in the config file is largely irrelevant -- the entire config of the main_server has been parsed when this final merging occurs. So even if a main_server definition appears after a vhost definition it might affect the vhost definition.

If the main_server has no `ServerName` at this point, then the hostname of the machine that *httpd* is running on is used instead. We will call the *main_server address set* those IP addresses returned by a DNS lookup on the `ServerName` of the main_server.

For any undefined `ServerName` fields, a name-based vhost defaults to the address given first in the `VirtualHost` statement defining the vhost.

Any vhost that includes the magic `_default_` wildcard is given the same `ServerName` as the main_server.

## 30.2. Virtual Host Matching

The server determines which vhost to use for a request as follows:

### Hash table lookup

When the connection is first made by a client, the IP address to which the client connected is looked up in the internal IP hash table.

If the lookup fails (the IP address wasn't found) the request is served from the `_default_` vhost if there is such a vhost for the port to which the client sent the request. If there is no matching `_default_` vhost the request is served from the main_server.

If the IP address is not found in the hash table then the match against the port number may also result in an entry corresponding to a `NameVirtualHost *`, which is subsequently handled like other name-based vhosts.

If the lookup succeeded (a corresponding list for the IP address was found) the next step is to decide if we have to deal with an IP-based or a name-base vhost.

## IP-based vhost

If the entry we found has an empty name list then we have found an IP-based vhost, no further actions are performed and the request is served from that vhost.

## Name-based vhost

If the entry corresponds to a name-based vhost the name list contains one or more vhost structures. This list contains the vhosts in the same order as the `VirtualHost` directives appear in the config file.

The first vhost on this list (the first vhost in the config file with the specified IP address) has the highest priority and catches any request to an unknown server name or a request without a `Host:` header field.

If the client provided a `Host:` header field the list is searched for a matching vhost and the first hit on a `ServerName` or `ServerAlias` is taken and the request is served from that vhost. A `Host:` header field can contain a port number, but Apache always matches against the real port to which the client sent the request.

If the client submitted a HTTP/1.0 request without `Host:` header field we don't know to what server the client tried to connect and any existing `ServerPath` is matched against the URI from the request. The first matching path on the list is used and the request is served from that vhost.

If no matching vhost could be found the request is served from the first vhost with a matching port number that is on the list for the IP to which the client connected (as already mentioned before).

## Persistent connections

The IP lookup described above is only done *once* for a particular TCP/IP session while the name lookup is done on *every* request during a KeepAlive/persistent connection. In other words a client may request pages from different name-based vhosts during a single persistent connection.

## Absolute URI

If the URI from the request is an absolute URI, and its hostname and port match the main server or one of the configured virtual hosts *and* match the address and port to which the client sent the request, then the scheme/hostname/port prefix is stripped off and the remaining relative URI is served by the corresponding main server or virtual host. If it does not match, then the URI remains untouched and the request is taken to be a proxy request.

## Observations

- A name-based vhost can never interfere with an IP-base vhost and vice versa. IP-based vhosts can only be reached through an IP address of its own address set and never through any other address. The same applies to name-based vhosts, they can only be reached through an IP address of the corresponding address set which must be defined with a NameVirtualHost directive.

- ServerAlias and ServerPath checks are never performed for an IP-based vhost.

- The order of name-/IP-based, the _default_ vhost and the NameVirtualHost directive within the config file is not important. Only the ordering of name-based vhosts for a specific address set is significant. The one name-based vhosts that comes first in the configuration file has the highest priority for its corresponding address set.

- The Host: header field is never used during the matching process. Apache always uses the real port to which the client sent the request.

- If a ServerPath directive exists which is a prefix of another ServerPath directive that appears later in the configuration file, then the former will always be matched and the latter will never be matched. (That is assuming that no Host: header field was available to disambiguate the two.)

- If two IP-based vhosts have an address in common, the vhost appearing first in the config file is always matched. Such a thing might happen inadvertently. The server will give a warning in the error logfile when it detects this.

- A _default_ vhost catches a request only if there is no other vhost with a matching IP address *and* a matching port number for the request. The request is only caught if the port number to which the client sent the request matches the port number of your _default_ vhost which is your standard Listen by default. A wildcard port can be specified (*i.e.,* _default_:*) to catch requests to any available port. This also applies to NameVirtualHost * vhosts. Note that this is simply an extension of the "best match" principle, as a specific and exact match is favored over a wildcard.

- The main_server is only used to serve a request if the IP address and port number to which the client connected is unspecified and does not match any other vhost (including a `_default_` vhost). In other words the main_server only catches a request for an unspecified address/port combination (unless there is a `_default_` vhost which matches that port).

- A `_default_` vhost or the main_server is *never* matched for a request with an unknown or missing `Host:` header field if the client connected to an address (and port) which is used for name-based vhosts, *e.g.*, in a `NameVirtualHost` directive.

- You should never specify DNS names in `VirtualHost` directives because it will force your server to rely on DNS to boot. Furthermore it poses a security threat if you do not control the DNS for all the domains listed. There's *more information* available on this and the next two topics.

- `ServerName` should always be set for each vhost. Otherwise A DNS lookup is required for each vhost.

## 30.3. Tips

In addition to the tips on the *DNS Issues* page, here are some further tips:

- Place all main_server definitions before any `VirtualHost` definitions. (This is to aid the readability of the configuration -- the post-config merging process makes it non-obvious that definitions mixed in around virtual hosts might affect all virtual hosts.)

- Group corresponding `NameVirtualHost` and `VirtualHost` definitions in your configuration to ensure better readability.

- Avoid `ServerPaths` which are prefixes of other `ServerPaths`. If you cannot avoid this then you have to ensure that the longer (more specific) prefix vhost appears earlier in the configuration file than the shorter (less specific) prefix (*i.e.*, "ServerPath /abc" should appear after "ServerPath /abc/def").

# Chapter 31.
# File Descriptor Limits

When using a large number of Virtual Hosts, Apache may run out of available file descriptors (sometimes called *file handles*) if each Virtual Host specifies different log files. The total number of file descriptors used by Apache is one for each distinct error log file, one for every other log file directive, plus 10-20 for internal use. Unix operating systems limit the number of file descriptors that may be used by a process; the limit is typically 64, and may usually be increased up to a large hard-limit.

Although Apache attempts to increase the limit as required, this may not work if:

- Your system does not provide the `setrlimit()` system call.
- The `setrlimit(RLIMIT_NOFILE)` call does not function on your system (such as Solaris 2.3)
- The number of file descriptors required exceeds the hard limit.
- Your system imposes other limits on file descriptors, such as a limit on stdio streams only using file descriptors below 256. (Solaris 2)

In the event of problems you can:

- Reduce the number of log files; don't specify log files in the `<VirtualHost>` sections, but only log to the main log files. (See *Splitting up your log files*, below, for more information on doing this.)
- If you system falls into 1 or 2 (above), then increase the file descriptor limit before starting Apache, using a script like

```
#!/bin/sh
ulimit -S -n 100
exec httpd
```

## 31.1. Splitting up your log files

If you want to log multiple virtual hosts to the same log file, you may want to split up the log files afterwards in order to run statistical analysis of the various virtual hosts. This can be accomplished in the following manner.

First, you will need to add the virtual host information to the log entries. This can be done using the LogFormat directive, and the %v variable. Add this to the beginning of your log format string:

```
LogFormat "%v %h %l %u %t \"%r\" %>s %b" vhost
CustomLog logs/multiple_vhost_log vhost
```

This will create a log file in the common log format, but with the canonical virtual host (whatever appears in the ServerName directive) prepended to each line. (See Custom Log Formats for more about customizing your log files.)

When you wish to split your log file into its component parts (one file per virtual host) you can use the program *split-logfile* to accomplish this. You'll find this program in the support directory of the Apache distribution.

Run this program with the command:

```
split-logfile < /logs/multiple_vhost_log
```

This program, when run with the name of your vhost log file, will generate one file for each virtual host that appears in your log file. Each file will be called hostname.log.

# Chapter 32.
# Issues Regarding DNS and Apache

This page could be summarized with the statement: don't configure Apache in such a way that it relies on DNS resolution for parsing of the configuration files. If Apache requires DNS resolution to parse the configuration files then your server may be subject to reliability problems (ie. it might not boot), or denial and theft of service attacks (including users able to steal hits from other users).

## 32.1.A Simple Example

```
<VirtualHost www.abc.dom>
ServerAdmin webgirl@abc.dom
DocumentRoot /www/abc
</VirtualHost>
```

In order for Apache to function properly, it absolutely needs to have two pieces of information about each virtual host: the `ServerName` and at least one IP address that the server will bind and respond to. The above example does not include the IP address, so Apache must use DNS to find the address of www.abc.dom. If for some reason DNS is not available at the time your server is parsing its config file, then this virtual host **will not be configured**. It won't be able to respond to any hits to this virtual host (prior to Apache version 1.2 the server would not even boot).

Suppose that www.abc.dom has address 192.0.2.1. Then consider this configuration snippet:

```
<VirtualHost 192.0.2.1>
ServerAdmin webgirl@abc.dom
DocumentRoot /www/abc
</VirtualHost>
```

This time Apache needs to use reverse DNS to find the `ServerName` for this virtualhost. If that reverse lookup fails then it will partially disable the virtualhost (prior to Apache version 1.2 the server would not even boot). If the virtual host is name-based then it will effectively be totally disabled, but if it is IP-based then it will mostly work. However, if Apache should ever have to generate a full URL for the server which includes the server name, then it will fail to generate a valid URL.

Here is a snippet that avoids both of these problems:

```
<VirtualHost 192.0.2.1>
ServerName www.abc.dom
ServerAdmin webgirl@abc.dom
DocumentRoot /www/abc
</VirtualHost>
```

## 32.2. Denial of Service

There are (at least) two forms that denial of service can come in. If you are running a version of Apache prior to version 1.2 then your server will not even boot if one of the two DNS lookups mentioned above fails for any of your virtual hosts. In some cases this DNS lookup may not even be under your control; for example, if abc.dom is one of your customers and they control their own DNS, they can force your (pre-1.2) server to fail while booting simply by deleting the www.abc.dom record.

Another form is far more insidious. Consider this configuration snippet:

```
<VirtualHost www.abc.dom>
ServerAdmin webgirl@abc.dom
DocumentRoot /www/abc
</VirtualHost>

<VirtualHost www.def.dom>
ServerAdmin webguy@def.dom
DocumentRoot /www/def
</VirtualHost>
```

Suppose that you've assigned 192.0.2.1 to www.abc.dom and 192.0.2.2 to www.def.dom. Furthermore, suppose that def.dom has control of their own DNS. With this config you have put def.dom into a position where they can steal all traffic destined to abc.dom. To do so, all they have to do is set www.def.dom to 192.0.2.1. Since they control their own DNS you can't stop them from pointing the www.def.dom record wherever they wish.

Requests coming in to 192.0.2.1 (including all those where users typed in URLs of the form http://www.abc.dom/whatever) will all be served by the def.dom virtual host. To better understand why this happens requires a more in-depth discussion of how Apache matches up incoming requests with the virtual host that will serve it. A rough document describing this *is available*.

## 32.3. The "main server" Address

The addition of *name-based virtual host support* in Apache 1.1 requires Apache to know the IP address(es) of the host that *httpd* is running on. To get this address it uses either the global <u>ServerName</u> (if present) or calls the C function gethostname (which should return the same as typing "hostname" at the command prompt). Then it performs a DNS lookup on this address. At present there is no way to avoid this lookup.

If you fear that this lookup might fail because your DNS server is down then you can insert the hostname in /etc/hosts (where you probably already have it so that the machine can boot properly). Then ensure that your machine is configured to use /etc/hosts in the event that DNS fails. Depending on what OS you are using this might be accomplished by editing /etc/resolv.conf, or maybe /etc/nsswitch.conf.

If your server doesn't have to perform DNS for any other reason then you might be able to get away with running Apache with the HOSTRESORDER environment variable set to "local". This all depends on what OS and resolver libraries you are using. It also affects CGIs unless you use mod_env to control the environment. It's best to consult the man pages or FAQs for your OS.

## 32.4. Tips to Avoid These Problems

- use IP addresses in VirtualHost
- use IP addresses in Listen
- ensure all virtual hosts have an explicit ServerName
- create a <VirtualHost _default_:*> server that has no pages to serve

## 32.5. Appendix: Future Directions

The situation regarding DNS is highly undesirable. For Apache 1.2 we've attempted to make the server at least continue booting in the event of failed DNS, but it might not be the best we can do. In any event, requiring the use of explicit IP addresses in configuration files is highly undesirable in today's Internet where renumbering is a necessity.

A possible work around to the theft of service attack described above would be to perform a reverse DNS lookup on the IP address returned by the forward lookup and compare the two names -- in the event of a mismatch, the virtualhost would be disabled. This would require reverse DNS to be configured properly (which is something that most admins are familiar with because of the common use of "double-reverse" DNS lookups by FTP servers and TCP wrappers).

In any event, it doesn't seem possible to reliably boot a virtual-hosted web server when DNS has failed unless IP addresses are used. Partial solutions such as disabling portions of the configuration might be worse than not booting at all depending on what the webserver is supposed to accomplish.

As HTTP/1.1 is deployed and browsers and proxies start issuing the Host header it will become possible to avoid the use of IP-based virtual hosts entirely. In this case, a webserver has no requirement to do DNS lookups during configuration. But as of March 1997 these features have not been deployed widely enough to be put into use on critical webservers.

# Part IV.
# URL Rewriting Guide

*"The great thing about mod_rewrite is it gives you all the configurability and flexibility of Sendmail. The downside to mod_rewrite is that it gives you all the configurability and flexibility of Sendmail."*

-- Brian Behlendorf
Apache Group

*"Despite the tons of examples and docs, mod_rewrite is voodoo. Damned cool voodoo, but still voodo."*

-- Brian Moore
*bem@news.cmc.net*

Welcome to mod_rewrite, the Swiss Army Knife of URL manipulation!

This module uses a rule-based rewriting engine (based on a regular-expression parser) to rewrite requested URLs on the fly. It supports an unlimited number of rules and an unlimited number of attached rule conditions for each rule to provide a really flexible and powerful URL manipulation mechanism. The URL manipulations can depend on various tests, for instance server variables, environment variables, HTTP headers, time stamps and even external database lookups in various formats can be used to achieve granular URL matching.

This module operates on the full URLs (including the path-info part) both in per-server context (`httpd.conf`) and per-directory context (`.htaccess` files and `<Directory>` blocks) and can even generate query-string parts on result. The rewritten result can lead to internal sub-processing, external request redirection or even to an internal proxy throughput.

But all this functionality and flexibility has its drawback: complexity. So don't expect to understand this entire module in just one day.

## Documentation

- *mod_rewrite reference documentation*
- *Introduction*
- *Flags*
- *Technical details*

- *Rewrite Guide - useful examples*
- *Advanced Rewrite Guide - more useful examples*

# Chapter 33.

# Apache Module mod_rewrite

| | |
|---|---|
| Description: | Provides a rule-based rewriting engine to rewrite requested URLs on the fly |
| Status: | Extension |
| Module Identifier: | rewrite_module |
| Source File: | mod_rewrite.c |
| Compatibility: | Available in Apache 1.3 and later |

## Summary

This module uses a rule-based rewriting engine (based on a regular-expression parser) to rewrite requested URLs on the fly. It supports an unlimited number of rules and an unlimited number of attached rule conditions for each rule, to provide a really flexible and powerful URL manipulation mechanism. The URL manipulations can depend on various tests, of server variables, environment variables, HTTP headers, or time stamps. Even external database lookups in various formats can be used to achieve highly granular URL matching.

This module operates on the full URLs (including the path-info part) both in per-server context (`httpd.conf`) and per-directory context (`.htaccess`) and can generate query-string parts on result. The rewritten result can lead to internal sub-processing, external request redirection or even to an internal proxy throughput.

Further details, discussion, and examples, are provided in the *detailed mod_rewrite documentation*.

## 33.1. Quoting Special Characters

As of Apache 1.3.20, special characters in *TestString* and *Substitution* strings can be escaped (that is, treated as normal characters without their usual special meaning) by prefixing them with a slash ('\') character. In other words, you can include an actual dollar-sign character in a *Substitution* string by using '\$'; this keeps mod_rewrite from trying to treat it as a backreference.

## 33.2. Environment Variables

This module keeps track of two additional (non-standard) CGI/SSI environment variables named SCRIPT_URL and SCRIPT_URI. These contain the *logical* Web-view to the current resource, while the standard CGI/SSI variables SCRIPT_NAME and SCRIPT_FILENAME contain the *physical* System-view.

Notice: These variables hold the URI/URL *as they were initially requested*, that is, *before* any rewriting. This is important to note because the rewriting process is primarily used to rewrite logical URLs to physical pathnames.

**Example**

```
SCRIPT_NAME=/sw/lib/w3s/tree/global/u/rse/.www/index.html
SCRIPT_FILENAME=/u/rse/.www/index.html
SCRIPT_URL=/u/rse/
SCRIPT_URI=http://en1.engelschall.com/u/rse/
```

## 33.3. Rewriting in Virtual Hosts

By default, mod_rewrite configuration settings from the main server context are not inherited by virtual hosts. To make the main server settings apply to virtual hosts, you must place the following directives in each <VirtualHost> section:

```
RewriteEngine On
RewriteOptions Inherit
```

## 33.4. Practical Solutions

For numerous examples of common, and not-so-common, uses for mod_rewrite, see the *Rewrite Guide*, and the *Advanced Rewrite Guide* documents.

### RewriteBase Directive

| | |
|---|---|
| Description: | Sets the base URL for per-directory rewrites |
| Syntax: | RewriteBase *URL-path* |
| Default: | See usage for information. |
| Context: | directory, .htaccess |
| Override: | FileInfo |
| Status: | Extension |
| Module: | mod_rewrite |

The RewriteBase directive explicitly sets the base URL for per-directory rewrites. As you will see below, RewriteRule can be used in per-directory config files (.htaccess). In such a case, it will act locally, stripping the local directory prefix before processing, and applying rewrite rules only to the remainder. When processing is complete, the prefix is automatically added back to the path. The default setting is; RewriteBase *physical-directory-path*

When a substitution occurs for a new URL, this module has to re-inject the URL into the server processing. To be able to do this it needs to know what the corresponding URL-prefix or URL-base is. By default this prefix is the corresponding filepath itself. **However, for most websites, URLs are NOT directly related to physical filename paths, so this assumption will often be wrong!** Therefore, you can use the RewriteBase directive to specify the correct URL-prefix.

> If your webserver's URLs are **not** directly related to physical file paths, you will need to use RewriteBase in every .htaccess file where you want to use <u>RewriteRule</u> directives.

For example, assume the following per-directory config file:

```
#
#   /abc/def/.htaccess -- per-dir config file for directory /abc/def
#   Remember: /abc/def is the physical path of /xyz, i.e., the server
#             has a 'Alias /xyz /abc/def' directive e.g.
#

RewriteEngine On

#  let the server know that we were reached via /xyz and not
#  via the physical path prefix /abc/def
RewriteBase    /xyz

#  now the rewriting rules
RewriteRule    ^oldstuff\.html$  newstuff.html
```

In the above example, a request to /xyz/oldstuff.html gets correctly rewritten to the physical file /abc/def/newstuff.html.

### For Apache Hackers

> The following list gives detailed information about the internal processing steps:
> ```
> Request:
>   /xyz/oldstuff.html
>
> Internal Processing:
>   /xyz/oldstuff.html      -> /abc/def/oldstuff.html  (per-server Alias)
>   /abc/def/oldstuff.html -> /abc/def/newstuff.html  (per-dir    RewriteRule)
>   /abc/def/newstuff.html -> /xyz/newstuff.html      (per-dir    RewriteBase)
>   /xyz/newstuff.html      -> /abc/def/newstuff.html  (per-server Alias)
> ```

```
Result:
  /abc/def/newstuff.html
```

This seems very complicated, but is in fact correct Apache internal processing. Because the per-directory rewriting comes late in the process, the rewritten request has to be re-injected into the Apache kernel, as if it were a new request. (See *mod_rewrite technical details*.) This is not the serious overhead it may seem to be - this re-injection is completely internal to the Apache server (and the same procedure is used by many other operations within Apache).

## RewriteCond Directive

| | |
|---|---|
| Description: | Defines a condition under which rewriting will take place |
| Syntax: | RewriteCond *TestString CondPattern* |
| Context: | server config, virtual host, directory, .htaccess |
| Override: | FileInfo |
| Status: | Extension |
| Module: | mod_rewrite |

The RewriteCond directive defines a rule condition. One or more RewriteCond can precede a RewriteRule directive. The following rule is then only used if both the current state of the URI matches its pattern, **and** if these conditions are met.

*TestString* is a string which can contain the following expanded constructs in addition to plain text:

- **RewriteRule backreferences**: These are backreferences of the form $N ($0 <= N <= 9$), which provide access to the grouped parts (in parentheses) of the pattern, from the RewriteRule which is subject to the current set of RewriteCond conditions..

- **RewriteCond backreferences**: These are backreferences of the form %N ($1 <= N <= 9$), which provide access to the grouped parts (again, in parentheses) of the pattern, from the last matched RewriteCond in the current set of conditions.

- **RewriteMap expansions**: These are expansions of the form ${mapname:key|default}. See *the documentation for RewriteMap* for more details.

- **Server-Variables**: These are variables of the form %{ *NAME_OF_VARIABLE* } where *NAME_OF_VARIABLE* can be a string taken from the following list:

| HTTP headers: | connection & request: |
|---|---|
| HTTP_USER_AGENT | REMOTE_ADDR |
| HTTP_REFERER | REMOTE_HOST |
| HTTP_COOKIE | REMOTE_PORT |
| HTTP_FORWARDED | REMOTE_USER |
| HTTP_HOST | REMOTE_IDENT |

| HTTP headers: | connection & request: | |
|---|---|---|
| HTTP_PROXY_CONNECTION | REQUEST_METHOD | |
| HTTP_ACCEPT | SCRIPT_FILENAME | |
| | PATH_INFO | |
| | QUERY_STRING | |
| | AUTH_TYPE | |
| **server internals:** | **date and time:** | **specials:** |
| DOCUMENT_ROOT | TIME_YEAR | API_VERSION |
| SERVER_ADMIN | TIME_MON | THE_REQUEST |
| SERVER_NAME | TIME_DAY | REQUEST_URI |
| SERVER_ADDR | TIME_HOUR | REQUEST_FILENAME |
| SERVER_PORT | TIME_MIN | IS_SUBREQ |
| SERVER_PROTOCOL | TIME_SEC | HTTPS |
| SERVER_SOFTWARE | TIME_WDAY | |
| | TIME | |

These variables all correspond to the similarly named HTTP MIME-headers, C variables of the Apache server or `struct tm` fields of the Unix system. Most are documented elsewhere in the Manual or in the CGI specification. Those that are special to mod_rewrite include those below.

IS_SUBREQ

Will contain the text "true" if the request currently being processed is a sub-request, "false" otherwise. Sub-requests may be generated by modules that need to resolve additional files or URIs in order to complete their tasks.

API_VERSION

This is the version of the Apache module API (the internal interface between server and module) in the current httpd build, as defined in include/ap_mmn.h. The module API version corresponds to the version of Apache in use (in the release version of Apache 1.3.14, for instance, it is 19990320:10), but is mainly of interest to module authors.

THE_REQUEST

The full HTTP request line sent by the browser to the server (e.g., "GET /index.html HTTP/1.1"). This does not include any additional headers sent by the browser.

REQUEST_URI

The resource requested in the HTTP request line. (In the example above, this would be "/index.html".)

REQUEST_FILENAME

> The full local filesystem path to the file or script matching the request, if this has already been determined by the server at the time REQUEST_FILENAME is referenced. Otherwise, such as when used in virtual host context, the same value as REQUEST_URI.

HTTPS

> Will contain the text "on" if the connection is using SSL/TLS, or "off" otherwise. (This variable can be safely used regardless of whether or not mod_ssl is loaded).

Other things you should be aware of:

1.  The variables SCRIPT_FILENAME and REQUEST_FILENAME contain the same value - the value of the filename field of the internal request_rec structure of the Apache server. The first name is the commonly known CGI variable name while the second is the appropriate counterpart of REQUEST_URI (which contains the value of the uri field of request_rec).

    If a substitution occurred and the rewriting continues, the value of both variables will be updated accordingly.

    If used in per-server context (*i.e.*, before the request is mapped to the filesystem) SCRIPT_FILENAME and REQUEST_FILENAME cannot contain the full local filesystem path since the path is unknown at this stage of processing. Both variables will initially contain the value of REQUEST_URI in that case. In order to obtain the full local filesystem path of the request in per-server context, use an URL-based look-ahead %{LA-U:REQUEST_FILENAME} to determine the final value of REQUEST_FILENAME.

2.  %{ENV:variable}, where *variable* can be any environment variable, is also available. This is looked-up via internal Apache structures and (if not found there) via getenv() from the Apache server process.

3.  %{SSL:variable}, where *variable* is the name of an *SSL environment variable*, can be used whether or not mod_ssl is loaded, but will always expand to the empty string if it is not. Example: %{SSL:SSL_CIPHER_USEKEYSIZE} may expand to 128.

4.  %{HTTP:header}, where *header* can be any HTTP MIME-header name, can always be used to obtain the value of a header sent in the HTTP request. Example: %{HTTP:Proxy-Connection} is the value of the HTTP header "Proxy-Connection:".

If a HTTP header is used in a condition this header is added to the Vary header of the response in case the condition evaluates to to true for the request. It is **not** added if the condition evaluates to false for the request. Adding the HTTP header to the Vary header of the response is needed for proper caching.

It has to be kept in mind that conditions follow a short circuit logic in the case of the '**ornext**|**OR**' flag so that certain conditions might not be evaluated at all.

5.  %{LA-U:variable} can be used for look-aheads which perform an internal (URL-based) sub-request to determine the final value of *variable*. This can be used to access variable for rewriting which is not available at the current stage, but will be set in a later phase.

    For instance, to rewrite according to the REMOTE_USER variable from within the per-server context (httpd.conf file) you must use %{LA-U:REMOTE_USER} - this variable is set by the authorization phases, which come *after* the URL translation phase (during which mod_rewrite operates).

    On the other hand, because mod_rewrite implements its per-directory context (.htaccess file) via the Fixup phase of the API and because the authorization phases come *before* this phase, you just can use %{REMOTE_USER} in that context.

6.  %{LA-F:variable} can be used to perform an internal (filename-based) sub-request, to determine the final value of *variable*. Most of the time, this is the same as LA-U above.

*CondPattern* is the condition pattern, a regular expression which is applied to the current instance of the *TestString*. *TestString* is first evaluated, before being matched against *CondPattern*.

**Remember:** *CondPattern* is a *perl compatible regular expression* with some additions:

1.  You can prefix the pattern string with a '**!**' character (exclamation mark) to specify a **non**-matching pattern.

2.  There are some special variants of *CondPatterns*. Instead of real regular expression strings you can also use one of the following:

    *   '**<CondPattern**' (lexicographically precedes)
        Treats the *CondPattern* as a plain string and compares it lexicographically to *TestString*. True if *TestString* lexicographically precedes *CondPattern*.

    *   '**>CondPattern**' (lexicographically follows)
        Treats the *CondPattern* as a plain string and compares it lexicographically to *TestString*. True if *TestString* lexicographically follows *CondPattern*.

    *   '**=CondPattern**' (lexicographically equal)
        Treats the *CondPattern* as a plain string and compares it lexicographically to

*TestString*. True if *TestString* is lexicographically equal to *CondPattern* (the two strings are exactly equal, character for character). If *CondPattern* is " " (two quotation marks) this compares *TestString* to the empty string.

- **'-d'** (is **d**irectory)
  Treats the *TestString* as a pathname and tests whether or not it exists, and is a directory.

- **'-f'** (is regular **f**ile)
  Treats the *TestString* as a pathname and tests whether or not it exists, and is a regular file.

- **'-s'** (is regular file, with **s**ize)
  Treats the *TestString* as a pathname and tests whether or not it exists, and is a regular file with size greater than zero.

- **'-l'** (is symbolic **l**ink)
  Treats the *TestString* as a pathname and tests whether or not it exists, and is a symbolic link.

- **'-x'** (has e**x**ecutable permissions)
  Treats the *TestString* as a pathname and tests whether or not it exists, and has executable permissions. These permissions are determined according to the underlying OS.

- **'-F'** (is existing **f**ile, via subrequest)
  Checks whether or not *TestString* is a valid file, accessible via all the server's currently-configured access controls for that path. This uses an internal subrequest to do the check, so use it with care - it can impact your server's performance!

- **'-U'** (is existing **U**RL, via subrequest)
  Checks whether or not *TestString* is a valid URL, accessible via all the server's currently-configured access controls for that path. This uses an internal subrequest to do the check, so use it with care - it can impact your server's performance!

 **Note**

All of these tests can also be prefixed by an exclamation mark ('!') to negate their meaning.

3. You can also set special flags for *CondPattern* by appending **[*flags*]** as the third argument to the RewriteCond directive, where *flags* is a comma-separated list of any of the following flags:

- **'nocase|NC'** (no case)
  This makes the test case-insensitive - differences between 'A-Z' and 'a-z' are ignored, both in the expanded *TestString* and the *CondPattern*. This flag is effective only for comparisons between *TestString* and *CondPattern*. It has no effect on filesystem and subrequest checks.

- **'ornext|OR'** (or next condition)
  Use this to combine rule conditions with a local OR instead of the implicit AND. Typical example:

```
RewriteCond %{REMOTE_HOST}  ^host1.*  [OR]
RewriteCond %{REMOTE_HOST}  ^host2.*  [OR]
RewriteCond %{REMOTE_HOST}  ^host3.*
RewriteRule ...some special stuff for any of these hosts...
```

  Without this flag you would have to write the condition/rule pair three times.

- **'novary|NV'** (no vary)
  If a HTTP header is used in the condition, this flag prevents this header from being added to the Vary header of the response.
  Using this flag might break proper caching of the response if the representation of this response varies on the value of this header. So this flag should be only used if the meaning of the Vary header is well understood.

**Example:**

To rewrite the Homepage of a site according to the "User-Agent:" header of the request, you can use the following:

```
RewriteCond  %{HTTP_USER_AGENT}  ^Mozilla.*
RewriteRule  ^/$               /homepage.max.html  [L]

RewriteCond  %{HTTP_USER_AGENT}  ^Lynx.*
RewriteRule  ^/$               /homepage.min.html  [L]

RewriteRule  ^/$               /homepage.std.html  [L]
```

Explanation: If you use a browser which identifies itself as 'Mozilla' (including Netscape Navigator, Mozilla etc), then you get the max homepage (which could include frames, or other special features). If you use the Lynx browser (which is terminal-based), then you get the min homepage (which could be a version designed for easy, text-only browsing). If neither of these conditions apply (you use any other browser, or your browser identifies itself as something non-standard), you get the std (standard) homepage.

## RewriteEngine Directive

| | |
|---|---|
| Description: | Enables or disables runtime rewriting engine |
| Syntax: | `RewriteEngine on|off` |
| Default: | `RewriteEngine off` |
| Context: | server config, virtual host, directory, .htaccess |
| Override: | FileInfo |
| Status: | Extension |
| Module: | mod_rewrite |

The `RewriteEngine` directive enables or disables the runtime rewriting engine. If it is set to `off` this module does no runtime processing at all. It does not even update the `SCRIPT_URx` environment variables.

Use this directive to disable the module instead of commenting out all the `RewriteRule` directives!

Note that rewrite configurations are not inherited by virtual hosts. This means that you need to have a `RewriteEngine on` directive for each virtual host in which you wish to use rewrite rules.

`RewriteMap` directives of the type `prg` are not started during server initialization if they're defined in a context that does not have `RewriteEngine` set to on

## RewriteLock Directive

| | |
|---|---|
| Description: | Sets the name of the lock file used for `RewriteMap` synchronization |
| Syntax: | `RewriteLock` *file-path* |
| Context: | server config |
| Status: | Extension |
| Module: | mod_rewrite |

This directive sets the filename for a synchronization lockfile which mod_rewrite needs to communicate with `RewriteMap` *programs*. Set this lockfile to a local path (not on a NFS-mounted device) when you want to use a rewriting map-program. It is not required for other types of rewriting maps.

## RewriteLog Directive

| | |
|---|---|
| Description: | Sets the name of the file used for logging rewrite engine processing |
| Syntax: | `RewriteLog` *file-path* |

| Context: | server config, virtual host |
|----------|------------------------------|
| Status:  | Extension                    |
| Module:  | mod_rewrite                  |

The RewriteLog directive sets the name of the file to which the server logs any rewriting actions it performs. If the name does not begin with a slash ('/') then it is assumed to be relative to the *Server Root*. The directive should occur only once per server config.

To disable the logging of rewriting actions it is not recommended to set *Filename* to /dev/null, because although the rewriting engine does not then output to a logfile it still creates the logfile output internally. **This will slow down the server with no advantage to the administrator!** To disable logging either remove or comment out the RewriteLog directive or use RewriteLogLevel 0!

**Security**

See the *Apache Security Tips* document for details on how your security could be compromised if the directory where logfiles are stored is writable by anyone other than the user that starts the server.

**Example**

RewriteLog "/usr/local/var/apache/logs/rewrite.log"

## RewriteLogLevel Directive

| Description: | Sets the verbosity of the log file used by the rewrite engine |
|--------------|---------------------------------------------------------------|
| Syntax:      | RewriteLogLevel *Level*                                        |
| Default:     | RewriteLogLevel 0                                              |
| Context:     | server config, virtual host                                   |
| Status:      | Extension                                                      |
| Module:      | mod_rewrite                                                    |

The RewriteLogLevel directive sets the verbosity level of the rewriting logfile. The default level 0 means no logging, while 9 or more means that practically all actions are logged.

To disable the logging of rewriting actions simply set *Level* to 0. This disables all rewrite action logs.

Using a high value for *Level* will slow down your Apache server dramatically! Use the rewriting logfile at a *Level* greater than 2 only for debugging!

**Example**

```
RewriteLogLevel 3
```

## RewriteMap Directive

| | |
|---|---|
| Description: | Defines a mapping function for key-lookup |
| Syntax: | RewriteMap *MapName* *MapType* : *MapSource* |
| Context: | server config, virtual host |
| Status: | Extension |
| Module: | mod_rewrite |
| Compatibility: | The choice of different dbm types is available in Apache 2.0.41 and later |

The RewriteMap directive defines a *Rewriting Map* which can be used inside rule substitution strings by the mapping-functions to insert/substitute fields through a key lookup. The source of this lookup can be of various types.

The *MapName* is the name of the map and will be used to specify a mapping-function for the substitution strings of a rewriting rule via one of the following constructs:

> ${ *MapName* : *LookupKey* }
> ${ *MapName* : *LookupKey* | *DefaultValue* }

When such a construct occurs, the map *MapName* is consulted and the key *LookupKey* is looked-up. If the key is found, the map-function construct is substituted by *SubstValue*. If the key is not found then it is substituted by *DefaultValue* or by the empty string if no *DefaultValue* was specified.

For example, you might define a RewriteMap as:

```
RewriteMap examplemap txt:/path/to/file/map.txt
```

You would then be able to use this map in a RewriteRule as follows:

```
RewriteRule ^/ex/(.*) ${examplemap:$1}
```

The following combinations for *MapType* and *MapSource* can be used:

- **Standard Plain Text**
  MapType: txt, MapSource: Unix filesystem path to valid regular file

  This is the standard rewriting map feature where the *MapSource* is a plain ASCII file containing either blank lines, comment lines (starting with a '#' character) or pairs like the following - one per line.

*MatchingKey SubstValue*

**Example**

```
##
##  map.txt -- rewriting map
##
Ralf.S.Engelschall    rse   # Bastard Operator From Hell
Mr.Joe.Average        joe   # Mr. Average
```

```
RewriteMap real-to-user txt:/path/to/file/map.txt
```

- **Randomized Plain Text**

  MapType: rnd, MapSource: Unix filesystem path to valid regular file

  This is identical to the Standard Plain Text variant above but with a special post-processing feature: After looking up a value it is parsed according to contained "|" characters which have the meaning of "or". In other words they indicate a set of alternatives from which the actual returned value is chosen randomly. For example, you might use the following map file and directives to provide a random load balancing between several back-end server, via a reverse-proxy. Images are sent to one of the servers in the 'static' pool, while everything else is sent to one of the 'dynamic' pool.

  **Example:**

  **Rewrite map file**

```
##
##  map.txt -- rewriting map
##
static    www1|www2|www3|www4
dynamic   www5|www6
```

  **Configuration directives**

```
RewriteMap servers rnd:/path/to/file/map.txt

RewriteRule ^/(.*\.(png|gif|jpg)) http://${servers:static}/$1 [NC,P,L]
RewriteRule ^/(.*) http://${servers:dynamic}/$1 [P,L]
```

- **Hash File**

  MapType: dbm [=*type*], MapSource: Unix filesystem path to valid regular file

  Here the source is a binary format DBM file containing the same contents as a *Plain Text* format file, but in a special representation which is optimized for really fast lookups. The *type* can be sdbm, gdbm, ndbm, or db depending on *compile-time settings*. If the *type* is omitted, the compile-time default will be chosen.

To create a dbm file from a source text file, use the *httxt2dbm* utility.

```
$ httxt2dbm -i mapfile.txt -o mapfile.map
```

- **Internal Function**
  MapType: `int`, MapSource: Internal Apache function

  Here, the source is an internal Apache function. Currently you cannot create your own, but the following functions already exist:

  - **toupper**:
    Converts the key to all upper case.

  - **tolower**:
    Converts the key to all lower case.

  - **escape**:
    Translates special characters in the key to hex-encodings.

  - **unescape**:
    Translates hex-encodings in the key back to special characters.

- **External Rewriting Program**
  MapType: `prg`, MapSource: Unix filesystem path to valid regular file

  Here the source is a program, not a map file. To create it you can use a language of your choice, but the result has to be an executable program (either object-code or a script with the magic cookie trick '`#!/path/to/interpreter`' as the first line).

  This program is started once, when the Apache server is started, and then communicates with the rewriting engine via its `stdin` and `stdout` file-handles. For each map-function lookup it will receive the key to lookup as a newline-terminated string on `stdin`. It then has to give back the looked-up value as a newline-terminated string on `stdout` or the four-character string "`NULL`" if it fails (*i.e.*, there is no corresponding value for the given key). A trivial program which will implement a 1:1 map (*i.e.*, key == value) could be:

  External rewriting programs are not started if they're defined in a context that does not have `RewriteEngine` set to on

```perl
#!/usr/bin/perl
$| = 1;
while (<STDIN>) {
    # ...put here any transformations or lookups...
    print $_;
}
```

But be very careful:

1. *"Keep it simple, stupid"* (KISS). If this program hangs, it will cause Apache to hang when trying to use the relevant rewrite rule.

2. A common mistake is to use buffered I/O on `stdout`. Avoid this, as it will cause a deadloop! "`$|=1`" is used above, to prevent this.

3. The `RewriteLock` directive can be used to define a lockfile which mod_rewrite can use to synchronize communication with the mapping program. By default no such synchronization takes place.

The `RewriteMap` directive can occur more than once. For each mapping-function use one `RewriteMap` directive to declare its rewriting mapfile. While you cannot **declare** a map in per-directory context it is of course possible to **use** this map in per-directory context.

 **Note**

For plain text and DBM format files the looked-up keys are cached in-core until the `mtime` of the mapfile changes or the server does a restart. This way you can have map-functions in rules which are used for **every** request. This is no problem, because the external lookup only happens once!

## RewriteOptions Directive

| Description: | Sets some special options for the rewrite engine |
|---|---|
| Syntax: | `RewriteOptions` *Options* |
| Context: | server config, virtual host, directory, .htaccess |
| Override: | FileInfo |
| Status: | Extension |
| Module: | mod_rewrite |
| Compatibility: | `MaxRedirects` is no longer available in version 2.1 and later |

The `RewriteOptions` directive sets some special options for the current per-server or per-directory configuration. The *Option* string can currently only be one of the following:

**inherit**

This forces the current configuration to inherit the configuration of the parent. In per-virtual-server context, this means that the maps, conditions and rules of the main server are inherited. In per-directory context this means that conditions and rules of the parent directory's `.htaccess` configuration are inherited.

## RewriteRule Directive

| | |
|---|---|
| Description: | Defines rules for the rewriting engine |
| Syntax: | RewriteRule *Pattern  Substitution*  [*flags*] |
| Context: | server config, virtual host, directory, .htaccess |
| Override: | FileInfo |
| Status: | Extension |
| Module: | mod_rewrite |

The `RewriteRule` directive is the real rewriting workhorse. The directive can occur more than once, with each instance defining a single rewrite rule. The order in which these rules are defined is important - this is the order in which they will be applied at run-time.

*Pattern* is a perl compatible regular expression. On the first RewriteRule it is applied to the *URL-path* of the request; subsequent patterns are applied to the output of the last matched RewriteRule.

---

**What is matched?**

The *Pattern* will initially be matched against the part of the URL after the hostname and port, and before the query string. If you wish to match against the hostname, port, or query string, use a `RewriteCond` with the `%{HTTP_HOST}`, `%{SERVER_PORT}`, or `%{QUERY_STRING}` variables respectively.

---

For some hints on *regular expressions*, see the *mod_rewrite Introduction*.

In mod_rewrite, the NOT character (`'!'`) is also available as a possible pattern prefix. This enables you to negate a pattern; to say, for instance: "*if the current URL does **NOT** match this pattern*". This can be used for exceptional cases, where it is easier to match the negative pattern, or as a last default rule.

 **Note**

> When using the NOT character to negate a pattern, you cannot include grouped wildcard parts in that pattern. This is because, when the pattern does NOT match (ie, the negation matches), there are no contents for the groups. Thus, if negated patterns are used, you cannot use $N in the substitution string!

The *Substitution* of a rewrite rule is the string that replaces the original URL-path that was matched by *Pattern*. The *Substitution* may be a:

**file-system path**

Designates the location on the file-system of the resource to be delivered to the client.

---

### URL-path

A <u>DocumentRoot</u>-relative path to the resource to be served. Note that `mod_rewrite` tries to guess whether you have specified a file-system path or a URL-path by checking to see if the first segment of the path exists at the root of the file-system. For example, if you specify a *Substitution* string of `/www/file.html`, then this will be treated as a URL-path *unless* a directory named www exists at the root or your file-system, in which case it will be treated as a file-system path. If you wish other URL-mapping directives (such as <u>Alias</u>) to be applied to the resulting URL-path, use the `[PT]` flag as described below.

### Absolute URL

If an absolute URL is specified, `mod_rewrite` checks to see whether the hostname matches the current host. If it does, the scheme and hostname are stripped out and the resulting path is treated as a URL-path. Otherwise, an external redirect is performed for the given URL. To force an external redirect back to the current host, see the `[R]` flag below.

### - (dash)

A dash indicates that no substitution should be performed (the existing path is passed through untouched). This is used when a flag (see below) needs to be applied without changing the path.

In addition to plain text, the *Substition* string can include

1. back-references ($N) to the RewriteRule pattern
2. back-references (%N) to the last matched RewriteCond pattern
3. server-variables as in rule condition test-strings (`%{VARNAME}`)
4. *mapping-function* calls (`${mapname:key|default}`)

Back-references are identifiers of the form $N (**N**=0..9), which will be replaced by the contents of the **N**th group of the matched *Pattern*. The server-variables are the same as for the *TestString* of a `RewriteCond` directive. The mapping-functions come from the `RewriteMap` directive and are explained there. These three types of variables are expanded in the order above.

As already mentioned, all rewrite rules are applied to the *Substitution* (in the order in which they are defined in the config file). The URL is **completely replaced** by the *Substitution* and the rewriting process continues until all rules have been applied, or it is explicitly terminated by a **L** flag.

**Modifying the Query String**

By default, the query string is passed through unchanged. You can, however, create URLs in the substitution string containing a query string part. Simply use a question mark inside the substitution string to indicate that the following text should be re-injected into the query string. When you want to erase an existing query string, end the substitution string with just a question mark. To combine new and old query strings, use the [QSA] flag.

Additionally you can set special actions to be performed by appending [*flags*] as the third argument to the `RewriteRule` directive. *Flags* is a comma-separated list, surround by square brackets, of any of the following flags:

**'B' (escape backreferences)**

Apache has to unescape URLs before mapping them, so backreferences will be unescaped at the time they are applied. Using the B flag, non-alphanumeric characters in backreferences will be escaped. For example, consider the rule:

```
RewriteRule ^(.*)$ index.php?show=$1
```

This will map /C++ to `index.php?show=/C++`. But it will also map /C%2b%2b to `index.php?show=/C++`, because the %2b has been unescaped. With the B flag, it will instead map to `index.php?show=/C%2b%2b`.

This escaping is particularly necessary in a proxy situation, when the backend may break if presented with an unescaped URL.

**'chain|C' (chained with next rule)**

This flag chains the current rule with the next rule (which itself can be chained with the following rule, and so on). This has the following effect: if a rule matches, then processing continues as usual - the flag has no effect. If the rule does **not** match, then all following chained rules are skipped. For instance, it can be used to remove the ".www" part, inside a per-directory rule set, when you let an external redirect happen (where the ".www" part should not occur!).

**'cookie|CO=*NAME:VAL:domain*[*:lifetime*[*:path*[*:secure*[*:httponly*]]]]' (set cookie)**

This sets a cookie in the client's browser. The cookie's name is specified by *NAME* and the value is *VAL*. The *domain* field is the domain of the cookie, such as '.apache.org', the optional *lifetime* is the lifetime of the cookie in minutes, and the optional *path* is the path of the cookie. If *secure* is set to 'secure', 'true' or '1', the cookie is only transmitted via secured connections. If *httponly* is set to 'HttpOnly', 'true' or '1', the `HttpOnly` flag is used, making the cookie not accessible to JavaScript code on browsers that support this feature.

### 'discardpathinfo|DPI' (discard PATH_INFO)

In per-directory context, the URI each `RewriteRule` compares against is the concatenation of the current values of the URI and PATH_INFO.

The current URI can be the initial URI as requested by the client, the result of a previous round of mod_rewrite processing, or the result of a prior rule in the current round of mod_rewrite processing.

In contrast, the PATH_INFO that is appended to the URI before each rule reflects only the value of PATH_INFO before this round of mod_rewrite processing. As a consequence, if large portions of the URI are matched and copied into a substitution in multiple `RewriteRule` directives, without regard for which parts of the URI came from the current PATH_INFO, the final URI may have multiple copies of PATH_INFO appended to it.

Use this flag on any substitution where the PATH_INFO that resulted from the previous mapping of this request to the filesystem is not of interest. This flag permanently forgets the PATH_INFO established before this round of mod_rewrite processing began. PATH_INFO will not be recalculated until the current round of mod_rewrite processing completes. Subsequent rules during this round of processing will see only the direct result of substitutions, without any PATH_INFO appended.

### 'env|E=*VAR:VAL*' (set environment variable)

This forces an environment variable named *VAR* to be set to the value *VAL*, where *VAL* can contain regexp backreferences ($N and %N) which will be expanded. You can use this flag more than once, to set more than one variable. The variables can later be dereferenced in many situations, most commonly from within XSSI (via `<!--#echo var="VAR"-->`) or CGI (`$ENV{'VAR'}`). You can also dereference the variable in a later RewriteCond pattern, using `%{ENV:VAR}`. Use this to strip information from URLs, while maintaining a record of that information.

### 'forbidden|F' (force URL to be forbidden)

This forces the current URL to be forbidden - it immediately sends back a HTTP response of 403 (FORBIDDEN). Use this flag in conjunction with appropriate RewriteConds to conditionally block some URLs.

### 'gone|G' (force URL to be gone)

This forces the current URL to be gone - it immediately sends back a HTTP response of 410 (GONE). Use this flag to mark pages which no longer exist as gone.

### 'handler|H=*Content-handler*' (force Content handler)

Force the Content-handler of the target file to be *Content-handler*. For instance, this can be used to simulate the mod_alias directive ScriptAlias, which internally forces all files inside the mapped directory to have a handler of "cgi-script".

### 'last|L' (last rule)

Stop the rewriting process here and don't apply any more rewrite rules. This corresponds to the Perl last command or the break command in C. Use this flag to prevent the currently rewritten URL from being rewritten further by following rules. Remember, however, that if the RewriteRule generates an internal redirect (which frequently occurs when rewriting in a per-directory context), this will reinject the request and will cause processing to be repeated starting from the first RewriteRule.

### 'next|N' (next round)

Re-run the rewriting process (starting again with the first rewriting rule). This time, the URL to match is no longer the original URL, but rather the URL returned by the last rewriting rule. This corresponds to the Perl next command or the continue command in C. Use this flag to restart the rewriting process - to immediately go to the top of the loop. **Be careful not to create an infinite loop!**

### 'nocase|NC' (no case)

This makes the *Pattern* case-insensitive, ignoring difference between 'A-Z' and 'a-z' when *Pattern* is matched against the current URL.

### 'noescape|NE' (no URI escaping of output)

This flag prevents mod_rewrite from applying the usual URI escaping rules to the result of a rewrite. Ordinarily, special characters (such as '%', '$', ';', and so on) will be escaped into their hexcode equivalents ('%25', '%24', and '%3B', respectively); this flag prevents this from happening. This allows percent symbols to appear in the output, as in

```
RewriteRule /foo/(.*) /bar?arg=P1\%3d$1 [R,NE]
```

which would turn '/foo/zed' into a safe request for '/bar?arg=P1=zed'.

### 'nosubreq|NS' (not for internal sub-requests)

This flag forces the rewriting engine to skip a rewriting rule if the current request is an internal sub-request. For instance, sub-requests occur internally in Apache when mod_include tries to find out information about possible directory default files (index.xxx files). On sub-requests it is not always useful, and can even cause errors, if the complete set of rules are applied. Use this flag to exclude some rules.

To decide whether or not to use this rule: if you prefix URLs with CGI-scripts, to force them to be processed by the CGI-script, it's likely that you will run into problems (or significant overhead) on sub-requests. In these cases, use this flag.

### 'proxy|P' (force proxy)

This flag forces the substitution part to be internally sent as a proxy request and immediately (rewrite processing stops here) put through the *proxy module*. You must make sure that the substitution string is a valid URI (typically starting with http://*hostname*) which can be handled by the Apache proxy module. If not, you will get an error from the proxy module. Use this flag to achieve a more powerful implementation of the *ProxyPass* directive, to map remote content into the namespace of the local server.

Note: mod_proxy must be enabled in order to use this flag.

### 'passthrough|PT' (pass through to next handler)

This flag forces the rewrite engine to set the uri field of the internal request_rec structure to the value of the filename field. This flag is just a hack to enable post-processing of the output of RewriteRule directives, using Alias, ScriptAlias, Redirect, and other directives from various URI-to-filename translators. For example, to rewrite /abc to /def using mod_rewrite, and then /def to /ghi using mod_alias:

```
RewriteRule ^/abc(.*) /def$1 [PT]
Alias /def /ghi
```

If you omit the PT flag, mod_rewrite will rewrite uri=/abc/... to filename=/def/... as a full API-compliant URI-to-filename translator should do. Then mod_alias will try to do a URI-to-filename transition, which will fail.

Note: **You must use this flag if you want to mix directives from different modules which allow URL-to-filename translators**. The typical example is the use of mod_alias and mod_rewrite.

The PT flag implies the L flag: rewriting will be stopped in order to pass the request to the next phase of processing.

### 'qsappend|QSA' (query string append)

This flag forces the rewrite engine to append a query string part of the substitution string to the existing string, instead of replacing it. Use this when you want to add more data to the query string via a rewrite rule.

### 'redirect|R [=*code*]' (force redirect)

Prefix *Substitution* with `http://thishost[:thisport]/` (which makes the new URL a URI) to force a external redirection. If no *code* is given, a HTTP response of 302 (MOVED TEMPORARILY) will be returned. If you want to use other response codes, simply specify the appropriate number or use one of the following symbolic names: `temp` (default), `permanent`, `seeother`. Use this for rules to canonicalize the URL and return it to the client - to translate "/~" into "/u/", or to always append a slash to /u/*user*, etc.

**Note:** When you use this flag, make sure that the substitution field is a valid URL! Otherwise, you will be redirecting to an invalid location. Remember that this flag on its own will only prepend `http://thishost[:thisport]/` to the URL, and rewriting will continue. Usually, you will want to stop rewriting at this point, and redirect immediately. To stop rewriting, you should add the 'L' flag.

While this is typically used for redirects, any valid status code can be given here. If the status code is outside the redirect range (300-399), then the *Substitution* string is dropped and rewriting is stopped as if the L flag was used.

### 'skip|S=*num*' (skip next rule(s))

This flag forces the rewriting engine to skip the next *num* rules in sequence, if the current rule matches. Use this to make pseudo if-then-else constructs: The last rule of the then-clause becomes skip=N, where N is the number of rules in the else-clause. (This is **not** the same as the 'chain|C' flag!)

### 'type|T=*MIME-type*' (force MIME type)

Force the MIME-type of the target file to be *MIME-type*. This can be used to set up the content-type based on some conditions. For example, the following snippet allows .php files to be *displayed* by mod_php if they are called with the .phps extension:

```
RewriteRule ^(.+\.php)s$ $1 [T=application/x-httpd-php-source]
```

---

**Home directory expansion**

When the substitution string begins with a string resembling "/~user" (via explicit text or backreferences), mod_rewrite performs home directory expansion independent of the presence or configuration of mod_userdir.

This expansion does not occur when the *PT* flag is used on the RewriteRule directive.

---

**Per-directory Rewrites**

The rewrite engine may be used in .*htaccess* files. To enable the rewrite engine for these files you need to set "RewriteEngine On" **and** "Options FollowSymLinks" must be enabled. If your administrator has disabled override of `FollowSymLinks` for a user's directory, then you cannot use the rewrite engine. This restriction is required for security reasons.

When using the rewrite engine in `.htaccess` files the per-directory prefix (which always is the same for a specific directory) is automatically *removed* for the pattern matching and automatically *added* after the substitution has been done. This feature is essential for many sorts of rewriting; without this, you would always have to match the parent directory, which is not always possible. There is one exception: If a substitution string starts with `http://`, then the directory prefix will **not** be added, and an external redirect (or proxy throughput, if using flag **P**) is forced. See the <u>RewriteBase</u> directive for more information.

The rewrite engine may also be used in `<Directory>` sections with the same prefix-matching rules as would be applied to `.htaccess` files. It is usually simpler, however, to avoid the prefix substitution complication by putting the rewrite rules in the main server or virtual host context, rather than in a `<Directory>` section.

Although rewrite rules are syntactically permitted in `<Location>` sections, this should never be necessary and is unsupported.

Here are all possible substitution combinations and their meanings:

**Inside per-server configuration (`httpd.conf`)
for request `"GET /somepath/pathinfo"`:**

```
Given Rule                                          Resulting Substitution
--------------------------------------------        ------------------------------------

^/somepath(.*)  otherpath$1                         invalid, not supported

^/somepath(.*)  otherpath$1   [R]                   invalid, not supported

^/somepath(.*)  otherpath$1   [P]                   invalid, not supported
--------------------------------------------        ------------------------------------
^/somepath(.*)  /otherpath$1                        /otherpath/pathinfo

^/somepath(.*)  /otherpath$1 [R]                    http://thishost/otherpath/pathinfo
                                                    via external redirection

^/somepath(.*)  /otherpath$1 [P]                    doesn't make sense, not supported
--------------------------------------------        ------------------------------------
^/somepath(.*)  http://thishost/otherpath$1         /otherpath/pathinfo

^/somepath(.*)  http://thishost/otherpath$1 [R]     http://thishost/otherpath/pathinfo
                                                    via external redirection

^/somepath(.*)  http://thishost/otherpath$1 [P]     doesn't make sense, not supported
--------------------------------------------        ------------------------------------
^/somepath(.*)  http://otherhost/otherpath$1        http://otherhost/otherpath/pathinfo
                                                    via external redirection
```

```
^/somepath(.*) http://otherhost/otherpath$1 [R] http://otherhost/otherpath/pathinfo
                                                 via external redirection
                                                 (the [R] flag is redundant)

^/somepath(.*) http://otherhost/otherpath$1 [P] http://otherhost/otherpath/pathinfo
                                                 via internal proxy
```

Inside per-directory configuration for `/somepath`
(`/physical/path/to/somepath/.htacccess`, with `RewriteBase /somepath`)
for request "`GET /somepath/localpath/pathinfo`":

```
Given Rule                                      Resulting Substitution
------------------------------------------      ----------------------------------
^localpath(.*) otherpath$1                      /somepath/otherpath/pathinfo

^localpath(.*) otherpath$1   [R]          http://thishost/somepath/otherpath/pathinfo
                                                via external redirection

^localpath(.*) otherpath$1   [P]                doesn't make sense, not supported
------------------------------------------      ----------------------------------
^localpath(.*) /otherpath$1                     /otherpath/pathinfo

^localpath(.*) /otherpath$1 [R]                 http://thishost/otherpath/pathinfo
                                                via external redirection

^localpath(.*) /otherpath$1 [P]                 doesn't make sense, not supported
------------------------------------------      ----------------------------------
^localpath(.*) http://thishost/otherpath$1      /otherpath/pathinfo

^localpath(.*) http://thishost/otherpath$1 [R]  http://thishost/otherpath/pathinfo
                                                via external redirection

^localpath(.*) http://thishost/otherpath$1 [P]  doesn't make sense, not supported
------------------------------------------      ----------------------------------
^localpath(.*) http://otherhost/otherpath$1     http://otherhost/otherpath/pathinfo
                                                via external redirection

^localpath(.*) http://otherhost/otherpath$1 [R] http://otherhost/otherpath/pathinfo
                                                via external redirection
                                                (the [R] flag is redundant)

^localpath(.*) http://otherhost/otherpath$1 [P] http://otherhost/otherpath/pathinfo
                                                via internal proxy
```

# Chapter 34.
# Apache mod_rewrite Introduction

This document supplements the `mod_rewrite` *reference documentation*. It describes the basic concepts necessary for use of `mod_rewrite`. Other documents go into greater detail, but this doc should help the beginner get their feet wet.

## 34.1. Introduction

The Apache module `mod_rewrite` is a very powerful and sophisticated module which provides a way to do URL manipulations. With it, you can do nearly all types of URL rewriting that you may need. It is, however, somewhat complex, and may be intimidating to the beginner. There is also a tendency to treat rewrite rules as magic incantation, using them without actually understanding what they do.

This document attempts to give sufficient background so that what follows is understood, rather than just copied blindly.

Remember that many common URL-manipulation tasks don't require the full power and complexity of `mod_rewrite`. For simple tasks, see `mod_alias` and the documentation on *mapping URLs to the filesystem*.

Finally, before proceeding, be sure to configure the `RewriteLog`. Although this log file can give an overwhelming amount of information, it is indispensable in debugging problems with `mod_rewrite` configuration, since it will tell you exactly how each rule is processed.

## 34.2. Regular Expressions

mod_rewrite uses the *Perl Compatible Regular Expression*[1] vocabulary. In this document, we do not attempt to provide a detailed reference to regular expressions. For that, we recommend the *PCRE man pages*[2], the *Perl regular expression man page*[3], and *Mastering Regular Expressions, by Jeffrey Friedl*[4].

---

[1] *http://pcre.org/*
[2] *http://pcre.org/pcre.txt*

In this document, we attempt to provide enough of a regex vocabulary to get you started, without being overwhelming, in the hope that `RewriteRules` will be scientific formulae, rather than magical incantations.

## 34.2.1. Regex vocabulary

The following are the minimal building blocks you will need, in order to write regular expressions and `RewriteRules`. They certainly do not represent a complete regular expression vocabulary, but they are a good place to start, and should help you read basic regular expressions, as well as write your own.

| Character | Meaning | Example |
|---|---|---|
| . | Matches any single character | `c.t` will match `cat`, `cot`, `cut`, etc. |
| + | Repeats the previous match one or more times | `a+` matches `a`, `aa`, `aaa`, etc |
| * | Repeats the previous match zero or more times. | `a*` matches all the same things `a+` matches, but will also match an empty string. |
| ? | Makes the match optional. | `colou?r` will match `color` and `colour`. |
| ^ | Called an anchor, matches the beginning of the string | `^a` matches a string that begins with a |
| $ | The other anchor, this matches the end of the string. | `a$` matches a string that ends with a. |
| ( ) | Groups several characters into a single unit, and captures a match for use in a backreference. | `(ab)+` matches `ababab` - that is, the + applies to the group. For more on backreferences see *below*. |
| [ ] | A character class - matches one of the characters | `c[uoa]t` matches `cut`, `cot` or `cat`. |
| [^ ] | Negative character class - matches any character not specified | `c[^/]t` matches `cat` or `c=t` but not `c/t` |

In `mod_rewrite` the ! character can be used before a regular expression to negate it. This is, a string will be considered to have matched only if it does not match the rest of the expression.

## 34.2.2. Regex Back-Reference Availability

One important thing here has to be remembered: Whenever you use parentheses in *Pattern* or in one of the *CondPattern*, back-references are internally created which can be used with

---

[3] *http://perldoc.perl.org/perlre.html*
[4] *http://www.oreilly.com/catalog/regex2/index.html*

---

the strings $N and %N (see below). These are available for creating the strings *Substitution* and *TestString*. *Figure 34.1* shows to which locations the back-references are transferred for expansion.

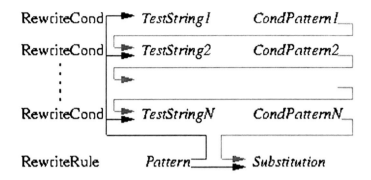

**Figure 34.1.** The back-reference flow through a rule

## 34.3. RewriteRule basics

A `RewriteRule` consists of three arguments separated by spaces. The arguments are

- *Pattern*: which incoming URLs should be affected by the rule;
- *Substitution*: where should the matching requests be sent;
- *[flags]*: options affecting the rewritten request.

The *Pattern* is always a *regular expression* matched against the URL-Path of the incoming request (the part after the hostname but before any question mark indicating the beginning of a query string).

The *Substitution* can itself be one of three things:

**A full filesystem path to a resource**

```
RewriteRule ^/games.* /usr/local/games/web
```

This maps a request to an arbitrary location on your filesystem, much like the `Alias` directive.

**A web-path to a resource**

```
RewriteRule ^/foo$ /bar
```

If `DocumentRoot` is set to /usr/local/apache2/htdocs, then this directive would map requests for http://example.com/foo to the path /usr/local/apache2/htdocs/bar.

**An absolute URL**

```
RewriteRule ^/product/view$ http://site2.example.com/seeproduct.html [R]
```

This tells the client to make a new request for the specified URL.

The *Substitution* can also contain *back-references* to parts of the incoming URL-path matched by the *Pattern*. Consider the following:

```
RewriteRule ^/product/(.*)/view$ /var/web/productdb/$1
```

The variable $1 will be replaced with whatever text was matched by the expression inside the parenthesis in the *Pattern*. For example, a request for `http://example.com/product/r14df/view` will be mapped to the path `/var/web/productdb/r14df`.

If there is more than one expression in parenthesis, they are available in order in the variables $1, $2, $3, and so on.

## 34.4. Rewrite Flags

The behavior of a `RewriteRule` can be modified by the application of one or more flags to the end of the rule. For example, the matching behavior of a rule can be made case-insensitive by the application of the [NC] flag:

```
RewriteRule ^puppy.html smalldog.html [NC]
```

For more details on the available flags, their meanings, and examples, see the *Rewrite Flags* document.

## 34.5. Rewrite conditions

One or more `RewriteCond` directives can be used to restrict the types of requests that will be subject to the following `RewriteRule`. The first argument is a variable describing a characteristic of the request, the second argument is a *regular expression* that must match the variable, and a third optional argument is a list of flags that modify how the match is evaluated.

For example, to send all requests from a particular IP range to a different server, you could use:

```
RewriteCond %{REMOTE_ADDR} ^10\.2\.
RewriteRule (.*) http://intranet.example.com$1
```

When more than one `RewriteCond` is specified, they must all match for the `RewriteRule` to be applied. For example, to deny requests that contain the word "hack" in their query string, except if they also contain a cookie containing the word "go", you could use:

```
RewriteCond %{QUERY_STRING} hack
RewriteCond %{HTTP_COOKIE} !go
RewriteRule .* - [F]
```

Notice that the exclamation mark specifies a negative match, so the rule is only applied if the cookie does not contain "go".

Matches in the regular expressions contained in the `RewriteCond`s can be used as part of the *Substitution* in the `RewriteRule` using the variables %1, %2, etc. For example, this will direct the request to a different directory depending on the hostname used to access the site:

```
RewriteCond %{HTTP_HOST} (.*)
RewriteRule ^/(.*) /sites/%1/$1
```

If the request was for `http://example.com/foo/bar`, then %1 would contain `example.com` and $1 would contain `foo/bar`.

## 34.6. Rewrite maps

See `RewriteMap`.

## 34.7. .htaccess files

Rewriting is typically configured in the main server configuration setting (outside any `<Directory>` section) or inside `<VirtualHost>` containers. This is the easiest way to do rewriting and is recommended. It is possible, however, to do rewriting inside `<Directory>` sections or `.htaccess` *files* at the expense of some additional complexity. This technique is called per-directory rewrites.

The main difference with per-server rewrites is that the path prefix of the directory containing the `.htaccess` file is stripped before matching in the `RewriteRule`. In addition, the `RewriteBase` should be used to assure the request is properly mapped.

# Chapter 35.

# Apache mod_rewrite Flags

This document discusses the flags which are available to the `RewriteRule` directive, providing detailed explanations and examples. This is not necessarily a comprehensive list of all flags available, so be sure to also consult the reference documentation.

## 35.1. Introduction

`RewriteRule`s can have their behavior modified by one or more flags. Flags are included in square brackets at the end of the rule, and multiple flags are separated by commas.

```
RewriteRule pattern target [Flag1,Flag2,Flag3]
```

The flags all have a short form, such as `CO`, as well as a longer form, such as `cookie`. Some flags take one or more arguments. Flags are not case sensitive.

## 35.2. The flags

Each flag has a long and short form. While it is most common to use the short form, it is recommended that you familiarize yourself with the long form, so that you remember what each flag is supposed to do.

Presented here are each of the available flags, along with an example of how you might use them.

### C|chain

The [C] or [chain] flag indicates that the `RewriteRule` is chained to the next rule. That is, if the rule matches, then it is processed as usual and control moves on to the next rule. However, if it does not match, then the next rule, and any other rules that are chained together, will be skipped.

### CO|cookie

The [CO], or [cookie] flag, allows you to set a cookie when a particular `RewriteRule` matches. The argument consists of three required fields and two optional fields.

You must declare a name and value for the cookie to be set, and the domain for which you wish the cookie to be valid. You may optionally set the lifetime of the cookie, and the path for which it should be returned.

By default, the lifetime of the cookie is the current browser session.

By default, the path for which the cookie will be valid is "/" - that is, the entire website.

Several examples are offered here:

```
RewriteEngine On
RewriteRule ^/index.html - [CO=frontdoor:yes:.apache.org:1440:/]
```

This rule doesn't rewrite the request (the "-" rewrite target tells mod_rewrite to pass the request through unchanged) but sets a cookie called 'frontdoor' to a value of 'yes'. The cookie is valid for any host in the .apache.org domain. It will be set to expire in 1440 minutes (24 hours) and will be returned for all URIs.

## E|env

With the [E], or [env] flag, you can set the value of an environment variable. Note that some environment variables may be set after the rule is run, thus unsetting what you have set. See *the Environment Variables document* for more details on how Environment variables work.

The following example sets an evironment variable called 'image' to a value of '1' if the requested URI is an image file. Then, that environment variable is used to exclude those requests from the access log.

```
RewriteRule \.(png|gif|jpg) - [E=image:1]
CustomLog logs/access_log combined env=!image
```

Note that this same effect can be obtained using SetEnvIf. This technique is offered as an example, not as a recommendation.

## F|forbidden

Using the [F] flag causes Apache to return a 403 Forbidden status code to the client. While the same behavior can be accomplished using the Deny directive, this allows more flexibility in assigning a Forbidden status.

The following rule will forbid .exe files from being downloaded from your server.

```
RewriteRule \.exe - [F]
```

This example uses the "-" syntax for the rewrite target, which means that the requested URI is not modified. There's no reason to rewrite to another URI, if you're going to forbid the request.

# G | gone

The [G] flag forces Apache to return a 410 Gone status with the response. This indicates that a resource used to be available, but is no longer available.

As with the [F] flag, you will typically use the "-" syntax for the rewrite target when using the [G] flag:

```
RewriteRule oldproduct - [G,NC]
```

# H | handler

Forces the resulting request to be handled with the specified handler. For example, one might use this to force all files without a file extension to be parsed by the php handler:

```
RewriteRule !\. - [H=application/x-httpd-php]
```

The regular expression above - ! \ . - will match any request that does not contain the literal . character.

# L | last

The [L] flag causes mod_rewrite to stop processing the rule set. In most contexts, this means that if the rule matches, no further rules will be processed.

If you are using RewriteRule in either .htaccess files or in <Directory> sections, it is important to have some understanding of how the rules are processed. The simplified form of this is that once the rules have been processed, the rewritten request is handed back to the URL parsing engine to do what it may with it. It is possible that as the rewritten request is handled, the .htaccess file or <Directory> section may be encountered again, and thus the ruleset may be run again from the start. Most commonly this will happen if one of the rules causes a redirect - either internal or external - causing the request process to start over.

It is therefore important, if you are using RewriteRule directives in one of these context that you take explicit steps to avoid rules looping, and not count solely on the [L] flag to terminate execution of a series of rules, as shown below.

The example given here will rewrite any request to index.php, giving the original request as a query string argument to index.php, however, if the request is already for index.php, this rule will be skipped.

```
RewriteCond %{REQUEST_URI} !index\.php
RewriteRule ^(.*) index.php?req=$1 [L]
```

## N|next

The [N] flag causes the ruleset to start over again from the top. Use with extreme caution, as it may result in loop.

The [Next] flag could be used, for example, if you wished to replace a certain string or letter repeatedly in a request. The example shown here will replace A with B everywhere in a request, and will continue doing so until there are no more As to be replaced.

```
RewriteRule (.*)A(.*) $1B$2 [N]
```

You can think of this as a `while` loop: While this pattern still matches, perform this substitution.

## NC|nocase

Use of the [NC] flag causes the `RewriteRule` to be matched in a case-insensitive manner. That is, it doesn't care whether letters appear as upper-case or lower-case in the matched URI.

In the example below, any request for an image file will be proxied to your dedicated image server. The match is case-insensitive, so that `.jpg` and `.JPG` files are both acceptable, for example.

```
RewriteRule (.*\.(jpg|gif|png))$ http://images.example.com$1 [P,NC]
```

## NE|noescape

By default, special characters, such as & and ?, for example, will be converted to their hexcode equivalent. Using the [NE] flag prevents that from happening.

```
RewriteRule ^/anchor/(.+) /bigpage.html#$1 [NE,R]
```

The above example will redirect /anchor/xyz to /bigpage.html#xyz. Omitting the [NE] will result in the # being converted to its hexcode equivalent, %23, which will then result in a 404 Not Found error condition.

## NS|nosubreq

Use of the [NS] flag prevents the rule from being used on subrequests. For example, a page which is included using an SSI (Server Side Include) is a subrequest, and you may want to avoid rewrites happening on those subrequests.

Images, javascript files, or css files, loaded as part of an HTML page, are not subrequests - the browser requests them as separate HTTP requests.

# P|proxy

Use of the [P] flag causes the request to be handled by mod_proxy, and handled via a proxy request. For example, if you wanted all image requests to be handled by a back-end image server, you might do something like the following:

```
RewriteRule (.*)\.(jpg|gif|png) http://images.example.com$1.$2 [P]
```

Use of the [P] flag implies [L] - that is, the request is immediatly pushed through the proxy, and any following rules will not be considered.

# PT|passthrough

The target (or substitution string) in a RewriteRule is assumed to be a file path, by default. The use of the [PT] flag causes it to be treated as a URI instead. That is to say, the use of the [PT] flag causes the result of the RewriteRule to be passed back through URL mapping, so that location-based mappings, such as Alias, for example, might have a chance to take effect.

If, for example, you have an Alias for /icons, and have a RewriteRule pointing there, you should use the [PT] flag to ensure that the Alias is evaluated.

```
Alias /icons /usr/local/apache/icons
RewriteRule /pics/(.+)\.jpg /icons/$1.gif [PT]
```

Omission of the [PT] flag in this case will cause the Alias to be ignored, resulting in a 'File not found' error being returned.

# QSA|qsappend

When the replacement URI contains a query string, the default behavior of RewriteRule is to discard the existing query string, and replace it with the newly generated one. Using the [QSA] flag causes the query strings to be combined.

Consider the following rule:

```
RewriteRule /pages/(.+) /page.php?page=$1 [QSA]
```

With the [QSA] flag, a request for /pages/123?one=two will be mapped to /page.php?page=123&one=two. Without the [QSA] flag, that same request will be mapped to /page.php?page=123 - that is, the existing query string will be discarded.

# R|redirect

Use of the [R] flag causes a HTTP redirect to be issued to the browser. If a fully-qualified URL is specified (that is, including http://servername/) then a redirect will be issued to that location. Otherwise, the current servername will be used to generate the URL sent with the redirect.

A status code may be specified, in the range 300-399, with a 302 status code being used by default if none is specified.

You will almost always want to use [R] in conjunction with [L] (that is, use [R,L]) because on its own, the [R] flag prepends `http://thishost[:thisport]` to the URI, but then passes this on to the next rule in the ruleset, which can often result in 'Invalid URI in request' warnings.

## S|skip

The [S] flag is used to skip rules that you don't want to run. This can be thought of as a `goto` statement in your rewrite ruleset. In the following example, we only want to run the `RewriteRule` if the requested URI doesn't correspond with an actual file.

```
# Is the request for a non-existent file?
RewriteCond %{REQUEST_FILENAME} !-f
RewriteCond %{REQUEST_FILENAME} !-d
# If so, skip these two RewriteRules
RewriteRule .? - [S=2]

RewriteRule (.*\.gif) images.php?$1
RewriteRule (.*\.html) docs.php?$1
```

This technique is useful because a `RewriteCond` only applies to the `RewriteRule` immediately following it. Thus, if you want to make a `RewriteCond` apply to several `RewriteRules`, one possible technique is to negate those conditions and use a [Skip] flag.

## T|type

Sets the MIME type with which the resulting response will be sent. This has the same effect as the `AddType` directive.

For example, you might use the following technique to serve Perl source code as plain text, if requested in a particular way:

```
# Serve .pl files as plain text
RewriteRule \.pl$ - [T=text/plain]
```

Or, perhaps, if you have a camera that produces jpeg images without file extensions, you could force those images to be served with the correct MIME type by virtue of their file names:

```
# Files with 'IMG' in the name are jpg images.
RewriteRule IMG - [T=image/jpg]
```

Please note that this is a trivial example, and could be better done using `<FilesMatch>` instead. Always consider the alternate solutions to a problem before resorting to rewrite, which will invariably be a less efficient solution than the alternatives.

If used in per-directory context, use only - (dash) as the substitution *for the entire round of mod_rewrite processing*, otherwise the MIME-type set with this flag is lost due to an internal re-processing (including subsequent rounds of mod_rewrite processing). The L flag can be useful in this context to end the *current* round of mod_rewrite processing.

# Chapter 36.
# Apache mod_rewrite Technical Details

This document discusses some of the technical details of mod_rewrite and URL matching.

## 36.1. Internal Processing

The internal processing of this module is very complex but needs to be explained once even to the average user to avoid common mistakes and to let you exploit its full functionality.

## 36.2. API Phases

First you have to understand that when Apache processes a HTTP request it does this in phases. A hook for each of these phases is provided by the Apache API. Mod_rewrite uses two of these hooks: the URL-to-filename translation hook which is used after the HTTP request has been read but before any authorization starts and the Fixup hook which is triggered after the authorization phases and after the per-directory config files (`.htaccess`) have been read, but before the content handler is activated.

So, after a request comes in and Apache has determined the corresponding server (or virtual server) the rewriting engine starts processing of all mod_rewrite directives from the per-server configuration in the URL-to-filename phase. A few steps later when the final data directories are found, the per-directory configuration directives of mod_rewrite are triggered in the Fixup phase. In both situations mod_rewrite rewrites URLs either to new URLs or to filenames, although there is no obvious distinction between them. This is a usage of the API which was not intended to be this way when the API was designed, but as of Apache 1.x this is the only way mod_rewrite can operate. To make this point more clear remember the following two points:

1.  Although mod_rewrite rewrites URLs to URLs, URLs to filenames and even filenames to filenames, the API currently provides only a URL-to-filename hook. In Apache 2.0 the two missing hooks will be added to make the processing more clear. But this point has no drawbacks for the user, it is just a fact which should be remembered: Apache does more in the URL-to-filename hook than the API intends for it.

2.  Unbelievably mod_rewrite provides URL manipulations in per-directory context, *i.e.,* within .htaccess files, although these are reached a very long time after the URLs have been translated to filenames. It has to be this way because .htaccess files live in the filesystem, so processing has already reached this stage. In other words: According to the API phases at this time it is too late for any URL manipulations. To overcome this chicken and egg problem mod_rewrite uses a trick: When you manipulate a URL/filename in per-directory context mod_rewrite first rewrites the filename back to its corresponding URL (which is usually impossible, but see the RewriteBase directive below for the trick to achieve this) and then initiates a new internal sub-request with the new URL. This restarts processing of the API phases.

    Again mod_rewrite tries hard to make this complicated step totally transparent to the user, but you should remember here: While URL manipulations in per-server context are really fast and efficient, per-directory rewrites are slow and inefficient due to this chicken and egg problem. But on the other hand this is the only way mod_rewrite can provide (locally restricted) URL manipulations to the average user.

Don't forget these two points!

## 36.3. Ruleset Processing

Now when mod_rewrite is triggered in these two API phases, it reads the configured rulesets from its configuration structure (which itself was either created on startup for per-server context or during the directory walk of the Apache kernel for per-directory context). Then the URL rewriting engine is started with the contained ruleset (one or more rules together with their conditions). The operation of the URL rewriting engine itself is exactly the same for both configuration contexts. Only the final result processing is different.

The order of rules in the ruleset is important because the rewriting engine processes them in a special (and not very obvious) order. The rule is this: The rewriting engine loops through the ruleset rule by rule (RewriteRule directives) and when a particular rule matches it optionally loops through existing corresponding conditions (RewriteCond directives). For historical reasons the conditions are given first, and so the control flow is a little bit long-winded. See *Figure 36.1* for more details.

As you can see, first the URL is matched against the *Pattern* of each rule. When it fails mod_rewrite immediately stops processing this rule and continues with the next rule. If the *Pattern* matches, mod_rewrite looks for corresponding rule conditions. If none are present, it just substitutes the URL with a new value which is constructed from the string *Substitution* and goes on with its rule-looping. But if conditions exist, it starts an inner loop for processing them in the order that they are listed. For conditions the logic is different: we don't match a pattern against the current URL. Instead we first create a string *TestString* by expanding variables, back-references, map lookups, *etc.* and then we try to match *CondPattern* against it. If the pattern doesn't match, the complete set of conditions and the corresponding rule fails. If the pattern matches, then the next condition is processed until no more conditions are available. If all conditions match, processing is continued with the substitution of the URL with *Substitution*.

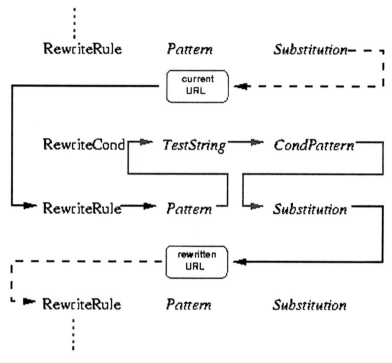

**Figure 36.1.** The control flow through the rewriting ruleset

# Chapter 37.
# URL Rewriting Guide

This document supplements the <u>mod_rewrite</u> *reference documentation.* It describes how one can use Apache's <u>mod_rewrite</u> to solve typical URL-based problems with which webmasters are commonly confronted. We give detailed descriptions on how to solve each problem by configuring URL rewriting rulesets.

> ATTENTION: Depending on your server configuration it may be necessary to slightly change the examples for your situation, e.g. adding the [PT] flag when additionally using <u>mod_alias</u> and <u>mod_userdir</u>, etc. Or rewriting a ruleset to fit in .htaccess context instead of per-server context. Always try to understand what a particular ruleset really does before you use it. This avoids many problems.

## 37.1. Canonical URLs

Description:

> On some webservers there are more than one URL for a resource. Usually there are canonical URLs (which should be actually used and distributed) and those which are just shortcuts, internal ones, etc. Independent of which URL the user supplied with the request he should finally see the canonical one only.

Solution:

> We do an external HTTP redirect for all non-canonical URLs to fix them in the location view of the Browser and for all subsequent requests. In the example ruleset below we replace /~user by the canonical /u/user and fix a missing trailing slash for /u/user.

```
RewriteRule   ^/~([^/]+)/?(.*)   /u/$1/$2   [R]
RewriteRule   ^/u/([^/]+)$   /$1/$2/   [R]
```

## 37.2. Canonical Hostnames

Description:

> The goal of this rule is to force the use of a particular hostname, in preference to other hostnames which may be used to reach the same site. For example, if you wish to force

the use of **www.example.com** instead of **example.com**, you might use a variant of the
following recipe.

**Solution:**

For sites running on a port other than 80:

```
RewriteCond %{HTTP_HOST}    !^www\.example\.com [NC]
RewriteCond %{HTTP_HOST}    !^$
RewriteCond %{SERVER_PORT}  !^80$
RewriteRule ^/?(.*)            http://www.example.com:%{SERVER_PORT}/$1 [L,R,NE]
```

And for a site running on port 80

```
RewriteCond %{HTTP_HOST}    !^www\.example\.com [NC]
RewriteCond %{HTTP_HOST}    !^$
RewriteRule ^/?(.*)            http://www.example.com/$1 [L,R,NE]
```

## 37.3. Moved `DocumentRoot`

**Description:**

Usually the `DocumentRoot` of the webserver directly relates to the URL "/". But often
this data is not really of top-level priority. For example, you may wish for visitors, on
first entering a site, to go to a particular subdirectory /about/. This may be
accomplished using the following ruleset:

**Solution:**

We redirect the URL / to /about/:

```
RewriteEngine on
RewriteRule   ^/$  /about/  [R]
```

Note that this can also be handled using the `RedirectMatch` directive:

```
RedirectMatch ^/$ http://example.com/e/www/
```

## 37.4. Trailing Slash Problem

**Description:**

The vast majority of "trailing slash" problems can be dealt with using the techniques
discussed in the *FAQ entry*[1]. However, occasionally, there is a need to use mod_rewrite
to handle a case where a missing trailing slash causes a URL to fail. This can happen, for
example, after a series of complex rewrite rules.

---

[1] *http://httpd.apache.org/docs/misc/FAQ-E.html#set-servername*

Solution:

The solution to this subtle problem is to let the server add the trailing slash automatically. To do this correctly we have to use an external redirect, so the browser correctly requests subsequent images etc. If we only did a internal rewrite, this would only work for the directory page, but would go wrong when any images are included into this page with relative URLs, because the browser would request an in-lined object. For instance, a request for `image.gif` in `/~quux/foo/index.html` would become `/~quux/image.gif` without the external redirect!

So, to do this trick we write:

```
RewriteEngine  on
RewriteBase    /~quux/
RewriteRule    ^foo$  foo/   [R]
```

Alternately, you can put the following in a top-level `.htaccess` file in the content directory. But note that this creates some processing overhead.

```
RewriteEngine  on
RewriteBase    /~quux/
RewriteCond    %{REQUEST_FILENAME}   -d
RewriteRule    ^(.+[^/])$            $1/   [R]
```

## 37.5. Move Homedirs to Different Webserver

Description:

Many webmasters have asked for a solution to the following situation: They wanted to redirect just all homedirs on a webserver to another webserver. They usually need such things when establishing a newer webserver which will replace the old one over time.

Solution:

The solution is trivial with `mod_rewrite`. On the old webserver we just redirect all `/~user/anypath` URLs to `http://newserver/~user/anypath`.

```
RewriteEngine on
RewriteRule    ^/~(.+)  http://newserver/~$1   [R,L]
```

## 37.6. Search pages in more than one directory

Description:

Sometimes it is necessary to let the webserver search for pages in more than one directory. Here MultiViews or other techniques cannot help.

Solution:

We program a explicit ruleset which searches for the files in the directories.

```
RewriteEngine on

#    first try to find it in dir1/...
#    ...and if found stop and be happy:
RewriteCond          /your/docroot/dir1/%{REQUEST_FILENAME}   -f
RewriteRule   ^(.+)  /your/docroot/dir1/$1   [L]

#    second try to find it in dir2/...
#    ...and if found stop and be happy:
RewriteCond          /your/docroot/dir2/%{REQUEST_FILENAME}   -f
RewriteRule   ^(.+)  /your/docroot/dir2/$1   [L]

#    else go on for other Alias or ScriptAlias directives,
#    etc.
RewriteRule   ^(.+)   -   [PT]
```

## 37.7. Set Environment Variables According To URL Parts

**Description:**

Perhaps you want to keep status information between requests and use the URL to
encode it. But you don't want to use a CGI wrapper for all pages just to strip out this
information.

**Solution:**

We use a rewrite rule to strip out the status information and remember it via an
environment variable which can be later dereferenced from within XSSI or CGI. This
way a URL /foo/S=java/bar/ gets translated to /foo/bar/ and the environment
variable named STATUS is set to the value "java".

```
RewriteEngine on
RewriteRule   ^(.*)/S=([^/]+)/(.*)    $1/$3  [E=STATUS:$2]
```

## 37.8. Virtual User Hosts

**Description:**

Assume that you want to provide www.**username**.host.domain.com for the
homepage of username via just DNS A records to the same machine and without any
virtualhosts on this machine.

**Solution:**

For HTTP/1.0 requests there is no solution, but for HTTP/1.1 requests which contain a
Host: HTTP header we can use the following ruleset to rewrite
http://www.username.host.com/anypath internally to
/home/username/anypath:

```
RewriteEngine  on
RewriteCond    %{HTTP_HOST}            ^www\.[^.]+\.host\.com$
RewriteRule    ^(.+)                   %{HTTP_HOST}$1          [C]
RewriteRule    ^www\.([^.]+)\.host\.com(.*)  /home/$1$2
```

## 37.9. Redirect Homedirs For Foreigners

### Description:

We want to redirect homedir URLs to another webserver www.somewhere.com when the requesting user does not stay in the local domain ourdomain.com. This is sometimes used in virtual host contexts.

### Solution:

Just a rewrite condition:

```
RewriteEngine  on
RewriteCond    %{REMOTE_HOST}  !^.+\.ourdomain\.com$
RewriteRule    ^(/~.+)         http://www.somewhere.com/$1 [R,L]
```

## 37.10. Redirecting Anchors

### Description:

By default, redirecting to an HTML anchor doesn't work, because mod_rewrite escapes the # character, turning it into %23. This, in turn, breaks the redirection.

### Solution:

Use the [NE] flag on the RewriteRule. NE stands for No Escape.

## 37.11. Time-Dependent Rewriting

### Description:

When tricks like time-dependent content should happen a lot of webmasters still use CGI scripts which do for instance redirects to specialized pages. How can it be done via mod_rewrite?

### Solution:

There are a lot of variables named TIME_xxx for rewrite conditions. In conjunction with the special lexicographic comparison patterns <STRING, >STRING and =STRING we can do time-dependent redirects:

```
RewriteEngine on
RewriteCond    %{TIME_HOUR}%{TIME_MIN}  >0700
RewriteCond    %{TIME_HOUR}%{TIME_MIN}  <1900
RewriteRule    ^foo\.html$              foo.day.html
RewriteRule    ^foo\.html$              foo.night.html
```

This provides the content of foo.day.html under the URL foo.html from 07:00-19:00 and at the remaining time the contents of foo.night.html. Just a nice feature for a homepage...

## 37.12. Backward Compatibility for YYYY to XXXX migration

**Description:**

How can we make URLs backward compatible (still existing virtually) after migrating document.YYYY to document.XXXX, e.g. after translating a bunch of .html files to .phtml?

**Solution:**

We just rewrite the name to its basename and test for existence of the new extension. If it exists, we take that name, else we rewrite the URL to its original state.

```
#     backward compatibility ruleset for
#     rewriting document.html to document.phtml
#     when and only when document.phtml exists
#     but no longer document.html
RewriteEngine on
RewriteBase    /~quux/
#    parse out basename, but remember the fact
RewriteRule    ^(.*)\.html$             $1         [C,E=WasHTML:yes]
#    rewrite to document.phtml if exists
RewriteCond    %{REQUEST_FILENAME}.phtml -f
RewriteRule    ^(.*)$ $1.phtml                      [S=1]
#    else reverse the previous basename cutout
RewriteCond    %{ENV:WasHTML}           ^yes$
RewriteRule    ^(.*)$ $1.html
```

## 37.13. From Old to New (intern)

**Description:**

Assume we have recently renamed the page foo.html to bar.html and now want to provide the old URL for backward compatibility. Actually we want that users of the old URL even not recognize that the pages was renamed.

**Solution:**

We rewrite the old URL to the new one internally via the following rule:

```
RewriteEngine   on
RewriteBase     /~quux/
RewriteRule     ^foo\.html$  bar.html
```

## 37.14. From Old to New (extern)

**Description:**

Assume again that we have recently renamed the page foo.html to bar.html and now want to provide the old URL for backward compatibility. But this time we want that the users of the old URL get hinted to the new one, i.e. their browsers Location field should change, too.

**Solution:**

We force a HTTP redirect to the new URL which leads to a change of the browsers and thus the users view:

```
RewriteEngine   on
RewriteBase     /~quux/
RewriteRule     ^foo\.html$  bar.html   [R]
```

## 37.15. From Static to Dynamic

**Description:**

How can we transform a static page foo.html into a dynamic variant foo.cgi in a seamless way, i.e. without notice by the browser/user.

**Solution:**

We just rewrite the URL to the CGI-script and force the handler to be **cgi-script** so that it is executed as a CGI program. This way a request to /~quux/foo.html internally leads to the invocation of /~quux/foo.cgi.

```
RewriteEngine   on
RewriteBase     /~quux/
RewriteRule     ^foo\.html$  foo.cgi   [H=cgi-script]
```

## 37.16. Blocking of Robots

**Description:**

How can we block a really annoying robot from retrieving pages of a specific webarea? A /robots.txt file containing entries of the "Robot Exclusion Protocol" is typically not enough to get rid of such a robot.

**Solution:**

We use a ruleset which forbids the URLs of the webarea /~quux/foo/arc/ (perhaps a very deep directory indexed area where the robot traversal would create big server load). We have to make sure that we forbid access only to the particular robot, i.e. just forbidding the host where the robot runs is not enough. This would block users from this host, too. We accomplish this by also matching the User-Agent HTTP header information.

```
RewriteCond %{HTTP_USER_AGENT}    ^NameOfBadRobot.*
RewriteCond %{REMOTE_ADDR}        ^123\.45\.67\.[8-9]$
RewriteRule ^/~quux/foo/arc/.+    -    [F]
```

## 37.17. Blocked Inline-Images

**Description:**

Assume we have under http://www.quux-corp.de/~quux/ some pages with inlined GIF graphics. These graphics are nice, so others directly incorporate them via hyperlinks to their pages. We don't like this practice because it adds useless traffic to our server.

**Solution:**

While we cannot 100% protect the images from inclusion, we can at least restrict the cases where the browser sends a HTTP Referer header.

```
RewriteCond %{HTTP_REFERER} !^$
RewriteCond %{HTTP_REFERER} !^http://www.quux-corp.de/~quux/.*$ [NC]
RewriteRule .*\.gif$        -                                   [F]
RewriteCond %{HTTP_REFERER}        !^$
RewriteCond %{HTTP_REFERER}        !.*/foo-with-gif\.html$
RewriteRule ^inlined-in-foo\.gif$  -                            [F]
```

## 37.18. Proxy Deny

**Description:**

How can we forbid a certain host or even a user of a special host from using the Apache proxy?

**Solution:**

We first have to make sure mod_rewrite is below(!) mod_proxy in the Configuration file when compiling the Apache webserver. This way it gets called *before* mod_proxy. Then we configure the following for a host-dependent deny...

```
RewriteCond %{REMOTE_HOST}  ^badhost\.mydomain\.com$
RewriteRule !^http://[^/.]\.mydomain.com.*  -  [F]
```

...and this one for a user@host-dependent deny:

```
RewriteCond %{REMOTE_IDENT}@%{REMOTE_HOST}   ^badguy@badhost\.mydomain\.com$
RewriteRule !^http://[^/.]\.mydomain.com.*  -  [F]
```

## 37.19. External Rewriting Engine

**Description:**

A FAQ: How can we solve the FOO/BAR/QUUX/etc. problem? There seems no solution by the use of mod_rewrite...

**Solution:**

Use an external RewriteMap, i.e. a program which acts like a RewriteMap. It is run once on startup of Apache receives the requested URLs on STDIN and has to put the resulting (usually rewritten) URL on STDOUT (same order!).

```
RewriteEngine on
RewriteMap     quux-map        prg:/path/to/map.quux.pl
RewriteRule    ^/~quux/(.*)$   /~quux/${quux-map:$1}
#!/path/to/perl

#    disable buffered I/O which would lead
#    to deadloops for the Apache server
$| = 1;

#    read URLs one per line from stdin and
#    generate substitution URL on stdout
while (<>) {
    s|^foo/|bar/|;
    print $_;
}
```

This is a demonstration-only example and just rewrites all URLs /~quux/foo/... to /~quux/bar/.... Actually you can program whatever you like. But notice that while such maps can be **used** also by an average user, only the system administrator can **define** it.

# Chapter 38.

# URL Rewriting Guide - Advanced topics

This document supplements the mod_rewrite reference documentation. It describes how one can use Apache's mod_rewrite to solve typical URL-based problems with which webmasters are commonly confronted. We give detailed descriptions on how to solve each problem by configuring URL rewriting rulesets.

ATTENTION: Depending on your server configuration it may be necessary to adjust the examples for your situation, e.g., adding the [PT] flag if using mod_alias and mod_userdir, etc. Or rewriting a ruleset to work in .htaccess context instead of per-server context. Always try to understand what a particular ruleset really does before you use it; this avoids many problems.

## 38.1. Web Cluster with Consistent URL Space

**Description:**

We want to create a homogeneous and consistent URL layout across all WWW servers on an Intranet web cluster, i.e., all URLs (by definition server-local and thus server-dependent!) become server *independent*! What we want is to give the WWW namespace a single consistent layout: no URL should refer to any particular target server. The cluster itself should connect users automatically to a physical target host as needed, invisibly.

**Solution:**

First, the knowledge of the target servers comes from (distributed) external maps which contain information on where our users, groups, and entities reside. They have the form:

```
user1   server_of_user1
user2   server_of_user2
:       :
```

We put them into files map.xxx-to-host. Second we need to instruct all servers to redirect URLs of the forms:

```
/u/user/anypath
/g/group/anypath
/e/entity/anypath
```

to

```
http://physical-host/u/user/anypath
http://physical-host/g/group/anypath
http://physical-host/e/entity/anypath
```

when any URL path need not be valid on every server. The following ruleset does this for us with the help of the map files (assuming that server0 is a default server which will be used if a user has no entry in the map):

```
RewriteEngine on

RewriteMap      user-to-host    txt:/path/to/map.user-to-host
RewriteMap     group-to-host    txt:/path/to/map.group-to-host
RewriteMap    entity-to-host    txt:/path/to/map.entity-to-host

RewriteRule    ^/u/([^/]+)/?(.*)    http://${user-to-host:$1|server0}/u/$1/$2
RewriteRule    ^/g/([^/]+)/?(.*)   http://${group-to-host:$1|server0}/g/$1/$2
RewriteRule    ^/e/([^/]+)/?(.*)  http://${entity-to-host:$1|server0}/e/$1/$2

RewriteRule    ^/([uge])/([^/]+)/?$          /$1/$2/.www/
RewriteRule    ^/([uge])/([^/]+)/([^.]+.+)   /$1/$2/.www/$3\
```

## 38.2. Structured Homedirs

**Description:**

Some sites with thousands of users use a structured homedir layout, *i.e.* each homedir is in a subdirectory which begins (for instance) with the first character of the username. So, /~foo/anypath is /home/**f**/foo/.www/anypath while /~bar/anypath is /home/**b**/bar/.www/anypath.

**Solution:**

We use the following ruleset to expand the tilde URLs into the above layout.

```
RewriteEngine on
RewriteRule    ^/~(([a-z])[a-z0-9]+)(.*)   /home/$2/$1/.www$3
```

## 38.3. Filesystem Reorganization

**Description:**

This really is a hardcore example: a killer application which heavily uses per-directory RewriteRules to get a smooth look and feel on the Web while its data structure is never touched or adjusted. Background: *net.sw* is my archive of freely available Unix software packages, which I started to collect in 1992. It is both my hobby and job to do this, because while I'm studying computer science I have also worked for many years as a system and network administrator in my spare time. Every week I need some sort of software so I created a deep hierarchy of directories where I stored the packages:

```
drwxrwxr-x    2 netsw   users      512 Aug   3 18:39 Audio/
drwxrwxr-x    2 netsw   users      512 Jul   9 14:37 Benchmark/
drwxrwxr-x   12 netsw   users      512 Jul   9 00:34 Crypto/
drwxrwxr-x    5 netsw   users      512 Jul   9 00:41 Database/
drwxrwxr-x    4 netsw   users      512 Jul  30 19:25 Dicts/
drwxrwxr-x   10 netsw   users      512 Jul   9 01:54 Graphic/
drwxrwxr-x    5 netsw   users      512 Jul   9 01:58 Hackers/
drwxrwxr-x    8 netsw   users      512 Jul   9 03:19 InfoSys/
drwxrwxr-x    3 netsw   users      512 Jul   9 03:21 Math/
drwxrwxr-x    3 netsw   users      512 Jul   9 03:24 Misc/
drwxrwxr-x    9 netsw   users      512 Aug   1 16:33 Network/
drwxrwxr-x    2 netsw   users      512 Jul   9 05:53 Office/
drwxrwxr-x    7 netsw   users      512 Jul   9 09:24 SoftEng/
drwxrwxr-x    7 netsw   users      512 Jul   9 12:17 System/
drwxrwxr-x   12 netsw   users      512 Aug   3 20:15 Typesetting/
drwxrwxr-x   10 netsw   users      512 Jul   9 14:08 X11/
```

In July 1996 I decided to make this archive public to the world via a nice Web interface. "Nice" means that I wanted to offer an interface where you can browse directly through the archive hierarchy. And "nice" means that I didn't want to change anything inside this hierarchy - not even by putting some CGI scripts at the top of it. Why? Because the above structure should later be accessible via FTP as well, and I didn't want any Web or CGI stuff mixed in there.

**Solution:**

The solution has two parts: The first is a set of CGI scripts which create all the pages at all directory levels on-the-fly. I put them under /e/netsw/.www/ as follows:

```
-rw-r--r--    1 netsw   users     1318 Aug   1 18:10 .wwwacl
drwxr-xr-x   18 netsw   users      512 Aug   5 15:51 DATA/
-rw-rw-rw-    1 netsw   users   372982 Aug   5 16:35 LOGFILE
-rw-r--r--    1 netsw   users      659 Aug   4 09:27 TODO
-rw-r--r--    1 netsw   users     5697 Aug   1 18:01 netsw-about.html
-rwxr-xr-x    1 netsw   users      579 Aug   2 10:33 netsw-access.pl
-rwxr-xr-x    1 netsw   users     1532 Aug   1 17:35 netsw-changes.cgi
-rwxr-xr-x    1 netsw   users     2866 Aug   5 14:49 netsw-home.cgi
drwxr-xr-x    2 netsw   users      512 Jul   8 23:47 netsw-img/
-rwxr-xr-x    1 netsw   users    24050 Aug   5 15:49 netsw-lsdir.cgi
-rwxr-xr-x    1 netsw   users     1589 Aug   3 18:43 netsw-search.cgi
-rwxr-xr-x    1 netsw   users     1885 Aug   1 17:41 netsw-tree.cgi
-rw-r--r--    1 netsw   users      234 Jul  30 16:35 netsw-unlimit.lst
```

The DATA/ subdirectory holds the above directory structure, *i.e.* the real ***net.sw*** stuff, and gets automatically updated via rdist from time to time. The second part of the problem remains: how to link these two structures together into one smooth-looking

URL tree? We want to hide the DATA/ directory from the user while running the appropriate CGI scripts for the various URLs. Here is the solution: first I put the following into the per-directory configuration file in the DocumentRoot of the server to rewrite the public URL path /net.sw/ to the internal path /e/netsw:

```
RewriteRule   ^net.sw$         net.sw/           [R]
RewriteRule   ^net.sw/(.*)$    e/netsw/$1
```

The first rule is for requests which miss the trailing slash! The second rule does the real thing. And then comes the killer configuration which stays in the per-directory config file /e/netsw/.www/.wwwacl:

```
Options       ExecCGI FollowSymLinks Includes MultiViews

RewriteEngine on

#   we are reached via /net.sw/ prefix
RewriteBase   /net.sw/

#   first we rewrite the root dir to
#   the handling cgi script
RewriteRule   ^$                      netsw-home.cgi     [L]
RewriteRule   ^index\.html$           netsw-home.cgi     [L]

#   strip out the subdirs when
#   the browser requests us from perdir pages
RewriteRule   ^.+/(netsw-[^/]+/.+)$   $1                 [L]

#   and now break the rewriting for local files
RewriteRule   ^netsw-home\.cgi.*      -                  [L]
RewriteRule   ^netsw-changes\.cgi.*   -                  [L]
RewriteRule   ^netsw-search\.cgi.*    -                  [L]
RewriteRule   ^netsw-tree\.cgi$       -                  [L]
RewriteRule   ^netsw-about\.html$     -                  [L]
RewriteRule   ^netsw-img/.*$          -                  [L]

#   anything else is a subdir which gets handled
#   by another cgi script
RewriteRule   !^netsw-lsdir\.cgi.*    -                  [C]
RewriteRule   (.*)                    netsw-lsdir.cgi/$1
```

Some hints for interpretation:

1.  Notice the L (last) flag and no substitution field ('-') in the fourth part

2.  Notice the ! (not) character and the C (chain) flag at the first rule in the last part

3.  Notice the catch-all pattern in the last rule

## 38.4. Redirect Failing URLs to Another Web Server

**Description:**

A typical FAQ about URL rewriting is how to redirect failing requests on webserver A to webserver B. Usually this is done via `ErrorDocument` CGI scripts in Perl, but there is also a `mod_rewrite` solution. But note that this performs more poorly than using an `ErrorDocument` CGI script!

**Solution:**

The first solution has the best performance but less flexibility, and is less safe:

```
RewriteEngine on
RewriteCond    /your/docroot/%{REQUEST_FILENAME} !-f
RewriteRule    ^(.+)                              http://webserverB.dom/$1
```

The problem here is that this will only work for pages inside the `DocumentRoot`. While you can add more Conditions (for instance to also handle homedirs, etc.) there is a better variant:

```
RewriteEngine on
RewriteCond    %{REQUEST_URI} !-U
RewriteRule    ^(.+)          http://webserverB.dom/$1
```

This uses the URL look-ahead feature of `mod_rewrite`. The result is that this will work for all types of URLs and is safe. But it does have a performance impact on the web server, because for every request there is one more internal subrequest. So, if your web server runs on a powerful CPU, use this one. If it is a slow machine, use the first approach or better an `ErrorDocument` CGI script.

## 38.5. Archive Access Multiplexer

**Description:**

Do you know the great CPAN (Comprehensive Perl Archive Network) under *http://www.perl.com/CPAN*? CPAN automatically redirects browsers to one of many FTP servers around the world (generally one near the requesting client); each server carries a full CPAN mirror. This is effectively an FTP access multiplexing service. CPAN runs via CGI scripts, but how could a similar approach be implemented via `mod_rewrite`?

**Solution:**

First we notice that as of version 3.0.0, `mod_rewrite` can also use the "ftp:" scheme on redirects. And second, the location approximation can be done by a `RewriteMap` over the top-level domain of the client. With a tricky chained ruleset we can use this top-level domain as a key to our multiplexing map.

```
RewriteEngine on
RewriteMap    multiplex            txt:/path/to/map.cxan
RewriteRule   ^/CxAN/(.*)          %{REMOTE_HOST}::$1                      [C]
RewriteRule   ^.+\.([a-zA-Z]+)::(.*)$ ${multiplex:$1|ftp.default.dom}$2   [R,L]
##
##  map.cxan -- Multiplexing Map for CxAN
##
de        ftp://ftp.cxan.de/CxAN/
uk        ftp://ftp.cxan.uk/CxAN/
com       ftp://ftp.cxan.com/CxAN/
 :
##EOF##
```

## 38.6. Browser Dependent Content

**Description:**

At least for important top-level pages it is sometimes necessary to provide the optimum of browser dependent content, i.e., one has to provide one version for current browsers, a different version for the Lynx and text-mode browsers, and another for other browsers.

**Solution:**

We cannot use content negotiation because the browsers do not provide their type in that form. Instead we have to act on the HTTP header "User-Agent". The following config does the following: If the HTTP header "User-Agent" begins with "Mozilla/3", the page foo.html is rewritten to foo.NS.html and the rewriting stops. If the browser is "Lynx" or "Mozilla" of version 1 or 2, the URL becomes foo.20.html. All other browsers receive page foo.32.html. This is done with the following ruleset:

```
RewriteCond %{HTTP_USER_AGENT}  ^Mozilla/3.*
RewriteRule ^foo\.html$         foo.NS.html        [L]

RewriteCond %{HTTP_USER_AGENT}  ^Lynx/.*          [OR]
RewriteCond %{HTTP_USER_AGENT}  ^Mozilla/[12].*
RewriteRule ^foo\.html$         foo.20.html        [L]

RewriteRule ^foo\.html$         foo.32.html        [L]
```

## 38.7. Dynamic Mirror

**Description:**

Assume there are nice web pages on remote hosts we want to bring into our namespace. For FTP servers we would use the mirror program which actually maintains an explicit

up-to-date copy of the remote data on the local machine. For a web server we could use
the program webcopy which runs via HTTP. But both techniques have a major
drawback: The local copy is always only as up-to-date as the last time we ran the
program. It would be much better if the mirror was not a static one we have to establish
explicitly. Instead we want a dynamic mirror with data which gets updated
automatically as needed on the remote host(s).

**Solution:**

To provide this feature we map the remote web page or even the complete remote web
area to our namespace by the use of the *Proxy Throughput* feature (flag [P]):

```
RewriteEngine   on
RewriteBase     /~quux/
RewriteRule     ^hotsheet/(.*)$  http://www.tstimpreso.com/hotsheet/$1   [P]
RewriteEngine   on
RewriteBase     /~quux/
RewriteRule     ^usa-news\.html$   http://www.quux-corp.com/news/index.html   [P]
```

# 38.8. Reverse Dynamic Mirror

**Description:**

...

**Solution:**

```
RewriteEngine on
RewriteCond    /mirror/of/remotesite/$1              -U
RewriteRule    ^http://www\.remotesite\.com/(.*)$ /mirror/of/remotesite/$1
```

# 38.9. Retrieve Missing Data from Intranet

**Description:**

This is a tricky way of virtually running a corporate (external) Internet web server
(www.quux-corp.dom), while actually keeping and maintaining its data on an
(internal) Intranet web server (www2.quux-corp.dom) which is protected by a firewall.
The trick is that the external web server retrieves the requested data on-the-fly from the
internal one.

**Solution:**

First, we must make sure that our firewall still protects the internal web server and only
the external web server is allowed to retrieve data from it. On a packet-filtering firewall,
for instance, we could configure a firewall ruleset like the following:

```
ALLOW Host www.quux-corp.dom Port >1024  --> Host www2.quux-corp.dom Port 80
DENY  Host *                 Port *      --> Host www2.quux-corp.dom Port 80
```

Just adjust it to your actual configuration syntax. Now we can establish the
mod_rewrite rules which request the missing data in the background through the
proxy throughput feature:

```
RewriteRule ^/~([^/]+)/?(.*)              /home/$1/.www/$2
RewriteCond %{REQUEST_FILENAME}           !-f
RewriteCond %{REQUEST_FILENAME}           !-d
RewriteRule ^/home/([^/]+)/.www/?(.*)  http://www2.quux-corp.dom/~$1/pub/$2 [P]
```

## 38.10. Load Balancing

**Description:**

Suppose we want to load balance the traffic to www.example.com over www[0-
5].example.com (a total of 6 servers). How can this be done?

**Solution:**

There are many possible solutions for this problem. We will first discuss a common
DNS-based method, and then one based on mod_rewrite:

1. **DNS Round-Robin**

   The simplest method for load-balancing is to use DNS round-robin. Here you just
   configure www[0-9].example.com as usual in your DNS with A (address)
   records, e.g.,

   ```
   www0    IN  A       1.2.3.1
   www1    IN  A       1.2.3.2
   www2    IN  A       1.2.3.3
   www3    IN  A       1.2.3.4
   www4    IN  A       1.2.3.5
   www5    IN  A       1.2.3.6
   ```

   Then you additionally add the following entries:

   ```
   www     IN  A       1.2.3.1
   www     IN  A       1.2.3.2
   www     IN  A       1.2.3.3
   www     IN  A       1.2.3.4
   www     IN  A       1.2.3.5
   ```

   Now when www.example.com gets resolved, BIND gives out www0-www5 - but in a
   permutated (rotated) order every time. This way the clients are spread over the

various servers. But notice that this is not a perfect load balancing scheme, because DNS resolutions are cached by clients and other nameservers, so once a client has resolved www.example.com to a particular wwwN.example.com, all its subsequent requests will continue to go to the same IP (and thus a single server), rather than being distributed across the other available servers. But the overall result is okay because the requests are collectively spread over the various web servers.

2. **DNS Load-Balancing**

A sophisticated DNS-based method for load-balancing is to use the program lbnamed which can be found at *http://www.stanford.edu/~riepel/lbnamed/*. It is a Perl 5 program which, in conjunction with auxilliary tools, provides real load-balancing via DNS.

3. **Proxy Throughput Round-Robin**

In this variant we use mod_rewrite and its proxy throughput feature. First we dedicate www0.example.com to be actually www.example.com by using a single

```
www    IN   CNAME    www0.example.com.
```

entry in the DNS. Then we convert www0.example.com to a proxy-only server, i.e., we configure this machine so all arriving URLs are simply passed through its internal proxy to one of the 5 other servers (www1-www5). To accomplish this we first establish a ruleset which contacts a load balancing script lb.pl for all URLs.

```
RewriteEngine on
RewriteMap     lb        prg:/path/to/lb.pl
RewriteRule    ^/(.+)$ ${lb:$1}              [P,L]
```

Then we write lb.pl:

```
#!/path/to/perl
##
##  lb.pl -- load balancing script
##

$| = 1;

$name   = "www";     # the hostname base
$first  = 1;         # the first server (not 0 here, because 0 is myself)
$last   = 5;         # the last server in the round-robin
$domain = "foo.dom"; # the domainname

$cnt = 0;
```

```
while (<STDIN>) {
    $cnt = (($cnt+1) % ($last+1-$first));
    $server = sprintf("%s%d.%s", $name, $cnt+$first, $domain);
    print "http://$server/$_";
}

##EOF##
```

A last notice: Why is this useful? Seems like www0.example.com still is overloaded? The answer is yes, it is overloaded, but with plain proxy throughput requests, only! All SSI, CGI, ePerl, etc. processing is handled done on the other machines. For a complicated site, this may work well. The biggest risk here is that www0 is now a single point of failure -- if it crashes, the other servers are inaccessible.

4. **Dedicated Load Balancers**

There are more sophisticated solutions, as well. Cisco, F5, and several other companies sell hardware load balancers (typically used in pairs for redundancy), which offer sophisticated load balancing and auto-failover features. There are software packages which offer similar features on commodity hardware, as well. If you have enough money or need, check these out. The *lb-l mailing list*[1] is a good place to research.

# 38.11. New MIME-type, New Service

**Description:**

On the net there are many nifty CGI programs. But their usage is usually boring, so a lot of webmasters don't use them. Even Apache's Action handler feature for MIME-types is only appropriate when the CGI programs don't need special URLs (actually PATH_INFO and QUERY_STRINGS) as their input. First, let us configure a new file type with extension .scgi (for secure CGI) which will be processed by the popular cgiwrap program. The problem here is that for instance if we use a Homogeneous URL Layout (see above) a file inside the user homedirs might have a URL like /u/user/foo/bar.scgi, but cgiwrap needs URLs in the form /~user/foo/bar.scgi/. The following rule solves the problem:

```
RewriteRule ^/[uge]/([^/]+)/\.www/(.+)\.scgi(.*) ...
... /internal/cgi/user/cgiwrap/~$1/$2.scgi$3   [NS,T=application/x-http-cgi]
```

---

[1] *http://vegan.net/lb/*

Or assume we have some more nifty programs: wwwlog (which displays the access.log for a URL subtree) and wwwidx (which runs Glimpse on a URL subtree). We have to provide the URL area to these programs so they know which area they are really working with. But usually this is complicated, because they may still be requested by the alternate URL form, i.e., typically we would run the swwidx program from within /u/user/foo/ via hyperlink to

```
/internal/cgi/user/swwidx?i=/u/user/foo/
```

which is ugly, because we have to hard-code **both** the location of the area **and** the location of the CGI inside the hyperlink. When we have to reorganize, we spend a lot of time changing the various hyperlinks.

**Solution:**

The solution here is to provide a special new URL format which automatically leads to the proper CGI invocation. We configure the following:

```
RewriteRule    ^/([uge])/([^/]+)(/?.*)/\*    /internal/cgi/user/wwwidx?i=/$1/$2$3/
RewriteRule    ^/([uge])/([^/]+)(/?.*):log /internal/cgi/user/wwwlog?f=/$1/$2$3
```

Now the hyperlink to search at /u/user/foo/ reads only

```
HREF="*"
```

which internally gets automatically transformed to

```
/internal/cgi/user/wwwidx?i=/u/user/foo/
```

The same approach leads to an invocation for the access log CGI program when the hyperlink :log gets used.

# 38.12. On-the-fly Content-Regeneration

**Description:**

Here comes a really esoteric feature: Dynamically generated but statically served pages, i.e., pages should be delivered as pure static pages (read from the filesystem and just passed through), but they have to be generated dynamically by the web server if missing. This way you can have CGI-generated pages which are statically served unless an admin (or a cron job) removes the static contents. Then the contents gets refreshed.

**Solution:**

This is done via the following ruleset:

```
RewriteCond %{REQUEST_FILENAME}    !-s
RewriteRule ^page\.html$           page.cgi    [T=application/x-httpd-cgi,L]
```

Here a request for page.html leads to an internal run of a corresponding page.cgi if page.html is missing or has filesize null. The trick here is that page.cgi is a CGI script which (additionally to its STDOUT) writes its output to the file page.html. Once it has completed, the server sends out page.html. When the webmaster wants to force a refresh of the contents, he just removes page.html (typically from cron).

## 38.13. Document With Autorefresh

### Description:

Wouldn't it be nice, while creating a complex web page, if the web browser would automatically refresh the page every time we save a new version from within our editor? Impossible?

### Solution:

No! We just combine the MIME multipart feature, the web server NPH feature, and the URL manipulation power of mod_rewrite. First, we establish a new URL feature: Adding just :refresh to any URL causes the 'page' to be refreshed every time it is updated on the filesystem.

```
RewriteRule  ^(/[uge]/[^/]+/?.*):refresh  /internal/cgi/apache/nph-refresh?f=$1
```

Now when we reference the URL

```
/u/foo/bar/page.html:refresh
```

this leads to the internal invocation of the URL

```
/internal/cgi/apache/nph-refresh?f=/u/foo/bar/page.html
```

The only missing part is the NPH-CGI script. Although one would usually say "left as an exercise to the reader" ;-) I will provide this, too.

```
#!/sw/bin/perl
##
##  nph-refresh -- NPH/CGI script for auto refreshing pages
##  Copyright (c) 1997 Ralf S. Engelschall, All Rights Reserved.
##
$| = 1;

#   split the QUERY_STRING variable
@pairs = split(/&/, $ENV{'QUERY_STRING'});
foreach $pair (@pairs) {
    ($name, $value) = split(/=/, $pair);
    $name =~ tr/A-Z/a-z/;
    $name = 'QS_' . $name;
```

```
        $value =~ s/%([a-fA-F0-9][a-fA-F0-9])/pack("C", hex($1))/eg;
        eval "\$$name = \"$value\"";
    }
$QS_s = 1 if ($QS_s eq ");
$QS_n = 3600 if ($QS_n eq ");
if ($QS_f eq ") {
    print "HTTP/1.0 200 OK\n";
    print "Content-type: text/html\n\n";
    print "&lt;b&gt;ERROR&lt;/b&gt;: No file given\n";
    exit(0);
}
if (! -f $QS_f) {
    print "HTTP/1.0 200 OK\n";
    print "Content-type: text/html\n\n";
    print "&lt;b&gt;ERROR&lt;/b&gt;: File $QS_f not found\n";
    exit(0);
}

sub print_http_headers_multipart_begin {
    print "HTTP/1.0 200 OK\n";
    $bound = "ThisRandomString12345";
    print "Content-type: multipart/x-mixed-replace;boundary=$bound\n";
    &print_http_headers_multipart_next;
}

sub print_http_headers_multipart_next {
    print "\n--$bound\n";
}

sub print_http_headers_multipart_end {
    print "\n-$bound--\n";
}

sub displayhtml {
    local($buffer) = @_;
    $len = length($buffer);
    print "Content-type: text/html\n";
    print "Content-length: $len\n\n";
    print $buffer;
}

sub readfile {
    local($file) = @_;
    local(*FP, $size, $buffer, $bytes);
    ($x, $x, $x, $x, $x, $x, $x, $size) = stat($file);
    $size = sprintf("%d", $size);
    open(FP, "&lt;$file");
    $bytes = sysread(FP, $buffer, $size);
    close(FP);
    return $buffer;
}
```

```
$buffer = &readfile($QS_f);
&print_http_headers_multipart_begin;
&displayhtml($buffer);

sub mystat {
    local($file) = $_[0];
    local($time);

    ($x, $x, $x, $x, $x, $x, $x, $x, $x, $mtime) = stat($file);
    return $mtime;
}

$mtimeL = &mystat($QS_f);
$mtime = $mtime;
for ($n = 0; $n &lt; $QS_n; $n++) {
    while (1) {
        $mtime = &mystat($QS_f);
        if ($mtime ne $mtimeL) {
            $mtimeL = $mtime;
            sleep(2);
            $buffer = &readfile($QS_f);
            &print_http_headers_multipart_next;
            &displayhtml($buffer);
            sleep(5);
            $mtimeL = &mystat($QS_f);
            last;
        }
        sleep($QS_s);
    }
}

&print_http_headers_multipart_end;

exit(0);

##EOF##
```

## 38.14. Mass Virtual Hosting

**Description:**

The <VirtualHost> feature of Apache is nice and works great when you just have a few dozen virtual hosts. But when you are an ISP and have hundreds of virtual hosts, this feature is suboptimal.

**Solution:**

To provide this feature we map the remote web page or even the complete remote web area to our namespace using the *Proxy Throughput* feature (flag [P]):

```
##
##   vhost.map
##
www.vhost1.dom:80   /path/to/docroot/vhost1
www.vhost2.dom:80   /path/to/docroot/vhost2
       :
www.vhostN.dom:80   /path/to/docroot/vhostN
##
##   httpd.conf
##
       :
#   use the canonical hostname on redirects, etc.
UseCanonicalName on
       :
#   add the virtual host in front of the CLF-format
CustomLog /path/to/access_log  "%{VHOST}e %h %l %u %t \"%r\" %>s %b"
       :
#   enable the rewriting engine in the main server
RewriteEngine on

#   define two maps: one for fixing the URL and one which defines
#   the available virtual hosts with their corresponding
#   DocumentRoot.
RewriteMap     lowercase     int:tolower
RewriteMap     vhost         txt:/path/to/vhost.map

#   Now do the actual virtual host mapping
#   via a huge and complicated single rule:
#
#   1. make sure we don't map for common locations
RewriteCond    %{REQUEST_URI}  !^/commonurl1/.*
RewriteCond    %{REQUEST_URI}  !^/commonurl2/.*
       :
RewriteCond    %{REQUEST_URI}  !^/commonurlN/.*
#
#   2. make sure we have a Host header, because
#      currently our approach only supports
#      virtual hosting through this header
RewriteCond    %{HTTP_HOST}  !^$
#
#   3. lowercase the hostname
RewriteCond    ${lowercase:%{HTTP_HOST}|NONE}  ^(.+)$
#
#   4. lookup this hostname in vhost.map and
#      remember it only when it is a path
#      (and not "NONE" from above)
RewriteCond    ${vhost:%1}  ^(/.*)$
#
#   5. finally we can map the URL to its docroot location
#      and remember the virtual host for logging purposes
RewriteRule    ^/(.*)$    %1/$1  [E=VHOST:${lowercase:%{HTTP_HOST}}]
       :
```

## 38.15. Host Deny

**Description:**

How can we forbid a list of externally configured hosts from using our server?

**Solution:**

For Apache >= 1.3b6:

```
RewriteEngine  on
RewriteMap     hosts-deny  txt:/path/to/hosts.deny
RewriteCond    ${hosts-deny:%{REMOTE_HOST}|NOT-FOUND}  !=NOT-FOUND [OR]
RewriteCond    ${hosts-deny:%{REMOTE_ADDR}|NOT-FOUND}  !=NOT-FOUND
RewriteRule    ^/.*  -  [F]
```

For Apache <= 1.3b6:

```
RewriteEngine  on
RewriteMap     hosts-deny  txt:/path/to/hosts.deny
RewriteRule    ^/(.*)$ ${hosts-deny:%{REMOTE_HOST}|NOT-FOUND}/$1
RewriteRule    !^NOT-FOUND/.* - [F]
RewriteRule    ^NOT-FOUND/(.*)$ ${hosts-deny:%{REMOTE_ADDR}|NOT-FOUND}/$1
RewriteRule    !^NOT-FOUND/.* - [F]
RewriteRule    ^NOT-FOUND/(.*)$ /$1
```

```
##
##   hosts.deny
##
##   ATTENTION! This is a map, not a list, even when we treat it as such.
##             mod_rewrite parses it for key/value pairs, so at least a
##             dummy value "-" must be present for each entry.
##

193.102.180.41 -
bsdti1.sdm.de  -
192.76.162.40  -
```

## 38.16. Proxy Deny

**Description:**

How can we forbid a certain host or even a user of a special host from using the Apache proxy?

**Solution:**

We first have to make sure <u>mod_rewrite</u> is below(!) <u>mod_proxy</u> in the Configuration file when compiling the Apache web server. This way it gets called *before* <u>mod_proxy</u>. Then we configure the following for a host-dependent deny...

```
RewriteCond %{REMOTE_HOST} ^badhost\.mydomain\.com$
RewriteRule !^http://[^/.]\.mydomain.com.*   -  [F]
```

...and this one for a user@host-dependent deny:

```
RewriteCond %{REMOTE_IDENT}@%{REMOTE_HOST}   ^badguy@badhost\.mydomain\.com$
RewriteRule !^http://[^/.]\.mydomain.com.*   -  [F]
```

## 38.17. Special Authentication Variant

Description:

Sometimes very special authentication is needed, for instance authentication which checks for a set of explicitly configured users. Only these should receive access and without explicit prompting (which would occur when using Basic Auth via mod_auth_basic).

Solution:

We use a list of rewrite conditions to exclude all except our friends:

```
RewriteCond %{REMOTE_IDENT}@%{REMOTE_HOST} !^friend1@client1.quux-corp\.com$
RewriteCond %{REMOTE_IDENT}@%{REMOTE_HOST} !^friend2@client2.quux-corp\.com$
RewriteCond %{REMOTE_IDENT}@%{REMOTE_HOST} !^friend3@client3.quux-corp\.com$
RewriteRule ^/~quux/only-for-friends/        -                          [F]
```

## 38.18. Referer-based Deflector

Description:

How can we program a flexible URL Deflector which acts on the "Referer" HTTP header and can be configured with as many referring pages as we like?

Solution:

Use the following really tricky ruleset...

```
RewriteMap  deflector  txt:/path/to/deflector.map

RewriteCond %{HTTP_REFERER} !=""
RewriteCond ${deflector:%{HTTP_REFERER}} ^-$
RewriteRule ^.* %{HTTP_REFERER} [R,L]

RewriteCond %{HTTP_REFERER} !=""
RewriteCond ${deflector:%{HTTP_REFERER}|NOT-FOUND} !=NOT-FOUND
RewriteRule ^.* ${deflector:%{HTTP_REFERER}} [R,L]
```

... in conjunction with a corresponding rewrite map:

```
##
##   deflector.map
##

http://www.badguys.com/bad/index.html    -
http://www.badguys.com/bad/index2.html    -
http://www.badguys.com/bad/index3.html    http://somewhere.com/
```

This automatically redirects the request back to the referring page (when "-" is used as the value in the map) or to a specific URL (when an URL is specified in the map as the second argument).

# Linbrary™ Advertising Club (LAC)

**Linbrary™** 🐧  **Official Docs as a Real Books**
http://www.linbrary.com  📚 Linux Library

## Linux Documentation Project - Machtelt Garrels

*http://www.tldp.org/*

| Version | Title | Edition | ISBN- 10 | ISBN- 13 |
|---------|-------|---------|----------|----------|
| **TLDP** | **Introduction to Linux** (Second Edition) | paperback | 1-59682-112-4 | 978-1-59682-112-5 |
| | | eBook (pdf) | 1-59682-114-0 | 978-1-59682-114-9 |
| | **Bash Guide for Beginners** | paperback | 0-9744339-4-2 | 978-0-97443-394-3 |
| | | eBook (pdf) | 1-59682-035-7 | 978-1-59682-035-7 |
| *http://www.linbrary.com/linux-tldp/* | | | | |

Linbrary Advertising Club

## Fedora Project Official Documentation

*http://fedoraproject.org/*

| Version | Title | Edition | ISBN-10 | ISBN-13 |
|---------|-------|---------|---------|---------|
| **Fedora 12** | Fedora 12 **Installation Guide** | paperback | 1-59682-179-5 | 978-1-59682-179-8 |
| | | eBook (pdf) | 1-59682-184-1 | 978-1-59682-184-2 |
| | Fedora 12 **User Guide** | paperback | 1-59682-180-9 | 978-1-59682-180-4 |
| | | eBook (pdf) | 1-59682-185-X | 978-1-59682-185-9 |
| | Fedora 12 **Security Guide** | paperback | 1-59682-181-7 | 978-1-59682-181-1 |
| | | eBook (pdf) | 1-59682-186-8 | 978-1-59682-186-6 |
| | Fedora 12 **SE Linux User Guide** | paperback | 1-59682-182-5 | 978-1-59682-182-8 |
| | | eBook (pdf) | 1-59682-187-6 | 978-1-59682-187-3 |
| | Fedora 12 **Virtualization Guide** | paperback | 1-59682-183-3 | 978-1-59682-183-5 |
| | | eBook (pdf) | 1-59682-188-4 | 978-1-59682-188-0 |
| **Fedora 11** | Fedora 12 **Installation Guide** | paperback | 1-59682-142-6 | 978-1-59682-142-2 |
| | | eBook (pdf) | 1-59682-146-9 | 978-1-59682-146-0 |
| | Fedora 12 **User Guide** | paperback | 1-59682-180-9 | 978-1-59682-180-4 |
| | | eBook (pdf) | 1-59682-185-X | 978-1-59682-185-9 |
| | Fedora 12 **Security Guide** | paperback | 1-59682-181-7 | 978-1-59682-181-1 |
| | | eBook (pdf) | 1-59682-186-8 | 978-1-59682-186-6 |
| | Fedora 12 **SE Linux User Guide** | paperback | 1-59682-182-5 | 978-1-59682-182-8 |
| | | eBook (pdf) | 1-59682-187-6 | 978-1-59682-187-3 |
| *http://www.linbrary.com/fedora/* | | | | |

Linbrary Advertising Club

## PostgreSQL Official Documentation

*http://www.postgresq.org/*

| Version | Title | Edition | ISBN-10 | ISBN-13 |
|---------|-------|---------|---------|---------|
| PostgreSQL 8.04 | PostgreSQL 8.04 **Volume I. The SQL Language** | paperback | 1-59682-158-2 | 978-1-59682-158-3 |
| | | eBook (pdf) | 1-59682-163-9 | 978-1-59682-163-7 |
| | PostgreSQL 8.04 **Volume II. Server Administration** | paperback | 1-59682-159-0 | 978-1-59682-159-0 |
| | | eBook (pdf) | 1-59682-164-7 | 978-1-59682-164-4 |
| | PostgreSQL 8.04 **Volume III. Server Programming** | paperback | 1-59682-160-4 | 978-1-59682-160-6 |
| | | eBook (pdf) | 1-59682-165-5 | 978-1-59682-165-1 |
| | PostgreSQL 8.04 **Volume IV. Reference** | paperback | 1-59682-161-2 | 978-1-59682-161-3 |
| | | eBook (pdf) | 1-59682-166-3 | 978-1-59682-166-8 |
| | PostgreSQL 8.04 **Volume V. Internals & Appendixes** | paperback | 1-59682-162-0 | 978-1-59682-162-0 |
| | | eBook (pdf) | 1-59682-167-1 | 978-1-59682-167-5 |

*http://www.linbrary.com/postgresql/*

Linbrary Advertising Club

CPSIA information can be obtained at www.ICGtesting.com
Printed in the USA
BVOW081503130112

280403BV00005B/12/P

9 781596 821910